Working Together
with Children and Families

Dr. Dana Fredebaugh
Nova Southeastern University
FGSEHS/GTEP
1750 NE 167th Street
North Miami Beach, FL   33162

This book is printed on recycled paper.

Working Together with Children and Families

Case Studies in Early Intervention

Edited by

P.J. McWilliam, Ph.D.
Investigator
Frank Porter Graham Child Development Center
The University of North Carolina at Chapel Hill

and

Donald B. Bailey, Jr., Ph.D.
Director
Frank Porter Graham Child Development Center
and
Associate Professor
Medical Allied Health
School of Medicine
The University of North Carolina at Chapel Hill

·P·A·U·L·H·
BROOKES
PUBLISHING C⁰

Baltimore · London · Toronto · Sydney

Paul H. Brookes Publishing Co.
P.O. Box 10624
Baltimore, Maryland 21285-0624

Typeset by Maple-Vail Composition Services, Binghamton, New York.
Manufactured in the United States of America by
BookCrafters, Falls Church, Virginia.

Second printing, April 1996.

Library of Congress Cataloging-in-Publication Data

Working together with children and families : case studies
  in early intervention / edited by P.J. McWilliam and
  Donald B. Bailey, Jr.
     p.   cm.
  Includes bibliographical references and index.
  ISBN 1-55766-123-5
  1. Parents of handicapped children—Services for—
Case studies. 2. Family social work—Case studies.
3. Social work with handicapped children—Case studies.
I. McWilliam, P.J., 1953–   . II. Bailey, Donald B.
HQ759.913.W67   1993
362.4′048′082—dc20   92-42852
                                  CIP

British Library Cataloguing-in-Publication data are available
from the British Library.

Contents

A premature birth unexpectedly introduces a
newborn's parents to the world of the neonatal
intensive care unit, newborn assessment, and
the challenges associated with caring for a
child with an unknown amount of brain
injury.

An early interventionist consultant assists the
frustrated staff of a child care program as they
work with a child whose mother enrolls him
without explaining the extent of his special
needs.

service providers who doubt her ability to
make sound decisions about her family's
welfare because of her previous drug use.

Situations for Problemsolving

About the Editors

P.J. McWilliam, Ph.D., Investigator, Frank Porter Graham Child Development Center, CB# 8180, The University of North Carolina at Chapel Hill, Chapel Hill, North Carolina 27599-8180

P.J. McWilliam completed her undergraduate work in psychology at the University of Maryland at Baltimore County. She received her master's degree in clinical psychology from West Virginia University and her doctorate in clinical psychology from The University of North Carolina at Greensboro. Much of her 15 years of experience in early intervention has been gained through her involvement with direct service agencies. This included serving as Assistant Director and Senior Coordinator of Child and Family Services for the Family, Infant and Preschool Program in Morganton, North Carolina, from 1982 to 1989. Dr. McWilliam has also served as director or investigator for a number of research and model demonstration grant projects. Her current work is in the area of early intervention personnel preparation, with particular emphasis on the development and evaluation of training strategies to assist others in implementing a family-centered approach to services. She has conducted numerous training events for early interventionists across the United States and Canada. A recent focus of her work in personnel preparation has been promoting the case method of instruction as an alternative or supplement to more traditional training strategies. Dr. McWilliam is currently principal investigator and director of a U.S. Department of Education Special Projects grant, the Case Method Instruction Project.

Donald B. Bailey, Jr., Ph.D., Director, Frank Porter Graham Child Development Center and Associate Professor, Medical Allied Health, School of Medicine, CB# 8180, The University of North Carolina at Chapel Hill, Chapel Hill, North Carolina 27599-8180

Donald B. Bailey, Jr., received his undergraduate degree in psychology from Davidson College and his master's degree in early childhood special education from The University of North Carolina at Chapel Hill. After working 3 years in a program for preschoolers and kindergarteners with disabilities, he attended The University of Washington, where he received his doctorate in special education in 1979. Since that time, he has served as a faculty member at The University of North Carolina at Chapel Hill. Dr. Bailey is nationally recognized for his research and writing related to services for infants and preschoolers with disabilities and their families. He has published numerous journal articles and is the co-author of several books on early intervention. From 1991 to 1994, he served as editor of the *Journal of Early Intervention*. Dr. Bailey has received a number of grants to support his work in the areas of family-centered service provision, early intervention personnel preparation, and innovative classroom-based practices. He is currently director of Frank Porter Graham Child Development Center of The University of North Carolina at Chapel Hill, a multidisciplinary center devoted to research, training, technical assistance, and policy analysis related to young children and their families.

About the Contributors

Virginia E. Bishop, Ph.D., Special Education Consultant for Visually Handicappèd Children, 4312 Duval Street, #206, Austin, Texas 78751

Virginia E. Bishop, Ph.D., is a private consultant in special education, specializing in children with visual impairments. She was an itinerant teacher of children with visual impairments for 30 years before becoming a private consultant. Dr. Bishop also teaches courses at the University of Texas at Austin to prepare teachers of children who have visual disabilities. She has written a number of journal articles and a textbook and has presented papers internationally.

Linda H. Carothers, M.S., Project Enlightenment, 501 South Boylan Avenue, Raleigh, North Carolina 27603

Linda H. Carothers, M.S., has had 15 years of experience as a child development specialist in rural and urban mental health programs in the southeast. For the past 8 years, she has worked as Infant/Parent Resource Consultant with Project Enlightenment, Wake County Public School System, which operates out of Raleigh, North Carolina. At Project Enlightenment, she provides direct services to families with premature infants. She has also been instrumental in implementing the Parents as Teachers (PAT) model program in Garner, North Carolina, and is a certified national trainer for the PAT program.

Karen E. Diamond, Ph.D., Assistant Professor, Department of Child Development and Family Studies, 1267 CDFS Building, Purdue University, West Lafayette, Indiana 47906-1267

Karen E. Diamond, Ph.D., a developmental psychologist, is an assistant professor and Director of the Child Development Laboratories in the Department of Child Development and Family Studies at Purdue University. She has more than 15 years of experience in early intervention, serving as both direct service provider and director of programs for young children with and without disabilities. Her interests are in the development of strategies for successfully integrating children with disabilities in regular early childhood education programs. A specific focus of her current work is the impact of inclusive education on children's awareness and understanding of disability in their peers.

Marilyn Espe-Sherwindt, M.A., Director, Project CAPABLE, Cincinnati Center for Developmental Disorders, Pavilion Building, Elland and Bethesda Avenues, Cincinnati, Ohio 45229-2899

Marilyn Espe-Sherwindt, M.A., serves as a project director at the University Affiliated Cincinnati Center for Developmental Disorders in Cincinnati, Ohio. For the past 10 years, she has been working in early intervention, first as a direct service provider to infants and families and, more recently, as a trainer in preservice, inservice, and outreach projects. Much of her research and writing has been in the area of families that are at risk, particularly parents with special needs or mental retardation.

Roy Grant, M.Ed., Associate Director, Pediatric Early Child Health Project, Mount Sinai Medical Center, Pediatric Ambulatory Care Division, One Gustave Levy Place, Box 1202, New York, New York 10029

Roy Grant, M.Ed., is Associate Director of the Mount Sinai Medical Center Pediatric Early Child Health Project, a comprehensive school-based early intervention program serving the East Harlem community of New York City. A psychotherapist and developmental specialist by training, Mr. Grant was formerly Director of Mental Health's largest clinical service project for homeless children and families in welfare hotels. He has extensive experience working with Head Start programs and is a member of the Advisory Committee of the Region II Head Start Resource Access Project at New York University.

Brandon F. Greene, Ph.D., Project 12-Ways, Southern Illinois University, Carbondale, Illinois 62901

Brandon F. Greene, Ph.D., is a professor of Behavior Analysis and Therapy at Southern Illinois University. He has considerable research, teaching, and practical experience in behavioral interventions with families affected by disability and by a history of child abuse and neglect. He currently directs Project 12-Ways, a program providing in-home behavioral interventions for these families.

Mary Frances Hanline, Ph.D., Assistant Professor, The Florida State University, Department of Special Education, B-172, Tallahassee, Florida 32306

Mary Frances Hanline, Ph.D., is an Assistant Professor in Early Childhood Special Education at The Florida State University. Her experiences in the field of early intervention and special education include classroom teaching, home visiting, and directing a Handicapped Children's Early Education Program (HCEEP) demonstration project that focuses on supporting families during their transition to preschool public school and on providing integration opportunities for preschool children. Research interests have centered around the social-emotional development of young children with disabilities, service delivery transitions, inclusion, play-based instruction, and the merging of early childhood special education and early childhood education in policies, personnel preparation, and practice.

James M. Helm, Ph.D., Wake Medical Center, Area Health Education Center–Pediatrics, Post Office Box 14465, Raleigh, North Carolina 27620-4465

James M. Helm, Ph.D., is a developmental specialist with Wake Medical Center and a clinical assistant professor in pediatrics and special education at the University of North Carolina at Chapel Hill. He has almost 20 years of experience working with families, infants, and young children in a variety of service settings. He currently works in the intensive care nursery and follow-up program of Wake Medical Center. His responsibilities include teaching and training related to providing developmentally appropriate care in NICUs. Dr. Helm is a consultant to a number of hospitals on issues related to NICU care, including environmental arrangements, infant assessment, developmental care, and family support.

Melissa R. Johnson, Ph.D., Wake Medical Center, Area Health Education Center and Departments of Pediatrics and Psychiatry, School of Medicine, University of North Carolina at Chapel Hill, Post Office Box 14465, Raleigh, North Carolina 27620-4465

Melissa R. Johnson, Ph.D., is a pediatric psychologist at Wake Medical Center and Wake Area Health Education Center, where she coordinates the developmental team that serves the Pediatric/Neonatology Teaching Service. She is Clinical Assistant Professor of Psychiatry at the University of North Carolina School of Medicine. The primary focus of her work is direct service and research with high-risk and chronically ill infants and young children and their families. She is certified in the Brazelton Neonatal Assessment Scale, the Assessment of Preterm Infant Behavior, and the Neonatal Individualized Developmental Care and Assessment Program, for which she is a trainer.

David E. Jones, M.A., The Beach Center on Families and Disability, % Life Span Institute, 3111 Haworth Hall, The University of Kansas, Lawrence, Kansas 66045

David E. Jones, M.A., is a doctoral candidate in counseling psychology and a researcher with the Beach Center on Families and Disability at the University of Kansas in Lawrence. His work is on the process of educational planning for young children who are ventilator assisted. He and his wife have four daughters, the oldest of whom is a child with mental retardation and special health care needs.

Hal C. Lewis, Ph.D., JFK Center for Developmental Disabilities, University of Colorado Health Sciences Center, 4200 East Ninth Avenue, Box C-234, Denver, Colorado 80262

Hal C. Lewis, Ph.D., is a clinical child psychologist with the JFK Center for Developmental Disabilities, University of Colorado Health Sciences Center and The Children's Hospital in Denver. Most of his 20 years of professional experience, as a school teacher and psychologist, has been with young children with developmental disabilities. His current work focuses on early intervention personnel preparation, services for young children with severe developmental psychopathology, and inclusion strategies for infants and toddlers with complex medical needs.

Jean Lowe, Ph.D., University of New Mexico, School of Medicine, Department of Pediatrics, Albuquerque, New Mexico 87131

Jean Lowe, Ph.D., is a developmental specialist at the University of New Mexico Children's Hospital. For the past 18 years, her work has focused on developmental evaluation of infants, toddlers, and school-age children. A number of model demonstration projects and research grants have supported her interest in extremely premature infants and infants who were exposed to drugs prenatally. Dr. Lowe is also involved in preservice and inservice training in the area of assessment and program planning for infants and toddlers who are at risk.

Roger C. Lubeck, Ph.D., Consultant, Corporate Behavior Analysts, Chicago, Illinois 60610

Roger C. Lubeck, Ph.D., spent 14 years as a university faculty and behavior analyst. His writing and research focused on parent training, child abuse, child social skills, and generalization. Dr. Lubeck now works for a Chicago-based firm that specializes in organizational change and management development.

K. Renee Norman, M.A., Program Coordinator, Spectrum Center, 879 Grant Avenue, San Lorenzo, California 94580

K. Renee Norman, M.A., is a program coordinator with Spectrum Center for Educational and Behavioral Development in San Lorenzo, California. She was the former clinical director of Project 12-Ways at Southern Illinois University at Carbondale. Her 8 years of direct service experience in early intervention have involved in-home and group parent training and early childhood education. Her current interests are in educational and clinical interventions with students with developmental disabilities and in providing effective staff training and development.

Charles A. Peck, M.A., Ph.D., Department of Counseling Psychology, 1800 East McLaughlin Boulevard, Washington State University, Vancouver, Washington 98655

Charles A. Peck, Ph.D., is a faculty member in special education and educational psychology at Washington State University—Vancouver. He has worked in a variety of roles in early intervention including classroom teacher, home visitor, consultant, inservice trainer, and researcher. His work now focuses on factors affecting the development and successful implementation of inclusive education programs.

Sandra Petersen, M.A., Special Education Unit, Colorado Department of Education, 201 East Colfax Avenue, Denver, Colorado 80203

Sandra Petersen, M.A., is an Early Childhood Special Educator and Coordinator of Training and Technical Assistance for Early Childhood for the Colorado Department of Education. Her area of interest is infant mental health and the effect of early relationships. She most values her experience as a Fellow of the National Center for Clinical Infant Programs. She has always combined academic and direct service experiences in a variety of early childhood settings and universities.

Marie Reilly, Ph.D., P.T., Wake Medical Center, Area Health Education Center and Division of Physical Therapy, Department of Medical Allied Health Professions, School of Medicine, University of North Carolina at Chapel Hill, Chapel Hill, North Carolina 27599

Marie Reilly, Ph.D., P.T., is a pediatric physical therapist for Wake Area Health Education Center and is a member of the clinical faculty at the University of North Carolina at Chapel Hill. Much of her 21 years of experience as a physical therapist has been in multidisciplinary early intervention programs. For the past 3 years, Dr. Reilly has coordinated an early intervention program at an outpatient pediatric facility in Raleigh, North Carolina. She also provides developmental assessment, consultation, and direct treatment in the neonatal intensive care nursery, special infant care clinic, and pediatric unit at Wake Medical Center.

Phyllis Spiegel-McGill, Ph.D., Director, New Family Project, Center for Child Study, Skidmore College, Saratoga Springs, New York 12866

Phyllis Spiegel-McGill, Ph.D., is the director of the New Family Project, an early intervention program located at Skidmore College in Saratoga Springs, New York. As a member of the Education Department, she also teaches courses on special education and early childhood. Dr. Spiegel-McGill is President-elect for New York State Division for Early Childhood of the Council for Exceptional Children. She has considerable experience in early intervention as a teacher, teacher–trainer, and as an administrator of a program that includes an inclusive preschool, home-based services for infants, and a parent support and information network. Her research in early childhood special education has focused on methods for facilitating social and cognitive development, inclusive education, and parent advocacy training. This work has been published and presented nationally and internationally.

Barbara Wagner-Siebauer, B.S., Birth to Three Program, 2855 North 79th Street, Milwaukee, Wisconsin 53222

Barbara Wagner-Siebauer, B.S., is an early intervention teacher in the Milwaukee Public School's Birth to Three program. The program provides home visits and center-based services to infants and toddlers with special needs and their teenage mothers. Ms. Wagner-Siebauer has provided direct services to infants and toddlers and their families for more than 18 years, working in both Delaware and Wisconsin. She has also participated in teacher training at the university level. Her current interests include working with infants who are born prematurely and providing appropriate support to teenage parents.

Mary R. Wandschneider, M.A., Department of Child, Consumer, and Family Studies, 101 White Hall, Washington State University, Pullman, Washington 99164-2010

Mary R. Wandschneider, M.A., is a researcher and professor with the Child, Consumer, and Family Studies Department at Washington State University in Pullman, Washington. Her experience in early intervention began more than 20 years ago when she was teaching in an early childhood setting that, although not labeled as such at the time, was an integrated program. Since then, Ms. Wandschneider has been involved in program development, consultation, and research regarding inclusive education for young children. A major emphasis of her work has been assisting parents and professionals to work together to improve services for children who are at risk. She sees her own parenting of her child with disabilities as an important part of her understanding of the field.

Eileen Ziesler, M.A., W 7425 Old 14, Ladysmith, Wisconsin 54848

Eileen Ziesler, M.A., is an early childhood special education teacher with the Ladysmith-Hawkins School District in Wisconsin. Beginning with the topic of her master's thesis in 1977, her special interest projects have centered on families of children with disabilities. She has been awarded three state discretionary grants for her school district, one of which resulted in a videotaped production of a modern dance work concerning the grieving process titled *When the Bough Breaks*. Ms. Ziesler currently serves as editor of the Wisconsin Division for Early Childhood newsletter and is a member of the Wisconsin Task Force on Autism.

Irene Nathan Zipper, M.S.W., School of Social Work, University of North Carolina, Chapel Hill, North Carolina 27599-3550

Irene Nathan Zipper, M.S.W., is a Clinical Instructor at the University of North Carolina School of Social Work. As a project coordinator for the Carolina Institute for Research in Infant Personnel Preparation at the Frank Porter Graham Child Development Center in Chapel Hill, she examined national implementation of the service coordination mandate under Part H and provided consultation to a number of states. She has been involved in training and curriculum development for case managers in child mental health systems, in training for Head Start personnel, and in counseling children and families in a variety of service settings.

Preface

In 1989 my co-editor, Don Bailey, invited me to be a part of the Carolina Institute for Research on Infant Personnel Preparation (CIRIPP) in Chapel Hill, North Carolina. He explained that my primary responsibility would be to explore the case method of instruction as a strategy for training early interventionists. Upon accepting Don's offer, I was handed a stack of journal articles and left to my own devices. I made my way through the stack and soon found myself at the university library poring over dusty old volumes on the case method of instruction that were written by professors at the Harvard Business School circa 1954. I was hooked. The method offered great promise for addressing many of the challenges encountered in early intervention personnel preparation. In particular, the case method provided a means of bridging the gap between theory and practice.

If this new method of instruction were to be adopted by the field, however, case studies for early interventionists would be needed. I began writing and gradually developed a small collection of case studies and related training materials entitled *The Families We Serve*. At the same time, the activities of CIRIPP provided opportunities to conduct preservice and inservice field testing of the case studies and the case method, and adaptations were made to suit the unique training content of our field.

Satisfied that the case studies were worthy of dissemination, Don and I decided to publish them. The last six cases in this book were among those originally appearing in the CIRIPP publication, *The Families We Serve*. We encouraged others to write additional case studies, and the majority of those included in this book came about as a result of an open invitation to the field. For each case study, we wrote a series of discussion questions. These questions were originally designed for use by instructors, but the independent reader may find them useful as a guide to the major issues addressed in each case.

All of the case studies in this book are based on actual experiences of professionals working in early intervention. The names of children, parents, and professionals have been changed, and certain aspects of the situations have been altered to mask the true identities of those whose lives are described. The stories, however, reflect the true nature of early intervention in the United States. Written in a narrative format, the case studies are more comparable to short stories than academic readings. The characteristics of the children and families are diverse, as are the settings in which services are provided. Many of the cases are supplemented with realistic dialogue or professionals' thoughts and emotions. In short, the characters and situations have a 3-dimensional quality, allowing readers to find common ground with the professionals featured in the stories and imagine themselves in the midst of the action. Anyone who ever thought that early intervention was easy will think differently after reading these stories. Anyone who ever thought the work was unfulfilling will probably have a change of heart.

If there is an overriding theme in this book, it is the celebration of the individual. Current academic writings about early intervention reverberate with messages about the importance of individualizing services for children and families. In the written transmission of theory, research, and recommended practices, however, clear pictures of individuals are seldom offered. It is hoped that this book will supplement the excellent work of our colleagues by offering clear pictures of children without labels, families with unique values, and professionals with feelings of their own. The case stories also provide images that demonstrate the distinctive nature of each community in which early intervention takes place. Most important, the stories provide specific examples of factors to consider in applying recommended practices on a case-by-case basis.

As this book goes into print, I reflect upon its content and contemplate its longevity. There have been great strides in early intervention theory and practice during the 15 years that I have been involved in the field. Will our current rate of progress continue? What new ideas and innovations lie ahead? I can only hope that at least some of the concerns of the families described in these case studies and the barriers they encounter will no longer exist for families of the future. I also hope that future advances in the field will continue to provide professionals with improved methods for working together with children and families. Perhaps one day this book will serve as a historical account of what early intervention services were like in the early 1990s. If so, I hope our progress is evident.

If any aspect of this book endures the test of time, it will be the concept of building relationships. Each of the case studies in this book tells a tale about the importance of relationships—between parents and their children, between parents and professionals, and between professionals and other professionals.

P.J. McWilliam

Acknowledgments

This book represents the combined efforts of many people. First and foremost, I would like to acknowledge those who were directly involved in the writing. I thank Don Bailey, my co-editor, for his obvious contributions to the book. During the 4 years I have had the privilege of working with Don, he has become a valued colleague and mentor. He has been an unflagging cheerleader for my work related to the case method of instruction, and his tolerance for my somewhat unorthodox workstyle is unsurpassed. I also extend my sincere appreciation to all of the authors who contributed case studies to this book. The quality of their work is obvious from the reading of their cases, and I thank them for giving their time and effort toward the production of this book. They have been a marvelous group to work with, and I have come away from this project with some new and talented colleagues. Finally, I would like to thank Kathy Boyd and Sarah Cheney of Paul H. Brookes Publishing Co. for their direct contributions to this publication. Their knowledge, skills, and style have made the writing of this book an enjoyable experience from start to finish.

The number of people who have had an indirect influence on this book are far too numerous to mention individually. There are, however, some groups and a few individuals who deserve special recognition. These are the people who have supported and promoted my work related to the case method of instruction during the past 4 years. I would first like to recognize the U.S. Department of Education, Office of Special Education Programs for funding of the Carolina Institute for Research on Infant Personnel Preparation (CIRIPP). It was through this project that the idea of the case method of instruction emerged as a viable method of training. The faculty, staff, and advisory board of CIRIPP were an unending source of support for my ideas and helped to disseminate them across the United States.

Special thanks is given to Pam Winton, Pat Snyder, Jeanette McCollum, and Mary Beth Bruder who showed their support through their actions. Not only did they support the idea of the case method and believe in the quality of my case studies, but they incorporated both into their own training of early interventionists. Without their encouragement and enthusiasm, this book may never have been written. I also thank Eileen McWilliam, who reviewed earlier versions of my case studies and encouraged me to write more. Not everyone is fortunate to have an editor in the family.

My greatest appreciation is extended to Robin McWilliam. Providing I put the kids to bed and packed their schoolbags, he was willing to provide feedback on drafts of several portions of this book. If you want someone to be brutally honest about the quality of your work—he's your man. I am fortunate to have Robin, not only as a colleague, but also as a husband and my best friend. Together we solve the riddles of early intervention research and practice over lunch at our kitchen table.

Lastly, I acknowledge the never-ending influence of my two daughters. Kirsten has taught me things I would rather not have known about the effects of disability on a family, because the price of that knowledge was too dear. Nevertheless, I am a better instructor because of her and she constantly reaffirms my belief in the importance of truly individualized and family-centered services. Sonny has taught me the differences I suspected all along. Both continually influence my work and enrich my life.

P.J. McWilliam

To Robin and Pam

Working Together
with Children and Families

DEFINING
AND DELIVERING
QUALITY SERVICES
IN EARLY
INTERVENTION

Not so many years ago, early intervention seemed so simple, so straightforward, and yet so wonderful. The idea was to identify at-risk children early in life, when brain growth was most rapid, and provide activities to facilitate developmental growth. We had developmental tests and checklists to guide our work and mark our progress with the children as well as a number of curricula that included activities designed to promote skill acquisition. We had rules to follow and recipes for success, and the job responsibilities were reasonably clear-cut.

Times have changed. We have realized that our old views were too simple and our focus on the child needed to be expanded to include the family and its complex support network. The child-focused recipes have been supplemented or even supplanted by family-centered approaches to services. The principle of inclusion now advocates that even the youngest children with disabilities, no matter how severe, have the right to participate in settings with their typically developing peers and can benefit from these experiences. Questions of developmentally appropriate practice have led others to develop and implement new methods of teaching and providing therapy. Naturalistic, or incidental, teaching strategies and integrated therapy are just a few among many proposed innovations. Equally important, we have come to realize the importance of collaboration among professionals and agencies working with young children and their families. Finally, many of us are now confronted with issues that did not exist in the past, such as the ever-increasing number of infants born to mothers who use illegal drugs and infants who are HIV-positive or have AIDS. It has all become complex and confusing, especially for those professionals trained in the old methods.

Recent advances in early intervention hold much promise for improving services to infants, toddlers, and preschoolers with disabilities and their families. But our new expectations for early intervention services call for a new breed of professional to turn that promise into a reality. Early interventionists of the future will be expected to have a much broader knowledge base than ever before. They will likewise be expected to have a broader array of skills, including skills for working with families and for working in concert with professionals from other disciplines and agencies.

Above all, the new early interventionist will need to be a thinker, a decisionmaker, and a problemsolver. The new and broadened definitions of early intervention require the interventionist to look beyond the immediate developmental or medical status of the child and to take into consideration a multitude of other factors that may influence or be influenced by the choice of intervention strategies. Among these factors are the family's values and priorities, the resources available within the family and their informal networks of support, and the structure, breadth, and availability of other community resources.

The chapters in this section are intended to provide readers with a basic understanding of these new perspectives on early intervention, where they came from, and their impact on direct services. Chapter 1 provides a description of how recommended practices in early intervention are formulated and their various sources. Also included in this chapter is a brief overview of some of the more commonly accepted notions of what constitutes appropriate and effective service delivery in early intervention. Chapter 2 presents the various challenges and potential barriers facing professionals as they attempt to incorporate recommended practices into their daily work with children and families.

Chapter 1

The Search for Quality Indicators

Donald B. Bailey, Jr. and P.J. McWilliam _____

For years, researchers in early intervention sought to answer the question, "Is early intervention effective?" This question was important in establishing early intervention legislation, programs, and services because advocates were arguing that the provision of early services would make a real difference in the lives of children with disabilities and their families. Legislators were presented with data from various projects, and a multitude of families and professionals testified to the powerful benefits of early intervention. The result of these efforts was the landmark passage of PL 99-457, the Education of the Handicapped Act Amendments of 1986. This legislation required states to provide services for all children with disabilities between the ages of 3 and 5 years. Services for infants and toddlers were not mandated, but Part H of the law provided substantial financial incentives for states offering services for children from birth through 2 years of age.

The quest for empirical verification of early intervention effectiveness led to considerable activity, discussion, and debate among researchers. The results of a number of studies are now available to document the benefits of early intervention for children from low-income families (e.g., Lazar, Darlington, Murray, Royce, & Snipper, 1992) and for children at risk for developmental delays because of low birth weight or prematurity (e.g., Infant Health and Development Program, 1990). Research on the effectiveness of early intervention for children with disabilities, however, has been less clear. Numerous reviews and analyses of this research were published in the 1980s (e.g., Casto & Mastropieri, 1986; Dunst & Rheingrover, 1981; Ottenbacher, 1989; Shonkoff & Hauser-Cram, 1987; Simeonsson, Cooper, & Scheiner, 1982), and most concluded that, although there is some evidence that early intervention is effective, the studies are not definitive, and evidence of highly powerful effects is certainly lacking.

Why has documentation of effectiveness been so elusive in early intervention for children with disabilities? It is likely that the question is far too complex for a simple answer. For example, "early" could mean providing services prenatally, immediately after birth, at 12 months of age, or at age 3. Definitions of "intervention" are equally diverse and include a range of philosophies and practices. As Bailey and Wolery (1992) point out, early intervention has multiple goals that include supporting families, promoting child development, helping children function independently and master environmental demands, building and supporting social competence, preparing for normalized life experiences, and preventing future problems or disabilities. Yet, the majority of studies have focused on a single measure of early intervention effectiveness—children's developmental or intellectual progress.

This conceptual confusion about early intervention effectiveness and the limited scope of existing research indicates the need for more and better studies. In some respects, however, it could be argued that the general question of effectiveness has lost much of its importance now that early intervention is a legislated national priority. Instead, researchers should focus their energies on identifying quality indicators of early intervention. Thus, the question has changed from "Is early intervention effective?" to "What are the characteristics of services that produce desired results for children and their families?" This question is even more complex, in that it calls for treatment comparison studies and seeks to determine the possibility of aptitude by treatment interactions.

The importance of identifying quality indicators was made evident in an article by Haskins (1989), who reviewed the research on early intervention effectiveness for children from low-income families. One interesting aspect of his analysis is that he separated the studies into two groups, those that were conducted in typical community-based child care programs and those that were conducted in "model" programs. He found that the long-term effectiveness of early intervention varied as a function of the type of setting in which the study was conducted. Predictably, model settings were much more likely to result in long-term benefits. This finding prompts the question of what practices constitute "model" early intervention.

The search for quality indicators has resulted in consensus on a number of recommended practices for conducting early intervention. In this chapter, we describe the sources from which recommended practices are derived and provide a brief overview of guidelines and principles for implementing some of the more highly promoted practices. Among these are family-centered practices, inclusion in mainstream settings, developmentally appropriate practice, and coordinated service delivery. Even highly recommended practices, however, may be inappropriate for some children and families. Repeated cautions are therefore made to consider the unique characteristics of each child and family in selecting practices.

THE ORIGINS OF RECOMMENDED PRACTICES

Recommended practices in early intervention are derived from a variety of sources including legislation, research, the standards and recommendations of professional organizations, and philosophical or advocacy movements originating in the field or in response to more global national priorities. The influence of these various sources are by no means independent of one another. Rather, each source has influence over the other, and the strength and direction of such influence may change. Likewise, recommended practices change or evolve as a consequence of new developments in the various sources of influence.

Legislation

PL 99-457 and the subsequent amendments provided in PL 102-119, the Individuals with Disabilities Education Act (IDEA) Amendments of 1991, provide specific guidelines for what constitutes appropriate practice. For example, Part H, which provides regulations and guidelines for services for infants and toddlers, calls for the establishment of an individualized family service plan (IFSP) for each eligible child and his or her family. To paraphrase the IFSP requirements, the following constitute appropriate practice:

1. Each child should have a comprehensive developmental assessment that, at minimum, determines present levels of physical, cognitive, communication, social-emotional, and adaptive behavior. In addition, health status should be documented. Although appropriate tests and other measures should be used, professionals should also use "informed clinical opinion" as the basis for determining developmental status.
2. When desired by the family, programs should assess family concerns, priorities, and resources related to enhancing the child's development. This assessment should be conducted by qualified professionals and must include information gathered

through a personal interview with one or more family members.

3. Outcomes for the child and family should be identified and written in the context of a formal document. Included in this document should be criteria for documenting attainment of outcomes and a predicted timeline for accomplishment.

4. The plan should include a detailed description of the array of services to be provided in order to meet the specified goals. This would include when and for how long services would be offered.

5. A service coordinator must be available to help the family gain access to services and to identify potential sources for payment of services.

6. Because transitions are often difficult times for children and families, an individualized transition plan (ITP) must be developed before the child reaches 36 months of age. The purpose of this plan is to make sure that the movement into preschool services is smooth and that there are no gaps in services.

7. To the greatest extent possible, children should be served in "natural" environments, those in which typically developing children would be placed, such as homes, family child care homes, or child care centers.

Thus, legislation serves as one basis for establishing recommended practices. Unfortunately, legislative regulations and guidelines, alone, usually cannot ensure that appropriate practices occur. One limitation is that most laws specify the minimum that must be done to ensure compliance, rather than what ought to be done to achieve optimum results. For example, because the legislation says nothing about the frequency or length of services that should be provided to a preschooler, a school could easily set up a play group one morning a week and meet the minimum guidelines of the legislation.

In addition, legislation rarely provides sufficient detail to ensure full implementation in a standard fashion. For example, Part H specifies that, in order to generate a statement of family concerns, priorities, and resources, family assessments must be available and be conducted if the family so desires. Few guidelines for family assessment are established, however, so the staff of each program are left to decide how they will comply with this important aspect of the law. The uncertain nature of this requirement has led to many concerns among both professionals and families (Bailey, 1991).

Finally, legislation is often limited because of vague or uncertain wording. For example, according to the law, children with disabilities should be served in natural environments, but only to "the greatest extent possible." This may leave open to a program the ability to make decisions about inclusion on the basis of administrative resources rather than on what is best for the child.

Research

Research provides important information for practitioners because it offers objective evidence of what works and the conditions under which certain practices are appropriate. It is clear, for example, that the quality of a child's physical and social environment exerts a significant influence on his or her behavior and long-term development. We also know that children with disabilities often have trouble generalizing from one situation to another. Therefore, intervention activities must be planned to help children demonstrate and use skills in a variety of settings. One example of an intervention procedure with effectiveness that has been widely documented is incidental teaching (Warren & Kaiser, 1988).

It is usually difficult to determine the effectiveness of a practice on the basis of a single study. It is only after a line of research has consistently pursued a topic that patterns of effects become clear. For example, Buysse and Bailey (1993) recently reviewed 22 studies comparing outcomes for young children with disabilities in inclusive and segregated settings. A consistent pattern of findings across the studies indicated that inclusive settings, in which children with disabilities were in the company of typically developing peers, almost always resulted in higher levels of social behavior. Children's developmental progress in areas such as cognitive, communication, and motor development over time, however, did not seem to vary as a function of inclusive versus segregated placement.

Thorough examination of research studies, however, often reveals that the findings do not pertain equally to all children. In fact, studies have demonstrated that some children benefit from one form of intervention while others benefit from another. For example, Cole, Mills, Dale, and Jenkins (1991) found that children with relatively mild disabilities made more language and cognitive gains in inclusive classrooms, whereas children with significant delays made more gains in segregated settings. Thus, although we can draw important conclusions from research and make recommendations about practices that are effective for most children, we must realize that children respond to interventions in different ways. The only way to be sure is to evaluate, on an individual basis, the effectiveness of interventions and services for each child and family.

Professional Organizations

Standards and recommendations put forth by professional organizations constitute another force in determining appropriate practices. While the impetus behind statements from such organizations may come from legislation, research, or other sources, the statement itself may have broader impact on actual practices than the original source due to the highly visible nature of some organizations and their realms of influence. Two examples are readily apparent in early intervention. The first was published as a position statement by the National Association for the Education of Young Children (NAEYC) (Bredekamp, 1986). This statement established guidelines for the education of young children and, as a whole, the principles and strategies outlined in the NAEYC statement are now commonly referred to as *developmentally appropriate practice* (DAP). Developmentally appropriate practice refers to learning activities that are consistent with a child's developmental age and a curriculum that is responsive to individual children's needs. It also refers to learning activities that are "child-initiated, child-directed, and teacher supported" (Bredekamp, 1986, p. 3). The guidelines for DAP have been incorporated into NAEYC's accreditation criteria and procedures (National Association for the Education of Young Children, 1984), and a document describing curriculum implications of developmentally appropriate practice is now available (Bredekamp & Rosegrant, 1992). It is safe to say that these practices have had a significant influence on the way early childhood programs are developed and organized for young children. They have also led to the development of instruments and procedures for evaluating the extent to which programs adhere to the recommended criteria (e.g., Hyson, Hirsh-Pasek, & Rescorla, 1990).

A second example of guidelines from professional organizations is a recent effort by the Division for Early Childhood of the Council for Exceptional Children (DEC-CEC). This extensive project began with the formation of small groups of experts and parents who developed preliminary drafts of recommended practices for each of a number of aspects of early intervention for young children with disabilities. These drafts of guidelines were then reviewed and evaluated by a second group of experts and revisions were made. The revised guidelines were disseminated to professionals and families across the United States who were asked to rate the extent to which each practice would be considered appropriate practice for working with young children and their families. This effort has resulted in a DEC-CEC publication describing recommended practices in early intervention (DEC Task Force on Recommended Practices, 1993).

It is clear, however, that guidelines such as these can spark considerable debate about whether they do, in fact, constitute appropriate practice. Fowell and Lawton (1992), for example, argue that the guidelines for developmentally appropriate practice ignore the important role of learning theory and teacher-directed activities in early education. Other authors have similarly suggested that the guidelines, although appropriate, may not be sufficient for many children with disabilities (Carta, Schwartz, Atwater, & McConnell, 1991; Mallory, 1992; Wolery, Strain, & Bailey, 1992). Thus, we have another example of how a widely accepted set of practices may not be appropriate, or at least may be insufficient, for some young children.

Philosophical or Advocacy Movements

A final, but no less important, source of information about appropriate practices comes from philosophical or advocacy movements. These movements may or may not be based in research. Their most important defining characteristic is that they are rooted in the values of a group of individuals who then advocate for their implementation. The most influential philosophy on current concepts of quality in early intervention may be the movement toward family-centered approaches in service delivery. At the heart of this movement is the firm belief that families should be the ultimate decisionmakers in the planning and implementation of methods to facilitate their child's development and that services should be individually tailored to address the unique concerns and priorities of each family. It is further believed that early intervention services should go beyond child-level interventions to include services or resources that are supportive of the broader family unit. The strength and scope of influence of this advocacy movement is exemplified by the inclusion of family-centered concepts in the federal regulations governing early intervention services, as well as by the burgeoning of research related to family support and family-centered practices in the 1980s and 1990s.

Another example of an advocacy movement is the effort directed toward full inclusion in regular education programs for children with disabilities. Although research evidence is continually accumulating and being brought to bear on this question, the movement fundamentally rests on the assumption that all children with disabilities have the right to participate in public-funded educational and recreational activities with their typically developing peers.

Advocates of full inclusion would argue that we should not question whether inclusion is a good idea, but simply ask how we can make it work.

Philosophical and advocacy movements are an important influence in establishing recommended practices. They are often the driving force behind legislation, research, and position statements by professional organizations. Whether by themselves, or in concert with these other sources of influence, advocacy movements can have far-reaching effects on what is considered appropriate and effective service provision.

In applying philosophical principles to their daily work, however, early interventionists must consider the unique aspects of each situation they encounter. The importance of doing so is demonstrated aptly in a study conducted by Affleck, Tennen, Rowe, Roscher, and Walker (1989). The study involved mothers of high-risk infants who had spent time in a neonatal intensive care unit (NICU). Based upon principles of family-centered care and the movement toward providing support during transitions, the authors developed a hospital-to-home transition program. The goals of the program included helping mothers adapt to stresses of the transition, encouraging enjoyable and facilitative mother–infant interactions, and enhancing parents' self-concepts. The program consisted of weekly 2-hour home visits by a public health nurse for 15 weeks following discharge from the NICU. During these visits, the nurses listened to mothers' feelings and concerns, described typical and atypical development, observed and described infant behavior, engaged the mother in mutual problemsolving, demonstrated therapeutic and caregiving procedures, and helped prepare for future events.

In evaluating the effects of the program, Affleck et al. (1989) found that positive outcomes were observed for mothers who felt they needed the program. At the end of the transition program, these mothers showed an improved sense of competence, had perceptions of greater control, and demonstrated improved responsiveness to their infants. However, for mothers who did not feel they needed the program, but participated anyway, the program had a negative effect. These mothers experienced a reduced sense of competence at the conclusion of services, perceived themselves as having less control, and demonstrated less responsiveness to their infants. This study demonstrates that intervention based on recommended practices can not only be ineffective, but may have negative effects on some families. In actuality, a crucial element of family-centered care was neglected. The individual concerns and priorities of each family were not considered in the selection and implementation of services.

AN OVERVIEW OF RECOMMENDED PRACTICES

An overview of what are considered to be exemplary practices in early intervention is provided next. What follows is not an exhaustive survey of principles and practices, for indeed entire volumes (e.g., Bailey & Wolery, 1992; Meisels & Shonkoff, 1990) have already been devoted to that purpose. Rather, the intention here is to provide a brief summary of current trends and issues that have received much attention since the passage of PL 99-457. The practices discussed are those that apply to the work of early interventionists across the many disciplines represented in the field. In addition, these practices apply to almost all of the children and families participating in early intervention services. Although these practices are heralded by most as being critical to quality services, their implementation by programs and individual clinicians has often been met with great difficulty. Finally, even for these important issues, coverage is incomplete and readers are referred to the recommended readings found at the end of this volume.

Family-Centered Practices

Since the mid 1980s, the concept of family-centered services has probably received the most attention in the establishment of quality indicators for early intervention. The importance of including caregivers in the development and implementation of intervention plans for infants and preschoolers with disabilities has long been recognized. In the past, however, parent involvement has often been limited and interventions have been focused exclusively on the child. For example, parents were often asked to sign intervention plans that were developed for their children by professionals (McGonigel & Garland, 1988; Turnbull & Turnbull, 1986) or were trained by professionals to implement therapy or educational activities in the same manner as they would be in a clinic or classroom setting. Such notions of parent involvement, however, have been challenged (e.g., Foster, Berger, & McLean, 1981; Wright, Granger, & Sameroff, 1984), and new approaches have been offered.

Leaders in the field (Bailey, 1987; Bailey & Simeonsson, 1988; Dunst, Trivette, & Deal, 1988) now advocate for a family-centered approach in which the central role the family plays in the development of the child is fully recognized. In this approach, the family, rather than the child, is the unit of assessment and intervention, and the parents are the ultimate decisionmakers in identifying goals and determining intervention strategies.

Using a family-centered approach, the complex relationships among all members of the family, as well as the relationships between the family and the community, are recognized (Dunst et al., 1988). The child, nuclear family, extended family, friends, neighbors, and the larger community are all viewed as different levels of a complex, interconnected system (Bronfenbrenner, 1979). Changes at any level of the system are likely to have a direct or indirect effect on other levels of the system. Programming to intervene in the development of the child should take into consideration the possible impact of such programming on other family members. It should also take into consideration possible sources of support for or interference with such programming on the part of people or institutions outside the nuclear family. In short, the goal of a family-centered approach is to maintain or improve the well-being of the family unit as a whole.

A major tenet of family-centered service provision is recognition and acceptance of differences among families. Families vary in terms of the structure of the family unit, the roles and expectations for family members, the values upheld by the family, the ways they use external resources and support, and the nature and consistency of daily routines. Interventions must be tailored to fit the unique characteristics of each family if they are to be effective (Kjerland & Kovach, 1990). Furthermore, the values and functions of families should not be judged or challenged by professionals.

A family-centered approach upholds the belief that every family has strengths. Family strengths may not be readily recognized by professionals owing to their divergence from mainstream notions of what constitutes a strong family. Families may also be unable to employ the skills and knowledge they possess as a result of any number of societal factors, including unemployment, lack of educational opportunities, or scarcity of appropriate resources. The role of the professional is to recognize and emphasize family strengths and resources in developing and implementing interventions rather than concentrating on family needs and deficits.

Finally, a family-centered approach involves respect for the autonomy of the family. The family determines what its needs and priorities are, and its members are the ultimate decisionmakers at every level of service delivery. The family decides what is important for their child with a disability as well as what is important for other family members. The ways in which these priorities are met are also decided by the family. This includes the right to refuse or postpone services.

The major role of the professional employing a family-centered approach becomes that of resource and supporter of family priorities. The professional is responsible for assisting the family in identifying goals for intervention and providing information to family members to ensure that they are informed decisionmakers. Information may include: 1) results of child assessments, 2) resources available in the community or elsewhere, 3) types of service delivery available, 4) how to gain access to resources or other sources of information, and 5) the types of intervention activities and strategies that may help them accomplish their goals. Thus, the professional provides a number of options from which a family may choose. The professional is also responsible for supporting the family's decisions. No doubt, this can be challenging when parents' decisions are not congruent with professionals' concepts of appropriate practice.

Child-Level Practices

Although much focus has been placed on issues and considerations in working with families, models and procedures for working with children have also undergone frequent review and change. As this book goes to press in 1993, there is considerable diversity in what professionals believe to be appropriate child-level interventions, and some significant controversies exist. Nevertheless, there is a high level of agreement on several key assumptions.

First is a recognition of the unique nature of each child's abilities, needs, and resources. The characteristics of children served in early intervention programs are highly diverse. The implication of this fact is that each child needs an individualized program of services. In order to individualize, a comprehensive interdisciplinary assessment is needed, and a monitoring system must be in place to determine whether services are effective. Parents should be involved in this assessment process and can help to ensure that programs and interventions fit their child's individual needs and styles as well as parent priorities.

Second, all children should be provided extensive opportunities to engage in developmentally appropriate activities. This requires an understanding of the rapid growth that occurs during the early childhood years and knowledge about the kinds of activities children of various developmental ages enjoy and can do. Of special significance is a recognition of the important role of social development and social relationships in the life of the child (Guralnick, 1990; Strain, 1990). We also know that children learn from concrete experiences in which they have frequent opportunities to be engaged with stimulating and appropriate materials and to receive meaningful feedback on their behavior.

Finally, researchers and practitioners alike are realizing more fully the importance of using play and the other activities that naturally occur throughout the day as the appropriate context for teaching and therapy. Because young children learn best when activities are meaningful for them, strategies such as incidental teaching, functional skills training, and integrated therapy are being advocated (McWilliam, 1992). Although these and other strategies differ in some ways, all are based on the assumption of teaching in the context of ongoing activities and routines, and, when possible, using children's interests and initiations as the context for teaching and therapy.

Inclusion in the Mainstream

Another key area of recommended practice is that of inclusion. Legislation, research, and advocacy movements suggest that, to the maximum extent possible, young children with disabilities ought to be provided opportunities to play and interact with typically developing children and to participate in the activities usually experienced by all young children. Beyond the fundamental argument that inclusion is a desirable social goal, there appear to be several other important reasons for its acceptance. For example, it is likely that the early years are the easiest time to promote inclusion because young children have not yet developed biases about children who differ from them. Experience in typical early childhood settings with typically developing peers ought to help children learn skills and behaviors appropriate to those settings and increase the chances of successful inclusion in the future. Research clearly demonstrates that inclusive settings have a positive effect on the social behavior of young children with disabilities (Buysse & Bailey, 1993), without adversely affecting their development in other domains.

It should be recognized, however, that inclusion presents specific challenges and concerns for many parents of young children with disabilities. Research has consistently shown that, although most parents believe that normalized experiences are important for their children, they are also concerned that their children might not receive the specialized help that could be available in special education settings. They may also feel that their child's inclusion is not well accepted by parents of typically developing children. Thus, early childhood interventionists should realize that families will want to be a part of the process for determining appropriate placements for their child and may need frequent opportunities to observe and determine whether an inclusive placement is working for their child.

Coordinated Service Delivery

Many children and families participating in early intervention require services from a number of professionals with diverse disciplinary backgrounds. Pediatricians and other medical specialists, social workers, special educators, speech-language pathologists, physical therapists, occupational therapists, audiologists, psychologists, nutritionists, and other professionals may be involved in addressing the concerns and priorities of families participating in early intervention. The constellation of professionals working with a child and family will be individually constituted and in accordance with both the characteristics of the child and the priorities established by the family. In some cases, the professionals may work together as a team within a single agency but, for other families, the professionals with whom they work may be dispersed across various agencies within the community. In either situation, it is important that the professionals working with a child and family coordinate their efforts to provide comprehensive and consistent service delivery that is aimed toward the accomplishment of the family's identified priorities. Failure to do so may result in fragmented or conflicting services that may be more stressful for families than they are beneficial.

The need for coordination and collaboration among professionals and agencies is well recognized in the legislation, as these words occur repeatedly throughout the regulations of PL 99-457 and PL 102-119. However, as previously stated, compliance with these mandates does not guarantee that appropriate or effective services are being offered. A variety of methods for conducting assessments, planning interventions, and providing services have been offered to guard against the fragmentation of services and attempt to ensure a coordinated effort for meeting family priorities. These range from the individual assessment and intervention planning for children in a single program (e.g., Linder, 1990, 1993; McWilliam, 1992) to the formation and functioning of interagency coordinating councils (Swan & Morgan, 1993).

At the heart of the many methods and guidelines offered is the concept of communication and cooperation among professionals. Only through ongoing awareness of the objectives and methods employed by all professionals involved with a child and family, in conjunction with the pooling of their resources and knowledge, can truly comprehensive and effective services be offered. To this end, Part H of IDEA stipulates that a service coordinator should be identified for each child and family. Although this measure may improve the quality of services that might otherwise be proffered, its effectiveness is limited without the committed effort of all professionals working with a child and family to communicate and work together toward a common set of goals.

SUMMARY

The passing of federal and state laws for services to infants, toddlers, and preschoolers with disabilities has eased the need for proving the effectiveness of early intervention. At the same time, these legal mandates have resulted in an increasing number of programs for infants and preschoolers and, with them, a sense of increased urgency to determine the best methods for providing these new services. The establishment of recommended practices, however, is a complicated and continuous process.

In this chapter, we have discussed how legislation, research, professional organizations, and philosophical or advocacy movements have influenced our definitions of appropriate and effective service provision. A growing body of empirical research in early intervention has provided us with the necessary support for recommending some practices over others in early intervention. Other practices, however, are recommended on the basis of current values in the field and the values of the United States as a whole. Family-centered service is a case in point. Alhough research in such areas is well under way, advocacy based on values has clearly preceded empirical support for these practices. This phenomenon, however, is not peculiar to early intervention, and the lack of scientific evidence should not deter professionals from incorporating such socially validated practices into their work with children and families (Peters & Heron, 1993).

Although the search for quality indicators has resulted in an impressive number of generally agreed upon principles and practices, the search has also been humbling. There is increasing recognition of the many questions that remain unanswered. For every practice that has been recommended, there seem to be exceptions. No practice appears to be appropriate or effective for all children and all families. This recognition led to the abandonment of the term "best practice" by the DEC task force (DEC Task Force on Recommended Practices, 1993) and its replacement of that term with "recommended practice" and "indicators of quality." In fact, premature claims of "best practice" are being cautioned against in all areas of special education (Peters & Heron, 1993).

The development and dissemination of recommended practices is important and even vital to the field of early intervention. These guidelines represent the accumulated wisdom and experience of a large number of researchers and practitioners and, as such, should be made available and put to good use. At the same time, it is incumbent upon every teacher, therapist, and other professional to carefully consider the unique characteristics of and circumstances surrounding every child and family they serve in deciding what is appropriate and effective.

REFERENCES

Affleck, G., Tennen, H., Rowe, J., Roscher, B., & Walker, L. (1989). Effects of formal support on mothers' adaptation to the hospital-to-home transition of high-risk infants: The benefits and costs of helping. *Child Development, 60,* 488–501.

Bailey, D.B. (1987). Collaborative goal-setting with families: Resolving differences in values and priorities for services. *Topics in Early Childhood Special Education, 7*(2), 59–71.

Bailey, D.B. (1991). Issues and perspectives on family assessment. *Infants and Young Children, 4*(1), 26–34.

Bailey, D.B., & Simeonsson, R.J. (Eds.). (1988). *Family assessment in early intervention.* Columbus, OH: Charles E. Merrill.

Bailey, D.B., & Wolery, M. (1992). *Teaching infants and preschoolers with disabilities.* Columbus, OH: Charles E. Merrill.

Bredekamp, S. (1986). *Developmentally appropriate practice.* Washington, DC: National Association for the Education of Young Children.

Bredekamp, S., & Rosegrant, T. (Eds.). (1992). *Reaching potentials: Appropriate curriculum and assessment for young children, Vol. 1.* Washington, DC: National Association for the Education of Young Children.

Bronfenbrenner, U. (1979). *The ecology of human development: Experiments by nature and design.* Cambridge: Harvard University Press.

Buysse, V., & Bailey, D.B. (1993). Behavioral and developmental outcomes in young children with disabilities in integrated and segregated settings: A review of comparative studies. *Journal of Special Education, 26*(4), 434–461.

Carta, J.J., Schwartz, I.S., Atwater, J.B., & McConnell, S.R. (1991). Developmentally appropriate practice: Appraising its usefulness for young children with disabilities. *Topics in Early Childhood Special Education, 11*(1), 1–20.

Casto, G., & Mastropieri, M.A. (1986). The efficacy of early intervention programs: A meta-analysis. *Exceptional Children, 52,* 417–424.

Cole, K.N., Mills, P.E., Dale, P.S., & Jenkins, J.R. (1991). Effects of preschool integration for children with disabilities. *Exceptional Children, 58,* 36–45.

DEC Task Force on Recommended Practices. (1993). *DEC recommended practices: Indicators of quality in programs for infants and young children with special needs and their families.* Reston, VA: Council for Exceptional Children.

Dunst, C., & Rheingrover, R.M. (1981). An analysis of the efficacy of infant intervention programs with organically handicapped children. *Evaluation and Program Planning, 4,* 287–323.

Dunst, C.J., Trivette, C.M., & Deal, A.G. (1988). *Enabling and empowering families: Principles and guidelines for practice.* Cambridge, MA: Brookline Books.

Education of the Handicapped Act Amendments of 1986. PL 99-457. (October 8, 1986). Title 20, U.S.C. 1400 et seq: *U.S. Statutes at Large, 100,* 1145–1177.

Foster, M., Berger, M., & McLean, M. (1981). Rethinking a good idea: A reassessment of parent involvement. *Topics in Early Childhood Special Education, 1*(3), 55–65.

Fowell, N., & Lawton, J. (1992). An alternative view of appropriate practice in early childhood education. *Early Childhood Research Quarterly, 7,* 53–73.

Guralnick, M.J. (1990). Social competence and early intervention. *Journal of Early Intervention, 14,* 3–14.

Haskins, R. (1989). Beyond metaphor: The efficacy of early childhood education. *American Psychologist, 44,* 274–282.

Hyson, M.C., Hirsh-Pasek, K., & Rescorla, L. (1990). The Classroom Practices Inventory: An observation instrument based on NAEYC's guidelines for developmentally appropriate practices for 4- and 5-year-old children. *Early Childhood Research Quarterly, 5,* 475–494.

Individuals with Disabilities Education Act Amendments of 1991, PL102-119. (October 7, 1991). Title 20, U.S.C. 1400 et seq: *U.S. Statutes at Large, 105,* 587–608.

Infant Health and Development Program. (1990). Enhancing the outcomes of low-birthweight, premature infants. *Journal of the American Medical Association, 263,* 3035–3042.

Kjerland, L., & Kovach, J. (1990). Family–staff collaboration for tailored infant assessment. In E.D. Gibbs & D.M. Teti (Eds.), *Interdisciplinary assessment of infants: A guide for early intervention professionals* (pp. 287–297). Baltimore: Paul H. Brookes Publishing Co.

Lazar, I., Darlington, R., Murray, H., Royce, I., & Snipper, A. (1992). Lasting effects of early education: A report from the Consortium for Longitudinal Studies. *Monographs of the Society for Research in Child Development, 47*(2–3, Serial No. 195).

Linder, T.W. (1990). *Transdisciplinary play-based assessment: A functional approach to working with young children.* Baltimore: Paul H. Brookes Publishing Co.

Linder, T.W. (1993). *Transdisciplinary play-based intervention: Guidelines for developing a meaningful curriculum for young children.* Baltimore: Paul H. Brookes Publishing Co.

Mallory, B.L. (1992). Is it always appropriate to be developmental? Convergent models for early intervention practice. *Topics in Early Childhood Special Education, 11*(4), 1–12.

McGonigel, M.J., & Garland, C.W. (1988). The individualized family service plan and the early intervention team: Team and family issues and recommended practices. *Infants and Young Children, 1*(1), 10–21.

McWilliam, R.A. (1992). *Family-centered intervention planning: A routines-based approach.* Tucson, AZ: Communication Skill Builders.

Meisels, S.J., & Shonkoff, J.P. (Eds.). (1990). *Handbook of early childhood intervention.* Cambridge: Cambridge University Press.

National Association for the Education of Young Children. (1984). *Accreditation criteria and procedures of the National Academy of Early Childhood Programs.* Washington, DC: Author.

Ottenbacher, K.J. (1989). Statistical conclusion validity of early intervention research with handicapped children. *Exceptional Children, 55,* 534–540.

Peters, M.T., & Heron, T.E. (1993). When the best is not good enough: An examination of best practice. *Journal of Special Education, 26*(4). 371–385.

Shonkoff, J.P., & Hauser-Cram, P. (1987). Early intervention for disabled infants and their families: A quantitative analysis. *Pediatrics, 80,* 650–658.

Simeonsson, R.J., Cooper, D.H., & Scheiner, A.P. (1982). A review and analysis of the effectiveness of early intervention programs. *Pediatrics, 69,* 635–641.

Strain, P.S. (1990). LRE for preschool children with handicaps: What we know, what we should be doing. *Journal of Early Intervention, 14,* 291–296.

Swan, W.W., & Morgan, J.L. (1993). *Collaborating for comprehensive services for young children and their families: The local interagency coordinating council.* Baltimore: Paul H. Brookes Publishing Co.

Turnbull, A.P., & Turnbull, H.R. (1986). *Families, professionals, and exceptionality: A special partnership.* Columbus, OH: Charles E. Merrill.

Warren, S.F., & Kaiser, A.P. (1988). Research in early language intervention. In S.L. Odom & M.B. Karnes (Eds.), *Early intervention for infants and children with handicaps: An empirical base* (pp. 89–108). Baltimore: Paul H. Brookes Publishing Co.

Wolery, M., Strain, P.S., & Bailey, D.B. (1992). Applying the framework of developmentally appropriate practice to children with special needs. In S. Bredekamp & T. Rosegrant (Eds.), *Reaching potentials: Appropriate curriculum and assessment for young Children, Vol. 1* (pp. 92–111). Washington, DC: National Association for the Education of Young Children.

Wright, J., Granger, R., & Sameroff, A. (1984). Parental acceptance and developmental handicap. In J. Blacher (Ed.), *Severely handicapped young children and their families: Research in review* (pp. 51–90). Orlando: Academic Press.

Chapter 2

Real-World Challenges to Achieving Quality

P.J. McWilliam

T he work of an early interventionist can be extremely rewarding, but it is not without challenges. Legislation, agency policies, research, professional organizations, and advocacy movements provide early interventionists with important guidelines for conducting work with children and families and ensuring that quality services are rendered. These guidelines or recommended practices, however, are of limited help to early interventionists when confronted with the frequently complex situations they encounter in their daily work. Variations in work environments, available resources, children's individual characteristics, their families' values and lifestyles, multiple and conflicting job requirements, the attitudes of colleagues, and the interventionist's personal values and beliefs will affect his or her decisions and ability to implement recommended practices. Even in the best programs, early interventionists are often faced with situations that have no easy answers.

Most recommended practices are qualified by the importance of individualizing services for each child and family. Although the concept of individualized services may sound obvious and simple, applying this concept in real-life situations can be exceedingly difficult. Even so, the ability to make sound decisions based on the unique circumstances surrounding each child and family is the key to achieving quality. The purpose of this chapter is to acknowledge the difficulties inherent in applying recommended practices due to the less than ideal circumstances in which the work of many early interventionists takes place. In the sections that follow, a number of factors and challenges are presented that may influence the decisionmaking of early interventionists and, at times, pose

21

as barriers to the achievement of quality services. These are the
following:

- The collision of principles
- The structure of communities
- The support of others
- Early interventionists' job requirements
- Professional skills and knowledge
- Personal values and beliefs

THE COLLISION OF PRINCIPLES

Perhaps the most difficult situations faced by professionals are those
in which recommended practices are pitted against each other. This
occurs when one principle or practice seems to be in direct viola-
tion of another. The most obvious examples are those in which
family-centered approaches result in less than desirable interventions for children. Suppose, for example, that a 3-year-old child is
showing significant delays in language development. The parents
express concern about the child's delays in expressive speech, and
these concerns are considered valid by the intervention team. In
keeping with recommended practices, the team uses incidental
teaching strategies and integrated therapy in the classroom and en-
courages similar, nondirective strategies in the home environment.
When these strategies are presented to the child's parents, however,
they do not agree. What the parents want is traditional, pull-out
therapy provided by a licensed speech-language pathologist. Ac-
quiescing to the parents' wishes would run counter to what the
intervention team might believe to be superior methods for facilitating language development. However, undue coercion of the family to accept the professionals' preferred methods of intervention
would violate basic principles of a family-centered approach. There
are no quick answers for handling such situations, yet the dilemma
must be resolved.

Early interventionists who spend the greater part of their professional education learning strategies for assessing and facilitating
children's development in their areas of expertise assume that they
will be called upon to share their knowledge and use their skills in
their work with children and families. In practice, however, there
are families who may not agree with professionals' perceptions of
what their child needs, may not follow through with professional
recommendations, or may decide upon strategies for intervening with
their child that are not in line with recommended practices. A family-

centered approach dictates that families should define their own priorities and early interventionists should support them in their decisions for themselves and their children. But when such differences of opinion exist, child progress may be reduced if family-centered practices are followed. Resolving such dilemmas is often not easy and requires thoughtful consideration and sensitive handling by professionals.

THE STRUCTURE OF COMMUNITIES

The characteristics of communities in which early intervention takes place may significantly influence how services are provided to children and families. One of the most obvious factors is the quantity and quality of services and resources available to families in the community. The need for a comprehensive and coordinated service delivery system is mentioned in nearly every listing of recommended practices. This includes the availability of resources to support families in meeting the priorities they define for themselves and providing options from which families may choose. In communities with limited resources, the support required for many family needs may not be available or the choices may be severely reduced.

Employment, financial assistance, specialized child care, transportation, medical or therapeutic equipment, and respite care are just a few of the many resources that a family may want or need in adjusting to life with a child with disabilities. If these services are not available in the community, the impact of overall services to a child and family may be diminished. In some cases, services may be available but they are fragmented, scattered among a variety of agencies, and difficult to obtain. The added stresses of locating and securing resources may reduce the overall effectiveness of service delivery.

The structure and functioning of services within programs also may affect an early interventionist's ability to implement recommended practices. More often than not, early intervention programs offer only one type of service. In the United States, the predominant model of service delivery for infants and toddlers (i.e., birth to 3 years of age) is home-based services; whereas, preschoolers (i.e., 3- to 5-year-olds) are more often served through classroom-based models. The extent to which the predominant model of a program is supplemented by other types of services is usually determined by the availability of additional funding. In rural areas and communities with limited budgets for early intervention, supplementary services may not exist. If additional or alternative services are desired by the family, they must be secured through other public agencies or through the private sector—often at the personal expense of the family.

Recommended practices stress the importance of individualizing services for children and families, offering choices from which families may choose, and coordinating services they receive. Working in programs or communities where few options are available and where existing services are fragmented poses a significant challenge for the early interventionist with good intentions. For example, how can one work toward inclusion when the predominant model of a program is a segregated classroom and all of the resources of that program are tied up in the operation of the classroom? After all, we know that successful outcomes for children in inclusive environments require much more than mere placement of the child in an environment with typically developing peers (e.g., Hundert & Houghton, 1992). However, suppose that a program's predominant model is inclusive education and all services are offered within community-based child care centers. If a family feels that its child is not benefiting from such a program and wants more intensive or structured intervention, how can we honor family preferences? Or suppose a child turns 3 years old and, by state law, becomes the responsibility of a different agency. If the receiving agency offers only classroom-based services, but the child would be better served through home-based services as he or she had been receiving, how can this situation be handled? Although there are no simple answers to such questions, creative problemsolving can lead to acceptable solutions.

THE SUPPORT OF OTHERS

As mentioned above, it is exceedingly rare for a child and family to receive all of their services from a single professional. It is far more common for a number of professionals to be involved in providing early intervention services for each child and family. Their involvement may be distributed across time, or they may provide services at the same time. Furthermore, the professionals working with a family may be affiliated with the same agency, work out of different agencies, or both. Thus, it might be said that early intervention is like a team sport, and the ability of one player to engage in recommended practices is determined, at least in part, by the attitudes and performance of other members.

The successful execution of many practices recommended for

classroom-based programs requires the joint efforts of a number of professionals and paraprofessionals. Inclusive education, incidental teaching, and integrated therapy are among such practices. When teachers, classroom aides, therapists, and administrators support the implementation of these practices and have the necessary skills, the results are usually positive. If, however, one or more members of the group is not in agreement or actively resists the implementation of the practice, the burden on the other members is increased and the chances of success may be lessened.

Interestingly, a recent nationwide survey (McWilliam, 1992) showed that the degree to which practitioners valued and implemented six recommended practices for center-based programs was significantly related to their professional discipline background. All of the six recommended practices included on the survey were related to integrated, coordinated, and contextually based or functional interventions. These practices were as follows:

- Therapy is conducted within the child's classroom.
- Other children are present during therapy.
- Interactions during therapy are child-initiated.
- The predominant role of the therapist is as consultant to classroom staff.
- Child goals have immediate, functional relevance (i.e., not prerequisite skills).
- Therapy is provided within the context of regular classroom routines.

The 773 respondents were asked which practices they typically used for various types of children, as well as what they considered to be ideal practices. Although respondents from all disciplines indicated that the more integrated practices were worthwhile, the special educators viewed them as significantly more worthwhile than did the other three disciplines (i.e., occupational therapy, speech-language therapy, and physical therapy) and used them more often in their daily work with children. In fact, the discipline background of respondents accounted for 40%–50% of the variance in ratings of actual and ideal practices. In contrast, the characteristics of children with whom the practices might be used accounted for only 10% of the variance in responses. Thus, the results of McWilliam's (1992) survey indicate that: 1) professionals from the various disciplines represented in early intervention differ significantly in their perspectives on what constitutes quality intervention in center-based programs, and 2) the discipline background of professionals may be more influential in determining whether recommended practices are used than the individual characteristics of the children for whom interventions are being developed.

The degree to which various team members will uphold a family-centered philosophy and engage in practices that are consistent with this philosophy also may be influenced by discipline background. In another survey of early intervention professionals (Bailey, Palsha, & Simeonsson, 1991), respondents were asked to indicate the relative importance of the various roles in their work with children and families. Half of the roles listed on the questionnaire were related to working with families and the other half were roles related to working with children. Although the majority of respondents rated more roles related to working with families as important (48%) or rated an equal number of child and family roles (22%), significant differences were found among disciplines. In particular, nurses and social workers endorsed more family roles than did educators or medical allied health professionals (i.e., speech-language pathologists, occupational therapists, physical therapists).

Together, the McWilliam (1992) and Bailey et al. (1991) surveys provide evidence that recommended practices for early intervention may not be equally valued or supported by all professionals. Early interventionists come from a variety of discipline backgrounds, and each instills in its members a different set of beliefs about how services should be provided. Coordination of services may be difficult when team members do not share a common philosophy about how their work should proceed. Strong leadership on the part of an administrator or supervisor may help to alleviate conflicts, enhance team cohesion, and facilitate collaboration with other agencies. Unfortunately, effective leadership is not always available (Johnson et al., 1992).

EARLY INTERVENTIONISTS' JOB REQUIREMENTS

The size of caseloads, range of responsibilities, and job flexibility of professionals may or may not be under their own control or even under the control of those who provide direct supervision. They are, however, often factors in professionals' ability to implement recommended practices. Time is often a major issue. For example, large caseloads or rural communities that require excessive travel may limit the time necessary to provide the best services possible for a given child or family. In order to distribute time fairly among those to whom they are responsible, early interventionists might not make telephone calls that would help, give a child a few additional minutes of individual attention, or spend time making extra home visits to a family. In fact, in a recent survey on job satisfaction (Kontos & File, 1992), early interventionists indicated that the possibility of lowered caseloads and smaller staff–child ratios might entice them to take new jobs.

The regulations of individual programs, as well as local and state bureaucratic requirements, also may pose barriers to the implementation of recommended practices. Barriers may be in the form of the scheduling of services, the types of services permitted, the type and amount of paperwork required, fee schedules, or any other number of rules imposed by those governing early intervention services. Suppose, for example, that an early interventionist works in a clinic-based or hospital-based outpatient program. The children and families served by the program always come to the center, but this interventionist realizes that he or she could better serve some families by providing an occasional home visit or by visiting a child care center. The interventionist's efforts to improve the quality of his or her services, however, may be thwarted if the administrator of the clinic denies the request to make these visits or the clinic's policies and procedures make no allowances for the reimbursement of travel expenses for such purposes.

Another factor that may affect the extent to which recommended practices may be implemented is the reimbursement policies of public and private insurance agencies. For example, some agencies that reimburse for speech-language therapy, occupational therapy, or physical therapy may only be willing to reimburse for time that the therapist spends with the child. Other time spent meeting the child's needs, such as team meetings and meetings with the parents, may not qualify as reimbursable hours.

PL 99-457 stipulates that Part H funds may be used only to pay for services if funds are not available from other public or private sources. These other sources are typically Medicaid and private health insurance agencies. Medicaid coverage varies from state to state, and each private health insurance agency has its own set of regulations. The rules for reimbursement of services by these agencies stipulate services that will be covered, where services can be provided, who provides specific services, and the frequency of service delivery or a maximum dollar limit of reimbursable services (Fox, Wicks, McManus, & Newacheck, 1992). Unfortunately, the types and amount of reimbursable services might not agree with recommended practices. For example, services are often only reimbursable if they are provided under the supervision of a physician or in a hospital or clinic setting (Fox et al., 1992). In programs and states with tight budgets, it is easy to see how the regulations of insurance agencies might influence practices.

PROFESSIONAL SKILLS AND KNOWLEDGE

The knowledge, skills, and accumulated experiences of each professional obviously influence his or her ability to provide quality services. Unfortunately, many early interventionists do not have the arsenal of knowledge and skills necessary in this field of work. For example, a statewide survey of colleges and universities in California (Hanson & Lovett, 1992) was conducted to determine the extent to which early intervention content was included in degree-granting programs offered by 11 different disciplines. The survey revealed that only 11% of the programs offered a specialized training program in early intervention. Only 18% reported having specific early intervention courses, and 42% indicated that early intervention content was infused into other coursework. In fact, 33% of the programs responding to the survey reported that they offered no training and, of these programs, 78% said they had no plans to add early intervention content to their existing curricula.

The Hanson and Lovett (1992) survey also requested information on the topics that were addressed when early intervention content was included in coursework. Although substantial variability was found across and within disciplines, the majority of early intervention content was child-focused and included topics such as typical and atypical child development or disabling and at-risk conditions and their effects on development. For the most part, topics related to working with families, cultural diversity, or team processes were given scant attention. The results of this California survey are mirrored by the results of a similar nationwide survey of colleges and universities that was conducted by Bailey and his colleagues (Bailey, Simeonsson, Yoder, & Huntington, 1990).

Given the relative dearth of knowledge and skills gained through preservice training programs, it is understandable that early interventionists may not feel competent to take on certain roles in early intervention or to perceive those roles as valuable. This seems especially true for roles related to working with families (Bailey et al., 1991). Issues and strategies related to inclusive education, naturalistic teaching, transitions, developmentally appropriate practice, coordinated service delivery, and other recommended practices in early intervention may also be unfamiliar and not valued by many professionals entering the field. Some may acquire new philosophies, skills, and knowledge on a learn-as-you-go basis after entering the workplace. For others, however, recommended practices in early intervention might conflict with what they were taught in their academic program or they might just be reluctant to learn and try out new methods. After all, it is difficult to abandon previously learned principles and practices and harder still to engage in unfamiliar practices.

PERSONAL VALUES AND BELIEFS

In addition to the external challenges faced in implementing recommended practices, decisions about services to children and families are influenced by personal values and beliefs. These are perhaps the most difficult to acknowledge and confront because they are the most invisible to the individual. Most people have fairly strong opinions about the importance of education, the qualities of a strong family, how children learn, the skills children need to succeed, and so forth. Values and opinions of individuals are shaped by their own personal histories, from how they were reared as children to the influences inherent in their professional educations. The beliefs that are held by each individual are often so well-ingrained that they may easily be mistaken for truths. The fact that colleagues, family, or friends hold the same or similar beliefs only adds to one's convictions.

Perhaps this is why it is often rewarding for early interventionists to work with children whose families are most similar to themselves. It is when they work with families whose values are significantly divergent from middle-class norms that they are most often challenged to question what is right or wrong and what is just different. Only when one understands or at least accepts the unique values and priorities of each family and designs interventions based on their perspective can a true family-centered approach be implemented (Hanson, Lynch, & Wayman, 1990; Vincent, 1992). Understanding one's own personal values assists in this task.

The blinding impact of our own values on our ability to provide quality service was pointed out by Lisbeth J. Vincent (1992) in her 1991 keynote address at the annual Division for Early Childhood of the Council of Exceptional Children conference in St. Louis, Missouri. She told of a family, newly arrived in Los Angeles from El Salvador, with an 18-month-old son with Down syndrome. The family found shelter in a one-room garage with a dirt floor and no running water or cooking facilities. The child was brought to the attention of an early intervention program in the area, and the family began receiving services. In addition to interventions for the child, the professionals found furniture, clothes, and extra food for the family and started to find public housing. Although initially pleased with the services provided by the program and eager to participate in activities, over time the family began to withdraw until all contact was stopped. Through the good fortune of a caring professional on the staff, the mystery was eventually unveiled. The family was proud of its success in coming to America. The dirt-floor garage was a vast improvement over the previous living arrangement in El Salvador. The continuous "helping" provided by the early intervention professionals was interpreted by the family as a message that they were "not good enough." Rather than face this judgment, they withdrew from the program.

The field of early intervention is only beginning to acknowledge and understand how interventionists' personal beliefs about services and their own values about children's and families' needs may prevent them from understanding what families want and, thus, may reduce the effectiveness of services. Every family involved in early intervention services has a different set of values and beliefs that deviates to some extent from the values of the professionals who are responsible for providing services. Discovering what a family's values are is only part of the challenge in achieving quality. Perhaps the greatest challenge to professionals is understanding their own values. For example, why do we think it is so important for children to sleep in their own beds? Why do we so disparage the use of baby walkers? How independent should a 3-year-old really be? Why are we aghast at the thought of a bottle-fed 2-year-old or a nursing 3-year-old? Is spanking abusive? More important, are parents judged harshly when their perspectives on such topics are different from those of service providers?

SUMMARY

This chapter has illustrated some of the challenges and barriers that early interventionists may face in attempting to incorporate recommended practices in their daily work with children and families. High-quality early intervention services require resources that may or may not be available in many of the communities in which services are offered. Services for children and families may be severely restricted or fragmented, and agencies may be unwilling to collaborate with one another. Other team members may not be aware of or support recommended practices. Job requirements or bureaucratic red tape may prevent the execution of preferred strategies for working with children and families. The educational background of interventionists may not have prepared them to engage in recommended practices. Finally, discordance between the values and lifestyles of professionals and those of families may interfere with effective communication and, hence, the delivery of meaningful services. This is reality and, if early interventionists are to deliver quality services to children and families, they must be adequately prepared to handle situations that may arise in less than ideal circumstances.

REFERENCES

Bailey, D.B., Palsha, S.A., & Simeonsson, R.J. (1991). Professional skills, concerns, and perceived importance of work with families in early intervention. *Exceptional Children, 58,* 156–165.

Bailey, D.B., Simeonsson, R.J., Yoder, D.E., & Huntington, G.S. (1990). Preparing professionals to serve infants and toddlers with handicaps and their families: An integrative analysis across eight disciplines. *Exceptional Children, 57,* 26–35.

Education of the Handicapped Act Amendments of 1986. PL 99-457. (October 8, 1986). Title 20, U.S.C. 1400 et seq: *U.S. Statutes at Large, 100,* 1145–1177.

Fox, H.B., Wicks, L.B., McManus, M.A., & Newacheck, P.W. (1992). Public and private health insurance for early intervention services. *Journal of Early Intervention, 16,* 109–122.

Hanson, M.J., & Lovett, D. (1992). Personnel preparation for early interventionists: A cross-disciplinary survey. *Journal of Early Intervention, 16,* 123–135.

Hanson, M.J., Lynch, E.W., & Wayman, K.I. (1990). Honoring the cultural diversity of families when gathering data. *Topics in Early Childhood Special Education, 10*(1), 112–131.

Hundert, J., & Houghton, A. (1992). Promoting social interaction of children with disabilities in integrated preschools: A failure to generalize. *Exceptional Children, 58,* 311–320.

Johnson, L.J., Kilgo, J., Cook, M.J., Hammitte, D.J., Beauchamp, K., & Finn, D. (1992). The skills needed by early intervention administrators/supervisors: A study across six states. *Journal of Early Intervention, 16,* 136–145.

Kontos, S., & File, N. (1992). Conditions of employment, job satisfaction, and job commitment among early intervention personnel. *Journal of Early Intervention, 16,* 155–165.

McWilliam, R.A. (1992). *Predictors of service delivery models in center-based early intervention.* Doctoral dissertation, University of North Carolina at Chapel Hill (UMI# 9302548).

Vincent, L.J. (1992). Families and early intervention: Diversity and competence. *Journal of Early Intervention, 16,* 166–172.

SECTION II

STORIES OF CHILDREN, FAMILIES, AND PROFESSIONALS

This section features a collection of stories about professionals working in early intervention. The first 15 cases provide examples of early interventionists struggling to apply recommended practices. Some of the stories are told by widely recognized leaders in the field, while others are told by professionals whose names are unfamiliar outside of their own communities. Many of the stories describe professionals in confusing situations, and the "right" thing to do is anything but clear-cut. Despite their uncertainty, these professionals are willing to try. Even when they feel confident about what should be done, they often face barriers that circumvent the execution of their plans. Although not always completely satisfied with the outcomes of their work, these professionals show a willingness to adhere to principles of recommended practices and to learn from their mistakes. Perhaps most inspiring are the stories of professionals who become aware of the influence their own personal values can have on the decisions they make in their work with children and families.

For students, these case studies offer a realistic picture of the types of situations they may some day face and forewarn them about the complexities and challenges inherent in direct service. These glimpses of real life may also help students to gain a better perspective on the usefulness of acquiring more theoretical and technical knowledge. For seasoned professionals, case studies are also a rich source of learning. Traditional workshop instruction and professional readings provide theoretical knowledge, facts, and technical skills devoid of context. The professional is expected to incorporate or apply such information to his or her direct service work independently. Stories of early intervention with which they can identify may serve as a bridge between theory and practice in that they demonstrate how others have applied knowledge and skills in real life.

Cases 16–21 in the collection serve a slightly different purpose. Unlike the other cases, they do not have endings. Instead, the reader is provided with the opportunity to decide what the professionals depicted in the cases should do. As pointed out elsewhere (McWilliam, 1992), very few early interventionists have ever received formal training in procedures for analyzing complex situations and making sound decisions based on the analyses, and yet the complex nature of early intervention demands that professionals have these skills if quality services are to be provided. Interventionists in every discipline must be able to pull from their accumulated repertoire the principles, knowledge, and skills that apply to a particular situation and use them to arrive at well-reasoned courses of action.

Instructional strategies based on the use of unsolved case situations have been used for teaching problemsolving and decisionmaking skills in a number of fields as diverse as business (Christensen & Hanson, 1987), reading instruction (Rasinski, 1989), organizational communication (Kreps & Lederman, 1985), nursing (Johnson & Purvis, 1987), political science (Lee, 1983), and pediatric psychopharmacology (Jackson, 1985). The potential benefits of these methods for training early interventionists have also been realized (McWilliam, 1992). Readers are encouraged to use the unsolved cases in this last section to develop and practice their own problemsolving and decisionmaking skills. A brief guide for decisionmaking is offered below to assist readers in their efforts.

- **Identify the problem.** Think carefully about the situation. Is there really a problem? Try to consider the situation from the perspectives of the various people involved in the situation. If a problem does exist, whose problem is it really? Does everyone involved perceive the same problem? Take the time to write down what the problem is or what must be changed or resolved to improve the situation. Be specific. This is a critical aspect of good decisionmaking.
- **Analyze contributing factors.** Consider the various factors that may have contributed to the present situation. What actions or circumstances occurred in the past or present that may have

caused the problem or are currently maintaining a less than desirable situation? In addition to overt actions and the quality or scope of available resources, take into consideration the possible contributions of the characters' cultural backgrounds, personal values or beliefs, and emotional needs. However, be cautious not to limit your analysis of the situation to the actions and feelings of one person in the case. Finally, guard against hasty conclusions regarding causation. Be open-minded and ask yourself if what you think is true might have an alternative explanation.

- **Identify available options.** It is often tempting to arrive at a solution quickly and begin taking action. This is especially true when you feel confident in your knowledge and skills related to the problem at hand. But, even in situations where a solution seems all too obvious, take some time to seriously consider alternative methods of dealing with the situation. Akin to the process of brainstorming, think broadly in identifying alternatives and don't dismiss any option until it has been fully explored. Remember, there are very few absolute rights or wrongs in our work. Although the first solution you think of is often what you will ultimately adopt, this is not always the case. Besides, if time is taken to develop alternatives, you will have available a Plan B and a Plan C if Plan A isn't successful. Developing a list of alternative solutions or courses of action to follow should also be good practice for ensuring that families have choices available to them in intervention planning.

- **Consider the potential outcomes of each option.** After a list of alternatives is completed, review each one in turn and consider its potential advantages and disadvantages. Think in terms of both the short-term and long-term consequences of following each course of action. What are the financial, emotional, time, or energy costs that may be incurred by each person involved if the solution in question is selected? Are the proposed outcomes of the solution in question worth the costs?

- **Decide on a course of action to follow.** Based upon the analyses described above, select the alternative that seems most promising for handling the situation. Then it is time to flesh out the details of the plan and put it into action. If you have followed the previous steps, you can feel confident that the decision you have reached is based on sound judgment. You have done the best you can and that is all that is expected of any professional in our field. Be mindful, however, that the course of action you choose may not have the anticipated effects. This doesn't mean that it was a wrong decision. You may have misinterpreted an important variable in the situation or may have misjudged the impact of the decision on others. It may also be that an unanticipated change took place while you were implementing your plan. When decisions or plans don't work out as you hoped they would, repeat the process and develop a new plan of action.

Readers may work through the case studies independently, but additional benefits may be gained when the situations are discussed with fellow students or colleagues. When decisionmaking is undertaken by a group, each person must communicate his or her ideas clearly to other group members. Each person is also called upon to listen carefully to the ideas proposed by others, to keep an open mind, and to respond in an appropriate manner. Practice in these skills may prove invaluable as a method of enhancing the interventionist's ability to communicate with families and other professionals in real life.

REFERENCES

Christensen, C.R., & Hanson, A.J. (1987). Teaching and the case method. Boston: Harvard Business School.

Jackson, A.H. (1985). Teaching pediatric psychopharmacology: An interdisciplinary model. Journal of the American Academy of Child Psychiatry, 24, 103–108.

Johnson, J., & Purvis, J. (1987). Case studies: An alternative learning/teaching method in nursing. Journal of Nursing Education, 26, 118–120.

Kreps, G.L., & Lederman, L.C. (1985). Using the case method in organizational communication education: Developing students' insight, knowledge, and creativity through experience-based learning and systematic debriefing. Communication Education, 34, 358–364.

Lee, Y.S. (1983). Public management and case study methods. Teaching Political Science: Politics in Perspective, 11(1), 6–14.

McWilliam, P.J. (1992). The case method of instruction: Teaching application and problem-solving skills to early interventionists. Journal of Early Intervention, 16, 360–373.

Rasinski, T.V. (1989). The case method approach in reading education. Reading Horizons, Fall, 5–14.

Applications
of Recommended
Practices

Little Things that Count

Melissa R. Johnson
and Marie Reilly

Dana and Barry envisioned a joyous arrival of their firstborn child, but their dreams were abruptly shattered by the premature onset of labor at 26 weeks gestation. Their newborn daughter, Megan, spends the first weeks of her life in the neonatal intensive care unit (NICU). She wins her fight for life, but does not escape an intraventricular hemorrhage and brain injury in the process. The residual effects of Megan's early trauma remain unknown as the parents prepare to take their little girl home. This story describes the parents' reactions to the unexpected crisis of a premature birth and beginning parenthood in the world of the NICU. The story also describes the sensitive approach of a psychologist and physical therapist as they conduct a newborn assessment (i.e., Assessment of Preterm Infants' Behavior [APIB]), communicate assessment information to the family, and restore the parents' confidence in their child and themselves.

Megan was born 3½ months prematurely, weighing 1¾ pounds. Her mother, Dana, and father, Barry, had been married for 2 years, and they had planned the pregnancy. Dana was 22 years old. She had worked as a secretary, but had planned to stay home after the birth of their first child. Barry was 25 years old. He worked as a telephone repairman and had been recently promoted to supervisor. Dana sought early and continuous prenatal care and had experienced a normal pregnancy until her membranes ruptured unexpectedly while she was at work. She was rushed to the hospital and found to be in early labor. Dana's cervix was fully dilated and her labor could not be stopped. Megan was delivered that day.

Megan cried immediately, but, because her respiratory efforts were feeble, she was promptly resuscitated by the neonatology team, who had arrived in the delivery room only moments before she did. Megan's Apgar scores were 3 at 1 minute and 6 at 5 minutes. Her parents saw a flurry of activity around their tiny, blue baby as she was taken from the delivery room to the NICU.

A FIGHT FOR LIFE

To Dana and Barry, it seemed like an eternity between Megan's birth and the call from the NICU nurse, who said that Megan was ready for them to visit. In fact, it was about 6 hours after Megan's birth when Barry wheeled Dana down the corridor from the maternity hall to the NICU. When they arrived, Dana and Barry felt they had entered a different world. Plate glass windows separated a spacious nurses' station from dimly lit rooms filled with small, high, warming tables and quilt-draped incubators, all obscured by a bewildering variety of medical equipment. As Dana and Barry tried to orient themselves, they were greeted by the charge nurse, who showed them how to wash their hands properly before they visited Megan. The nurse caring for Megan then helped Barry to navigate the wheelchair through the heavy glass door and into the six-bed NICU room where Megan lay.

Dana sobbed as she absorbed the sight of her baby daughter attached to a respirator, with the endotracheal tube tape obscuring most of her wizened, red face. Intravenous fluids were connected to a tube that was sewn into her naval, and another tube disappeared into a large board on her left foot. Numerous heart rate and respiratory monitors were attached to her small body. The nurse heard Dana murmur to her husband that Megan didn't look like a baby and, indeed, the lack of body fat and the limbs smaller than her father's fingers bore no resemblance to a typical full-term infant, who would weigh four times Megan's weight.

Barry and Dana were too overwhelmed to focus on the environment surrounding their child, but they later learned that the dim lights in the room, the closed blinds, and the hushed staff voices were part of a conscious effort to support Megan's efforts to rest and conserve energy. They did notice that, rather than lying on her back as they had expected, she was placed on her side with her tiny limbs gently flexed on a fluffy sheepskin pad that had been built up on all four sides so that she looked as if she were cradled in a white nest. Both Barry and Dana felt frozen at first, longing to reach out to Megan but feeling that she would be injured by the slightest touch. Noting their anxiety, the nurse gently guided their hands to surround and hold Megan's hands and feet. Megan startled at their first touch, but soon relaxed as Dana's hands touched her fingertips and then gradually moved to allow her tiny fingers to curl around one of her mother's fingers.

During the next week, the family experienced more stresses as Megan's condition worsened. The rate of her ventilator had to be increased so that it would effectively breathe for her. She received blood transfusions to keep her blood pressure normal and to provide the red blood cells needed to carry oxygen to her body tissues. On the seventh day of Megan's life, a picture was taken of her brain with a portable ultrasound machine. The pediatric resident found Dana, who was leaving the lactation room after pumping her breast milk, and told her that the ultrasound had revealed bleeding in the ventricles on both sides of Megan's brain. Terrified, Dana paged Barry on his company beeper. He left his job, to which he had just returned the day before, and 2 hours later, the couple sat in the office of the attending neonatologist. Dana and Barry struggled to comprehend the doctor's explanation—that the bleeding, an intra-ventricular hemorrhage, could stabilize, improve, or worsen. The bleeding could lead to hydrocephalus, which might need to be surgically drained with a shunt, or it could represent the early stages of periventricular leukomalacia, which is the scarring seen after the death of cells in the white matter of the brain. The next day, Dana began to cry while she was talking with Megan's nurse. Barry had told her the night before that he couldn't deal with raising a child with a disability. Dana told the nurse that, regardless of how Barry felt about it, nothing would keep her from taking care of her baby.

The developmental team observed this family from a distance, as they were receiving much support from Megan's nurses and the unit social worker. The primary nurses were skilled in developmental care and shared with nurses from other shifts their observations about Megan's need for a quiet environment, nested positioning, and extremely gentle handling. The nurses asked me, the team psychologist, to be aware of this family's needs and to begin work with them.

Early in Megan's third week, I found Dana in the parents' room. She was waiting for a nursing report to end so she could visit her baby. I introduced myself and we began to chat. Dana told me how terrified she had been for the last 2 weeks, but that she was encouraged by the lowered ventilator settings achieved in the last several days. I wondered how Barry, who was now visiting regularly in the evenings, was doing. Dana volunteered that, although Barry had initially felt he couldn't deal with a child with a disability, he recently told her that together they would cope with whatever the future held. Dana sadly noted that it was a good thing because the second ultrasound had just been completed and it indicated that Megan's ventricles were continuing to enlarge. I asked Dana what she thought had changed Barry's feelings. Dana said simply, "She's his baby now."

HOMEWARD BOUND

Megan won her fight for life. She was able to breathe more on her own and was weaned off the ventilator. Her oxygen requirement also gradually diminished. She was first placed under an oxygen hood and then weaned to a nasal cannula. At 35 weeks gestation, she was breathing room air. After many setbacks with tube feedings, she began to feed from a bottle and finally was able to breast-feed when her mother visited. Even so, Megan's ventricles continued to increase in size until they stabilized at a level just below the point at which the neonatologists would recommend a shunt. The words brain damage were used more than once. The physicians and I offered to talk with Dana and Barry about Megan's future development, but they preferred that we address their questions about more immediate concerns, such as Megan's nursing care or possible discharge dates.

As Megan approached 37 weeks postconceptional age, a discharge date was set. Her parents were clearly attached to her and spent many hours in the NICU. Dana had patiently worked with the unit's lactation consultant, and breastfeeding was going well. Serial ultrasounds, however, continued to show progressive hydrocephalus.

Although Dana and Barry rarely discussed Megan's prognosis, I sensed their anxiety during their regular evening visits with their daughter. Megan tended to be a quiet infant who slept peacefully in her open bassinet and who cuddled with her parents. According to the nurses, however, Megan demonstrated few awake or alert periods. Her parents interacted sensitively and protectively with her, but with timidity.

Until Megan's discharge date was set, the developmental team had only limited interactions with the family because of their evening visiting pattern. One week before discharge, the medical and developmental team decided to address Megan's developmental and behavioral capacities more directly. The first step toward dealing with these issues was to administer an Assessment of Preterm Infants' Behavior[1], which would be helpful in both assessing Megan's abilities and providing direction for intervention strategies. The APIB, an extension and modification of the Brazelton Neonatal Behavioral Assessment Scale, is designed especially for preterm infants. It provides a detailed scoring system reflecting the infants' organization with regard to the autonomic, motor, and state subsystems of behavior.

I suggested that Dana and Barry observe while the APIB was performed. I hoped their attendance would accomplish several goals. First, we could highlight and clarify for Megan's parents her organizational competencies and strengths as well as facilitate a discussion of realistic concerns about her future development. Second, the APIB would provide a framework for encouraging Dana and Barry to feel confident in their ability to care for Megan. This was especially important in light of her imminent discharge. Third, scoring the APIB would provide the team with data about Megan's neurobehavioral functioning at discharge, a baseline from which to monitor and track her progress during the coming months.

When I talked with Dana about the exam over the telephone, she was enthusiastic and readily agreed to come to the nursery to participate. Dana also explained that Barry would not be able to come because he had signed up for extra shifts at work so he could take time off when Megan came home. Dana and I tried to think of a way for Barry to participate, but were unsuccessful. In light of the little time available, we decided to go ahead with just Dana. Although it was a less than perfect solution, Dana seemed satisfied with the decision.

Janet, the physical therapist, and I decided to work together in conducting Megan's APIB. Because I was certified in the use of the APIB, I would conduct the actual exam and scoring. Janet would observe and pay particular attention to Megan's motor functioning because she was at high risk for developing motor problems. Janet

[1]Als, H. (1982). Toward a synactive theory of development: Promise for the assessment of preterm infants' behavior (APIB). In H.E. Fitzgerald, B.M. Lester, & M.W. Yogman (Eds.), *Theory and research in behavioral pediatrics, Vol. 1* (pp. 64–133). New York: Plenum. Als, H., Lester, B.M., Tronick, E., & Brazelton, T.B. (1982). Towards a research instrument for the assessment of preterm infants' behavior (APIB). In H.E. Fitzgerald, B.M. Lester, & M.W. Yogman (Eds.), *Theory and research in behavioral pediatrics, Vol. 1* (pp. 35–63). New York: Plenum. Als, H., Lester, B.M., Tronick, E., & Brazelton, T.B. (1982). Manual for the assessment of preterm infants' behavior (APIB). In H.E. Fitzgerald, B.M. Lester, & M.W. Yogman (Eds.), *Theory and research in behavioral pediatrics, Vol. 1* (pp. 64–133). New York: Plenum.

would also be there to support Dana and attend to her reactions and concerns.

A SHOW OF STRENGTH

Megan was being fed on a flexible 4-hour schedule, usually eating at around 6 A.M. and 10 A.M., so Dana met with Janet and me at 8:30 the next morning. I gave Dana a brief introduction to the APIB, explaining that we would be able to learn how Megan organized input from her environment and what kind of help she needed to organize herself most effectively. With the approval of her nurse, Megan's monitors were disconnected and her bassinet was wheeled into the isolation room adjoining the intermediate care nursery. Baseline observations revealed a pale, delicate-appearing infant swaddled cozily in a blanket and snuggled into a sheepskin nest. She was lying on her tummy with her hands tucked under her chin. We commented on how pretty Megan was and how quietly and comfortably she was sleeping.

When I proceeded to shine a flashlight over Megan's closed eyes, she responded with a startle the first few times but, with repetition, her startle gradually decreased in intensity. Even so, she never shut out the stimulus altogether. Dana commented with pleasure about how Megan noticed the light even with her eyes closed. I agreed and added that, although Megan couldn't ignore the light completely, her ability to respond more calmly over the 10 administrations showed that she was learning about her environment. She was learning what was significant and what was "old news." Megan's responses were similar when a rattle was presented 10 times. Megan had already passed her hearing screening, but again Dana expressed pleasure that she so clearly responded to the sound.

When Megan was gently uncovered and placed on her back, she responded with increased and poorly organized motor activity. She showed marked hyperextension of her legs. All three observers commented that she seemed to be asking for help in containing her limbs and Dana remarked that she knew Megan hated being on her back. I gently cupped my hands around Megan's feet and we discussed alternative approaches to diapering. Throughout such discussions, Janet and I were careful to avoid offering pronouncements about how Dana and Barry should do things. Instead, we asked for Dana's opinions and ideas, based on both her current and past observations of Megan, and we supported and validated her wisdom.

The exam progressed through the assessment of more distal reflexes, such as foot and hand grasp, Babinski, clonus, resistance
and recoil of arms and legs, and so forth. Dana was pleased by the
normalcy of many of these responses. Megan's lack of resistance to
extension, especially in her legs, and the strong hyperextension that
she maintained when her legs were released concerned us. Janet
described this finding as *stiffness,* and we decided to monitor Megan's reflexes and muscle tone during clinic visits so that we could
provide any help she might need in this area. No specific interventions were recommended at that moment, but Janet made a mental
note to assess leg extensor tone during future visits. Dana already
demonstrated her understanding that Megan needed support through
blanket swaddling or caregivers' hands to maintain flexion, and the
focus of this exam was on competencies and confidence building.
The goal for Megan and her parents in the coming days would be a
smooth and happy transition to home, without the anxiety of instituting a new exercise program immediately.

As the exam moved to more active handling, we noted that,
despite mild autonomic reactivity (i.e., increased "webbing" of Megan's color), she was making efforts to wake up and become alert.
As I prepared to pull Megan to sitting, I explained what I was about
to do. Janet noticed Dana cringe and squeezed her shoulder as she
assured her that Megan would be all right. To everyone's delight,
Megan's eyes opened and brightened and she made a clear effort to
use her shoulder and neck muscles to lift her head for several seconds after she was seated. Dana gasped with excitement and said,
"I never dreamed she could do that. She's so much stronger than I
thought. Wait until I tell her daddy!"

The tension I had previously sensed among the three of us sub-
sided. The next portion of the exam proceeded smoothly with continued signs of lower body extensor tone, but Megan seemed to gain,
rather than lose, energy. I made a special effort to prepare Dana for
the spin maneuver and elicitation of the Moro reflex, but she was
much more relaxed and teased me about not getting dizzy as I slowly
spun Megan. Dana then interpreted Megan's robust response to the
Moro with pride as Janet pointed out how Megan had a clear signal
to tell us when she felt loss of support.

At this point, Megan's alertness was peaking. I moved to a rocker,
with Dana seated next to us, and began to assess Megan's ability to
orient. Megan followed my face and voice with shiny-eyed alertness as I quietly talked to her, and she focused on my face when I
was quiet. To assess her ability to locate a voice, Janet coached

Dana to call Megan from both her left and right sides, whereupon Megan searched and located the source of her mother's voice.

Megan began to tire somewhat and her gaze dulled slightly as a chiming apple was presented. Her efforts to follow the apple, as well as several occasions when she averted her gaze, could be seen in light of her efforts to both receive and regulate visual input. During this period, Dana asked with her voice trembling, "This means my baby can see, doesn't it?"

Upon completion, all four of the test participants were fatigued, and the adults felt satisfied. After Megan was settled in the nursery, I made some notes while Dana went to the parents' lounge. When I rejoined her a few minutes later to provide some closure on what had transpired, I found Dana talking to another parent whose extremely low birth weight infant had received a similar assessment the previous week. I heard Dana joyfully describe how Megan became wide awake and how she moved her head around to see what was happening. I asked Dana what that meant to her, as Megan's mother. She explained that, for her, it meant Megan would eat, cuddle, and sleep. She went on to say that Megan had never wakened up so much and never followed her face like she had followed mine today. I suggested that perhaps Megan had not been called upon to engage in such behavior before and that she might have been responding differently because I was a stranger who aroused her curiosity. In contrast, Dana and Barry were more familiar to Megan and, thereby, served as signals for comfort, cuddling, food, and relaxed loving. This interpretation seemed to please Dana, and she beamed as she reviewed what Megan could do. Perhaps her most telling comment was "She's seemed so fragile . . . so sick. Now I realize she's stronger than I thought. She's growing up! I'll still worry a little, because I know she could have brain damage, but now I feel ready to take her home."

As Dana reviewed how she would describe the exam to Barry, she said that he had commented before leaving for work, "I hope she passes her test." Dana had told him that she didn't think it was a test you could pass or fail, but thought that she would now tell him that Megan did indeed pass. "I never dreamed she could do so much," concluded Dana, "The way she could get her head up . . . the way she could turn her head so she could breathe. Well, there's just so much she can do!"

DISCUSSION QUESTIONS

1. In this case, the NICU is different from many others around the country. How is it different and how may these differences contribute to the well-being of newborns who are critically ill? How might these differences affect the parents of these infants?

2. Delivering "bad news" is a common responsibility for professionals in NICUs and other hospital environments. Is the delivery of "bad news" about Megan's intraventricular hemorrhage handled appropriately? Should this situation have been handled differently? What would you have said if it were your responsibility to tell Megan's parents about her enlarged ventricles?

3. If you were Megan's nurse, how would you have responded to Dana's comments and tears when she said that Barry didn't want to deal with rearing a child with a disability?

4. In general, what responsibility, if any, should NICU nurses have in providing information to parents and helping them through such emotional times?

5. Was it appropriate for the developmental team to get involved in Megan's case when it did? Should they have been involved sooner? Later? Who decides?

6. Dana and Barry did not appear to be interested in discussing the issue of Megan's capabilities and prognosis. Do you think they were denying that she had problems? Was it appropriate for the developmental team to decide that these issues should be addressed anyway?

7. If you were the psychologist, how would you have approached the topic of administering the APIB with Dana? What words might you have used? What would you have done if Dana said she did not want to have the APIB administered?

8. Could or should more have been done to involve Barry in administering the APIB? Should more have been done to include him in discussions about the results and conclusions following its administration?

9. Was the joint effort of the psychologist and the physical therapist the best way to handle the assessment of Megan's abilities? Were there any distinct advantages or would as much have been achieved if they had conducted their work separately?

10. One of the goals of administering the APIB was to increase the parents' confidence in themselves and in Megan. What specifically was said or done that might have accomplished this goal?

11. As this case demonstrates, a number of professionals have contact with infants and their parents in NICUs. If you were in charge, what methods would you use to ensure that the efforts of doctors, nurses, social workers, other specialists, and technicians were well-coordinated and sensitive to families?

12. Although Megan is going home, her future development is far from certain. What, if anything, would you do to further ensure a smooth transition home and the availability of needed information or resources in the months that follow? Who would be responsible?

Jack and Jill—and Sam?

Mary R. Wandschneider
and Charles A. Peck

The situation had already reached crisis proportions when Barbara, director of the Jack and Jill Child Care Center, decided to call for assistance. Sam's mother, desperate for summer child care, had enrolled him at Jack and Jill without explaining the extent of his special needs. His persistent misbehavior was infuriating to the staff, and serious consideration was being given to dismissing him from the program. The telephone call for help was Sam's last chance to remain at Jack and Jill. This story describes the efforts of a consultant, Monica, to assist the child care staff and support Sam's inclusion in this less-than-perfect integrated setting.

"This is Barbara Wheeler over at Jack and Jill Child Care Center. Look, we have a new kid in our program this summer. His name is Sam, and he's absolutely impossible! We know he got special services during the school year because his mother told us, but he's making things really hard here. We just can't have him in our program unless he gets better. Somebody said you might be able to help us with him. I certainly hope so, because if you can't, I'm afraid he'll have to leave. It's just not fair to the staff or the other children to have to deal with him every day."

This telephone call from Barbara Wheeler marked the beginning of a 15-month consulting relationship between our program and the Jack and Jill Child Care Center. Our program is designed to help community early childhood programs include young children with disabilities, but the call from Jack and Jill posed a very different kind of challenge from those we had been facing in our other consulting work. Our staff had been working with community child care and preschool programs for a year, hammering out the details, training, and making plans before actually including children with disabilities. We had prepared programs for integration by carefully facilitating dialogue among all of the critical "stakeholders" in the process—parents, school district special education personnel, community early childhood directors, and other community leaders. In short, we had worked in the relative luxury of having time and resources available to support planning and preparation in what were already outstanding early childhood programs.

The Jack and Jill Child Care Center was another story. This was a program with which we had never planned. Suddenly, it was confronted with a child who had special needs, and the staff felt entirely unequipped to respond to this child. In addition, the program had done little, if any, general staff training, much less any staff training specifically related to inclusion. Moreover, the Jack and Jill Child Care Center had numerous difficulties with many of the typically developing children they served. Finally, the program director was clearly on the verge of excluding Sam. Her patience and resources were already wearing thin.

Sam had been enrolled during the regular school year in a local special education preschool. We later learned from Sam's teachers that his mother was desperate to find summer child care that she could afford and that would accept a child with special needs. Sam's mother had pursued all of the obvious center-based options and some family child care options as well. Her efforts, however, had been unsuccessful. The Jack and Jill Child Care Center seemed to be the only remaining choice in this small rural area.

It was clear that many things about this center would make inclusion particularly difficult. The class sizes were very large, and many of the staff members were inexperienced college students who usually worked 2-hour shifts 2 or 3 days a week. Fortunately, during the summer, the staff consisted of fewer students who worked longer shifts. Even so, there were still about 18 staff members working in Sam's classroom throughout the week. Barbara, the director, made it very clear that managing the center was difficult enough without the extra hassle of dealing with Sam.

Although we were not legally bound to provide consultation to the Jack and Jill Child Care Center, we felt an ethical obligation to do what we could to support the inclusion of this child. But where should we start? This was definitely a more difficult situation than we had encountered in our work with other child care centers. In addition to class size and staff scheduling problems, other issues included the long distance to the outdoor play space, the use of an outdated curriculum, and the lack of qualified teachers. To further complicate our work, the staff had already developed negative attitudes about Sam's inclusion. Among ourselves, we discussed the possibilities of an alternative placement for Sam, but we came to the same conclusion his mother had—Jack and Jill Child Care Center was the only choice.

We knew it was not feasible to "fix" the center's problems. We had neither the resources nor the power to make extensive changes in the program. We had to somehow give the center's staff a sense of their own power to solve the difficulties of including Sam, so that they might begin to feel more competent and less overwhelmed by their difficulties with him. One of our staff members, Monica, was elected to take on this challenge. She began with a telephone call to Barbara Wheeler in the hopes of gaining a clearer understanding of the problem.

AN IMPOSSIBLE KID

Barbara answered the telephone when Monica called. Monica introduced herself and summarized what she had been told about the situation with Sam before asking Barbara for more details.

"Can you tell me more about what Sam is like when he's at your center?" asked Monica.

"All I can say is that he's really awful!" began Barbara. She seemed to be a woman who spoke what was on her mind. "He acts like a particularly obnoxious 2-year-old with lots of 'no's' and temper tantrums, but he's actually 4 years old." She took a deep breath and continued, "I don't care what other people say about him, that kid's a lot smarter than people think he is. He knows exactly what he's doing. He'll get what he wants one way or the other."

"It sounds like it's been pretty rough working with him," Monica sympathized. Then she tried once again to get more detailed information. "Perhaps you could tell me about the specific things he does in the classroom that pose problems. What does he do during morning circle, free play, lunch, or other times of the day?"

"Well, during circle he's impossible. He won't sit down. He wanders around the room. We can't get him to sit in the circle, so sometimes we let him just wander. When we do make him sit in the circle, he screams and disrupts everything. We don't know if we should expect him to sit or not. Whenever an adult asks him to do something, he starts kicking, scratching, and butting his head into the teacher who's with him."

"How frustrating that must be for everyone," replied Monica. "Is there anything else?"

"Are you kidding!" exclaimed Barbara. "He causes giant hassles around going to the bathroom. Mostly he just wets in his pants. What's frustrating is that staff will take Sam and some of the other beginners to the bathroom at their regular scheduled times, and Sam starts yelling and kicking and screaming, 'No, no, no!' He'll refuse to even pull down his pants, but not 5 minutes later he wets in his pants."

Barbara stopped her ranting and there was an uncomfortable moment of silence. Monica didn't know whether Barbara was catching her breath, or if the silence indicated it was Monica's turn to talk. Even worse, Monica wasn't sure how to respond to what Barbara just said. It sounded as though Sam had passed the point of no return as far as Barbara was concerned. Monica was still contemplating a response when Barbara resumed talking.

"Well, actually it was a lot worse the first week he was here," said Barbara. Her voice was softer and less frantic than it had been a moment before. "Now he'll go to the bathroom without quite as much fussing, but he still won't urinate in the toilet. He just stands there without doing anything, and 5 minutes later he has wet pants."

For the first time, Monica was encouraged. "It sounds like that first week was a nightmare," she said, "but you seem to have made some real progress with him in a short amount of time. I'm impressed! Whatever you and your staff have decided to do seems to be working. At least it sounds as though he's become a bit more cooperative."

"Well I guess so, but mostly I'm very frustrated," said Barbara. "Some of my teachers say they don't like him—that he's impossible and shouldn't be in a regular child care center. They don't have the special skills to take care of him, and he's taking their time away from other children." It sounded as if Barbara wasn't the only one who was exasperated by Sam's behavior.

"What really infuriates me," continued Barbara, "is that his mother didn't tell us how bad he was. If things don't get better soon we're going to have to tell her we can't have him in our program. Really, you should see how it is in the classroom! It's not fair to the staff or to the other children."

"I can appreciate how frustrating this must be for you and your staff," replied Monica. "He sounds like a real handful, but it also sounds as though you've had some success in dealing with him. I'm glad you called us because we'd certainly like to support you in trying to make this work."

"We have fewer children here in the summer, so we are willing to give it another try. But the fall is another story," cautioned Barbara. "He'll have to improve a lot if he's going to stay in our program then."

"I see," said Monica. "Well, perhaps I could visit the classroom and then recommend how we might work together. Could I come and watch him in the classroom and then meet with you afterward?"

"That sounds good," answered Barbara. "Could you come tomorrow?"

It seemed important to be responsive at this point, so Monica rescheduled the meeting she was supposed to have with her supervisor the next morning. She would go to the center to observe Sam and take notes.

Although not quite the terror that was described over the telephone the day before, Monica could see that Sam was indeed a difficult child to manage. As she suspected, Monica noted that the staff were inconsistent in how they dealt with Sam, and having different staff members in charge throughout the morning only aggravated the problem. Sam seemed to try out each new person who entered the room only to get a different response from each of them. The only consistent management of Sam was during toileting. Although the staff had taken a rather strong-armed approach with him in the matter of going to the bathroom, it was consistent.

Soon after lunch, the children went outside to play, and Monica met briefly with Barbara Wheeler and one of the lead teachers, Rita. Monica went over the notes she had taken and summarized her observations in terms of the inconsistencies in staff responses to Sam's behavior. Barbara and Rita acknowledged the inconsistencies that Monica described and agreed that it probably contributed to their difficulties in managing Sam's behavior. They talked further about how difficult it would be to ensure that everyone responded to Sam in the same way because there were so many staff members involved and their schedules were so varied. Nevertheless, Barbara made it clear that the number of staff members and their schedules were aspects of the program that could not be changed to accommodate Sam.

Barbara and Rita discussed ways they had tried to communicate with the large staff on other issues and described their frustration with their previous methods. Even so, Monica asked if they could think of any ideas for improving communication among the staff in deciding on and implementing methods for handling Sam. After much discussion about the difficulties of getting the whole group together, Barbara and Rita decided they would try to assemble the entire staff for a meeting. This had never been done before. Their hope was to come to an agreement on a plan and carry it out consistently. When Barbara asked, Monica agreed to facilitate the meeting.

Before leaving the center that day, the three women worked out a plan for the meeting so Barbara could better explain to the staff why she was asking them to get together. First, everyone would discuss the problems in handling Sam and decide what needed to be attended to first. They would also share the various methods everyone had tried with Sam and how well they had worked in controlling his behavior. The group would then decide on strategies for everyone to follow in responding to Sam's specific problem behaviors. Finally, the group would decide how to monitor its progress and maintain consistency in responding to Sam.

Monica suggested that Sam's mother might be included in the meeting, but this idea was met with resistance. Barbara and Rita agreed that consistency between home and child care was important, but they said that Sam's mother was not very cooperative. Furthermore, they thought the staff would be uncomfortable with her presence at the meeting. Monica was not pleased with their attitude toward Sam's mother, but kept her feelings to herself. If the staff could experience some success in changing Sam's behavior at the center, they might feel more confident and consequently be more willing to involve Sam's mother in the future.

In discussing who else should be included in the meeting, Barbara and Rita mentioned that it would be helpful if they knew how Sam's previous teacher had handled him in the classroom. Barbara talked about where he had been enrolled and Monica realized that his previous teacher must have been a woman named Rhonda, whom she had met on several occasions through her work on an interagency committee. Although Rhonda would be on summer vacation now, Monica offered to try to call her at home and see if she would be willing to come to a meeting about Sam.

WHAT IS THE PROBLEM?

The meeting was held on a Tuesday evening after the center closed and, of the 20 people invited to the meeting, 15 attended. Monica had succeeded in contacting Rhonda, and she was among those who attended. Following a brief introduction by Barbara, Monica opened the meeting. She began by saying how impressed she was with the group's dedication, as demonstrated by their willingness to get together in the evening to talk about Sam. She also talked about the positive things she had seen during her recent observation in the child care center, emphasizing their successful beginning in overcoming Sam's resistance to toileting. Then Monica outlined the purpose of the meeting and opened the floor to a general discussion of the problems they were experiencing with Sam and strategies for dealing with his misbehavior. For an hour and a half, the group engaged in animated storytelling of their experiences with Sam and lively discussion about what needed to be done.

"Well, the hardest thing for me to handle is Sam's yelling, flailing his arms around, and hitting me when I ask him to do something," said one of the child care workers. "It's so frustrating! It's gotten to the point where I try to avoid asking him to do anything—but sometimes I just have to."

"I think those spells are the hardest thing for a lot of us," agreed Rita. "They seem so out of proportion to what he's been asked to do. It's especially bad when it's time to go to the bathroom or to the kitchen to eat."

"Yeah," someone else chimed in, "I hate it when he has a fit about going to the bathroom."

"Well, how about when he's in the bathroom?" interjected a male college student. "It takes him forever, so he's usually late going to lunch. Then he's late finishing lunch and. . . ."

"That's a problem," said another student, "because the confusion of other kids finishing and putting their dishes away distracts Sam, and he ends up barely eating anything."

"And I'm irritated that with the problems at lunch time you can almost count on him wetting his pants even though you've just taken him to the bathroom," Rita added, rolling her eyes in exasperation.

"I just hate it when he starts yelling," said a small voice from the back of the room. The woman, a student, couldn't have been more than 17 or 18 years old. "He yells when I take him to the bathroom, he yells at lunch, and he yells when it's time to go outside. He had a real tantrum one day when I told him it was time to go to circle." She paused a moment and scanned the room for indications of agreement. "Now I just let him do what he wants during circle. Sometimes he comes on his own and sometimes he doesn't."

"And if he comes to circle," said someone else, "he usually only stays a minute or two. Then he goes wandering off. Of course, then the other kids want to wander, too."

"I'm not sure what to do with circle either," added another

student. "I tend to just let him do what he wants, too. . . . Believe me, I regret it if I don't!"

At this point, Monica felt that enough time had been devoted to descriptions of Sam's misbehavior and staff members had had adequate opportunity to vent their frustration. She wanted to help them clarify and focus the problem. She asked whether others had found that Sam became upset when he was asked to move to a new activity. Everyone agreed that he seemed to be set off by transitions.

"Are there any other kinds of concerns you have about these situations?" asked Monica.

"Well, one of the things I find to be difficult," began one of the workers, "is that whenever there is a transition, but particularly with the big transitions, he doesn't do the appropriate thing. For instance, he might go into the pantry instead of the free play area after snack."

Another worker nodded her head and said, "I've seen that a lot. For instance, on his first day here, when we were walking to the playground, he started wandering upstairs."

"Yeah," agreed a student, "it doesn't seem like he's deliberately trying to disobey the plan—he just wanders off."

"I've seen that too," said another, "and it makes me worry that he could easily get himself into a dangerous situation. It makes it more difficult to have him in the group because I have to pay attention to him every second. Sometimes it seems like it isn't fair to the other kids."

Rhonda, who had not said a word up to this point, finally spoke. "We see that same wandering off in our preschool," she said. "We take turns being the one responsible for keeping close tabs on what he's doing. We list whose turn it is on the daily schedule and we try to make sure he knows the routine."

"That's a good idea," someone said.

"That does sound like a good way to relieve the pressure," said Monica. "Have any of the rest of you seen this behavior of wandering off during transitions?" Her question was met with vigorous head nodding and murmurs of affirmation among the group. This did, indeed, seem to be one of the major difficulties in working with Sam. Monica thought she would check out other issues. "Are there any other concerns?" she asked.

The young woman in the back of the room spoke again. "I just feel uncertain with Sam. Sometimes I expect the same things I do of the other children and he does well. Other times I expect the same and it's totally unrealistic for him."

Two other group members agreed. They didn't know what was fair to expect of Sam either.

"Well, we've been working with him for a year now," said Rhonda. "Maybe we could share some of our experiences and testing results."

"That would be very helpful," said Rita.

"Yes, that would be helpful," said Monica. "Let's talk about those strategies as soon as we finish identifying what we think the major issues are, okay? Are the rest of you also uncertain of what is reasonable to expect of Sam?" Again, there was vigorous nodding from the group. Another major issue had been identified. "Are there any other concerns?" asked Monica.

Barbara, who had been looking at her watch with increasing frequency during the past 20 minutes, spoke up. "I think we have other problems," she said, "but some of them are related to the ones we've already talked about. I think we should figure out some strategies to deal with these first and deal with the others later."

Following Barbara's lead, Monica summarized the concerns the staff had identified: 1) Sam often yells, screams, scratches, and hits when he's asked to change activities, particularly at major transition times; 2) Sam often wanders into an inappropriate activity during transition times, particularly when going to and from meals and the bathroom; and 3) staff are uncertain about the level of behavior they should expect of Sam. The group agreed that these were the major concerns, and Monica turned the discussion in the direction of developing a plan of action.

A PLAN OF ACTION

Monica began by having the group discuss strategies they had tried and had seemed to hold some promise for the future. The group members discussed some of their successes in working with Sam. Individuals often identified things that few in the group had tried or known about. Approaches that had helped for two or more care providers included:

- When Sam was informed ahead of time about transitions and had some direct assistance, he seemed to have somewhat fewer outbreaks of screaming.
- If Sam was taken to a quiet place when he was screaming, kicking, and flailing, he often calmed down and could do the proposed activity with assistance.

- When Sam sat near an adult during circle time, he seemed to attend somewhat longer in circle.
- Sometimes Sam responded to a direct contingency statement such as, "You can go to the water table after you eat one bite."
- When Sam's behavior was dealt with in the same way across days and among all staff members, he seemed to eventually catch on to the rules.
- When Sam was chosen to be one of the first children to do an activity, he did better than when he had to wait.

Everyone agreed that it was important to establish a plan and be consistent in following through with it. Each of the major problems that had been identified were listed on a small chalkboard, and ideas were generated for dealing with each. Although Monica facilitated the discussion and helped the group to clarify its decisions, only ideas developed by the staff were included in the plan of action. At the close of the meeting, Monica agreed to write up the plan of action that they had developed.

A MEASURE OF SUCCESS

Barbara Wheeler and her staff left the meeting feeling good about the plan they had developed. Several staff members commented that it felt good just to talk about the things with which they had been struggling. Others said that it felt good to know how they would respond to Sam, even if their strategies proved unsuccessful.

Sam remained enrolled in the center for the next 15 months. The initial plan of action was not completely successful, but Sam did show clear progress in several areas. His screaming almost entirely disappeared, and the cues staff used at transition times greatly reduced his wandering. Monica monitored Sam's progress and took care to reflect his gains back to the staff. The staff began to take real pride in what they had accomplished with Sam.

During the next few months, Monica facilitated three more meetings, and Barbara and her staff began to view getting together to clarify problems, share ideas, and plan a common "approach" as a strategy they could use to address other problems at the center. As they began to say things like, "maybe we need to get together to deal with this," Monica knew her major goal had been attained.

All of the problems at the Jack and Jill Child Care Center were not resolved. Barbara faced a continuing dilemma about the time

PLAN OF ACTION FOR SAM

Transition to Circle Time

Expectation: Sam will come to circle, sit down, and initially stay for 3–4 minutes. Depending on his progress, each week he will stay for a longer period of time, up to the full time of circle (10–15 minutes). If the circle time is more lengthy, he will be permitted to move to free play as the younger children are.

Approaches

- The head teacher will alert Sam once, prior to the start of circle, that circle is about to begin. She will assist Sam in cleaning up or finishing his activity. She will tell him personally when it is time to come to circle, take his hand, and walk him to circle.
- A designated adult will sit near Sam and remind him of the rule: "We all stay in circle until it's time for _____."
- If Sam begins to scream, kick, or otherwise act out, the designated adult will take him to the book corner on the other side of the room and explain that he cannot return to the group until he has quieted. The adult will then turn away from Sam, but stay nearby.

Transition to Bathroom

Expectation: Sam will wash his hands and urinate at the times that the group does, and he will leave the bathroom at the appropriate times.

Approaches

- The first adult leaving circle with a group going to the bathroom will ask Sam to join his or her group and take his hand to walk with him.
- This adult will be very matter-of-fact. If Sam doesn't do the expected actions once in the bathroom, the adult will give him cues about appropriate behavior such as, "Sam, what do you do first?", "Remember to pull your pants down next," "Now what, Sam?", "Remember, you need to wash your hands next, Sam," and so forth.
- If Sam urinates in his pants, the adult will encourage him to try to urinate again in the toilet before assisting him in changing his clothes.
- When Sam finishes using the bathroom, the same adult will ask him, "Where do you go next, Sam?" He or she will monitor Sam as he leaves the bathroom, will assist him in finding a seat at the snack table, and will sit at his table and ensure that he begins eating, in the same way he or she handled the bathroom routine.

Reasonable Levels of Behavior To Expect of Sam

Expectation: The staff will be more aware of Sam's capabilities and what is reasonable to expect of him in daily routines.

(continued)

Plan of Action for Sam (*continued*)

Approaches
- Sam's special education teacher, Rhonda, will come to a staff meeting next week and describe what she believes are reasonable expectations of Sam based on her testing and experience with him.
- Rhonda will also bring a written sheet she has developed for her staff, listing what Sam can do, and what he's working to accomplish.

Follow-Up Plan
- Monica will observe Sam and the staff three times weekly for 20 minutes during the next 3 weeks. She will focus her observations on the expectations and approaches identified by the group.
- Staff members will report directly to Barbara to inform her of any difficulties they may be having in following through with the plan of action, and whether they are seeing any changes in Sam's behavior.
- Monica will meet with Barbara and Rita once a week to report her observations and to discuss the staff's experiences and Sam's progress. If necessary, this group will suggest possible modifications of the plan.
- Monica will meet with the entire staff in 1 month to discuss progress and make modifications in the plan.

---

and expense of calling staff meetings, and therefore meetings were often delayed until problems reached crisis proportions. Several of the behavior problems staff saw with Sam were never completely resolved. For example, he never did sit very well during circle time. Nevertheless, Barbara Wheeler and the staff became more aware of their own capacity to solve problems related to including children with special needs in their program—and Sam's mother maintained the child care she so badly needed.

DISCUSSION QUESTIONS

1. At the end of the case, the authors write, "Monica knew her major goal had been attained." What was Monica's major goal in working with the Jack and Jill Child Care Center? What strategies did she use to attain her goal?

2. Review the first telephone conversation that Monica had with Barbara Wheeler, the director of the child care center. Find at least four quotations from Monica that exemplify her overall approach to providing consultation to the child care center. Briefly discuss how each quotation you selected was intended to attain her goal.

3. Should Monica have been more directive in her consultation? That is, should she have offered some suggestions of her own about methods for dealing with Sam or provided written information for the staff to read?

4. In general, what factors should be considered in determining whether a directive, nondirective, or combination approach is employed in providing consultation to program staff?

5. The staff did not want the mother involved in the staff meeting about Sam. Although Monica did not agree, she quietly accepted their decision. Should she have expressed her concerns to the staff and attempted to influence their attitude toward Sam's mother?

6. What responsibility, if any, does Monica have for informing the mother about plans that are made for dealing with Sam at the child care center, or the results of the implementation of those plans?

7. Thinking about your experiences, in what ways can you identify with this situation from the viewpoint of the child care staff? From Barbara's point of view? From Monica's?

8. In your own community, what resources are available to assist the staff of regular child care centers in the inclusion of young children with special needs? What additional resources are needed for successful outcomes?

9. In many ways, the Jack and Jill Child Care Center represents a large percentage of child care settings in the United States. Should we promote the inclusion of children with disabilities in these less-than-ideal environments?

Thank You for Your Time

Barbara Wagner-Siebauer _____

Jessie was 15 years old and already the mother of two young boys, Jerome and Lamont, both of whom appeared to have developmental delays. She was also pregnant, expecting her third child in a matter of weeks. Jessie's questionable parenting skills resulted in the family's referral to a combination home-based and center-based intervention program. This case describes the efforts of the interventionist who visited Jessie and her two sons in their inner-city home. Under less than ideal circumstances, the interventionist attempts to foster Jessie's interest and involvement in the boys' development. Potentially sensitive issues, such as birth control and completing high school, are also addressed through the interventionist's work with this young mother.

Jessie's reputation preceded her. Her next door neighbor described Jessie as "out of control," noting that she frequently entertained male friends and called out to young men on the street. The neighbor expressed concern about Jessie's two sons, saying that they often ran around unsupervised. It wasn't too long before our social worker received a telephone call. As a result of that call, a new family was referred to our birth-to-three program: a 15-year-old, single mother with two sons, ages 14 months and 24 months. Both children appeared to be delayed enough to warrant early intervention services. Several weeks later, I climbed the broken stairs to their inner-city home.

As the only early intervention teacher working for this 7-year-old program for teenage mothers and their infants and toddlers with developmental delays, I have faced many challenges. The population we serve is almost exclusively from our midwestern city's north side, the area referred to as our *inner city*. Most of the families we

63

serve live in impoverished conditions, and the majority are on welfare. The problems these families face are numerous and complex. Solutions are rarely simple. My philosophy has been to focus on the child and family and to deal with the problems of the environment only as they interfere with the parent–child relationship. When I begin to work with a teenage mother, I attempt to remain nonjudgmental, fitting myself into the home environment as comfortably as I can, even if doing this means pretending to ignore my surroundings. This is important because I have frequently seen well-meaning professionals turn a family off when they first visit a home. I remember a speech-language therapist who stared at cockroaches as they scurried up and down a bedroom wall and a social worker who gasped in disbelief as a mother of three children said that she and her children slept in the living room because their tiny apartment had no bedroom. These professionals tended to be poorly received by the families. The first visit is critical to the establishment of rapport with the family and laying the foundation for future contacts.

A DARK CHALLENGE

When I knocked on Jessie's door for the first time, it opened by itself. Peering into the darkness, I called out to Jessie, who I hoped had gotten my letter and was expecting me. I identified myself as the "baby teacher," a nonthreatening title that has gotten me through doors that might otherwise not have opened. After a minute or two, a voice called, "Come in." I found that the front door only opened about half way, so I had to squeeze through with my test kit. My test kit is a big red basket, filled to the top with the necessary materials and a few colorful toys just for play. Its appearance has also helped to get me in doors. It looks like something fun, instead of something threatening, is about to take place.

The voice turned out to be that of Jesssie's mother, a woman in her 30s, wearing a robe and carrying a can of beer. "Come in and sit down," she said, gesturing to the cushionless chair in the corner of the room. I did, and then saw Jerome and Lamont standing by the two mattresses on the other side of the room. I smiled at them, but they ran out of the room, heading toward the back of the house. My eyes had become accustomed to the dim lighting in the room. The shades were pulled down, allowing little sunlight into the room. The only real light was from a bare bulb that hung from a ceiling fixture in the adjacent hall.

Jessie's mother, Maxine, said she knew I was there to check on how the boys were doing and that she knew they were behind most other children their ages. She said that Jessie didn't spend enough time teaching them things. Maxine walked over to the mattresses and shook the figure under the sheets, saying, "Jessie, get up. There's a baby nurse here to check on the boys." Jessie rolled over, but did not get up.

A child was crying in a back room, and Maxine went to check on the boys. Jessie rolled over, opened her eyes, and said, "Hi." I introduced myself as she sat up on the edge of the mattress. Jessie looked about 7 months pregnant, and I asked her when the baby was due.

"In a month or two," she answered, "and it better be a girl 'cause I don't want no more boys. Boys get into too much trouble." At that moment, Jerome and Lamont came back into the room, climbed up on the mattress, and sat beside Jessie.

I began to get a brief developmental history from Jessie and found she was quite willing to fill me in on the details she could remember about the boys. Both boys had been low birth weight babies and had been sickly as infants. Jerome, at 24 months, was still not talking. Lamont's vocabulary, at 14 months, consisted of "Stop it" and "No." Lamont had been hospitalized when he was 10 months old because Jerome had stuck a hairpin in his ear, puncturing the eardrum.

I allowed the boys to explore the toys in my test kit and observed their play skills. I observed a lot of manipulation, but little functional play. Jessie was interested in the toys herself, but fairly punitive toward the boys' attempts to handle them. She made comments like, "That's not how you do it," but did not provide them with appropriate alternatives. Based on what I heard and saw, I decided to recommend a visit by our transdisciplinary team. Because Jessie was attending school only sporadically, she readily agreed to a follow-up visit the next week. I suggested that, if she did go to school and the boys were left in the care of another trusted adult, the evaluations could still take place.

A week later, three of us arrived at Jessie's door at the designated time. We knocked on the door, and Jerome opened it. Peering inside, we could see a man sleeping on the floor. We called out, identifying ourselves, but the man didn't move and no other adult appeared. We have learned to be cautious in such situations, so we waited at the door as Jerome and Lamont pounced on the sleeping man. The boys eventually persuaded him to wake up. Upon seeing

us at the door, he stood and we immediately offered an explanation, "We're here to test the boys to see if they can get into our
program." He motioned for us to come inside.

"Jessie told me you would be coming," he said. "I'm Jessie's
stepfather, and I'm watching the boys while she's at school."

We went in and got comfortable on the floor where the boys
were already sitting in anticipation. Jessie's stepfather pulled one
of the mattresses over to a corner of the room, where he stayed for
the remainder of our hour-long visit. For the most part, he appeared
to be sleeping, but he opened his eyes periodically and glanced in
the direction of the boys. Jerome and Lamont were reasonably cooperative, appearing comfortable with the idea that three strangers
were asking them to play with a lot of new toys.

By the end of the hour, our psychologist had obtained enough
information to determine some specific areas of delay. I had been
able to score two developmental checklists. Our speech-language
pathologist gained enough information to report significant expressive and receptive language delays and a case of ringworm! This is
one of the hazards of the job and doesn't stop us from holding children on our laps.

OFF TO SCHOOL

An offer was extended for the boys to be enrolled in our program,
and Jessie accepted. "Can you take them to school every day, all
day?" she asked.

I explained that our program was both home-based and center-
based, with children attending our classroom one, two, or three
mornings a week and with home visits scheduled once a week
whenever possible. Jessie opted for three mornings a week and said
that weekly home visits were fine as well.

Jessie's input in our goal-setting procedure was clear-cut. "I want
them toilet trained so I don't have to keep buying them Pampers,
especially after the baby comes. And I want them to stop fighting
with each other."

I helped Jessie to translate her concerns into a goal of toilet
training for 2-year-old Jerome, a goal of awareness of a wet diaper
for Lamont, and several goals of sharing and improved play skills
for both boys. We then suggested a few additional goals in areas
that were explained to Jessie as, "getting ready to talk," "understanding what you say," "learning to think while playing," and
"learning to dress and eat by themselves." She agreed to these as

well, but made it clear that her priorities were getting the boys out of diapers and stopping the fights they had with each other.

The boys' first day to attend our program was the first Tuesday of December. In our state, December is cold regardless of whether the sun is shining. With the temperature hovering at approximately 32 degrees, Jerome and Lamont stepped off our bus in winter jackets and shorts. We got the boys into the classroom as quickly as possible, removed their jackets, and there they stood in matching, tropical print, short-sleeved shirts and shorts!

We settled into a routine of weekly home visits on the same day each week after school. Jessie was usually there and showed at least some interest in the activities I brought for the boys. She rarely participated in the activities, but her interest was enough to sustain my efforts. Then the baby was born. Jessie had a girl, healthy and at full term. She and the baby became inseparable. As Jessie became very attached to her new daughter, Sara, her interest in the boys seemed to wane. We tried various approaches to helping Jessie strike a balance among her three children's needs for attention.

Jessie dropped out of school. How do you convince a 15-year-old mother of three that going back to school is important? We tried, but soon realized that we had little chance of persuading her. Jessie's mother tried as well, but eventually laughed off her failure to get her daughter to stay in school. Rather than continuing to pressure Jessie about school, we decided to take advantage of the time she had at home and invited her to come to school with Jerome and Lamont. We encouraged Jessie to ride along on our bus with them in the mornings. We saw this as an opportunity for Jessie to spend some quality time with her sons. Jessie must have seen it differently because, on her first visit to the program, she got off the bus with Sara in her arms. We tried to make the best of the situation, but the baby was not only Jessie's focus, but also the children's. I asked Jessie if there was anyone who could watch Sara at home so she could help us in the classroom when she came.

On her next visit, Jessie did not bring the baby, and we treated her as a parent volunteer. We gave her specific activities to carry out with individual children, including Jerome and Lamont. We were surprised by her enthusiasm in working with the children and the effectiveness of her interactions with them. In fact, we were so impressed that we made up a parent volunteer award, personalized with her name on it, and presented it to her during our end of the morning group time. Jessie beamed with pride and pointed out her name to Jerome and Lamont, who sat on either side of her in the circle. "Look," she said, "it has Momma's name on it. It says your

Momma did a good job." Her response to our praise was a lesson we have never forgotten in dealing with Jessie or other teenage parents.

PRIDE AND PROGRESS

As the weeks passed, we began to see progress in Jerome and Lamont. A few functional words were emerging, and they were developing basic cognitive, social, and adaptive skills. To Jessie's delight, Jerome was making some progress in becoming toilet trained.

One day the boys were absent with no explanation. A visit to their home revealed that the family was packing and would be moving the next day. Luckily, we caught Jessie and her mother still at home and were able to get the new address, which was about 20 blocks away. Visits to the new home, an apartment in a six-family building, were often chaotic and confusing. Numerous family members and visitors came and went during our visits. The living room, where Jessie preferred to meet, was between a kitchen and two bedrooms and was the major pathway through the home. I wanted to draw Jessie into the visits more, but she was as distracted by all of the activity as Jerome and Lamont were. Then, one week I brought my camera.

I told Jessie that I was taking pictures of mothers playing with their children to demonstrate to other professionals that parents in our program really learn how to interact with their children and help them to progress. Quite unexpectedly, Jessie firmly reprimanded the first passerby for interrupting. She announced to all of the members of the household that they were not to bother us when Jerome and Lamont were having their "learning time." The camera became a catalyst for Jessie to attend to what the boys were doing. For the camera, she first began to implement suggestions that she had been aware of for months. She used simple, clear directions, got down on her children's level, interacted face-to-face, and elicited beautiful cooperation as she and the boys put pieces in a puzzle and played an object-matching game. I praised her lavishly as she continued her role as parent–teacher for the camera. The following week I showed Jessie the pictures and gave her a set to keep. From that time, she was much more focused during activities with the boys, and they were less distracted as well.

The months passed with Jerome and Lamont making steady progress. Jessie remained generally enthusiastic about what they were learning. She stayed out of school another semester despite our encouragement to return. The motivation and family support to do so simply was not there. We find this to be a pattern with many of our parents, especially after several children are born. We still felt that for Jessie, maintaining a supportive interest in all three children was an accomplishment in itself.

HANDLING A THREAT

That spring, we got news that a teenage mother we were working with was expecting her fourth child, and my thoughts turned immediately to Jessie. Jessie's boyfriend had recently moved into the house with her family's approval, and it was entirely possible that she would become pregnant again. Some positive things were happening in her life, and the possibility of another baby seemed to threaten this progress. I wondered what preventative role I could or should play. My teacher assistant and I discussed the issue and decided that I could bring up the topic with Jessie and then let her decide whether my involvement was appropriate.

On my next visit, I told Jessie that we really cared about her and her children and knew how difficult it could be for her if she were to have another baby. Jessie agreed that another baby would be difficult to handle and accepted my offer to help her avoid another pregnancy. Jessie had a means of birth control, but she wasn't consistent in using it. My assistant and I decided that we would try designing a simple, catchy phrase, printed on colorful paper to encourage her. Our "Hang tough—you can avoid another pregnancy" message was printed on fluorescent pink and orange paper, and I took one of these on each visit to Jessie. At first, Jessie laughed. I brought them for 4 or 5 weeks and then one week I forgot. Jessie asked, "Where's my pregnancy reminder?" almost as soon as I sat down. Jessie had noticed that I was consistently demonstrating to her that someone did care whether she got pregnant again, and, so far, the caring was working. The weekly reminders have continued and, as this is being written, Jessie has not had any "baby news." It is the longest she has gone without carrying a child in 3 years.

LETTERS OF SUPPORT

Last year, our program was placed in the position of having to find out whether the teenage parents we served appreciated the services we provided. We were notified in May that, due to severe budget cuts, there would be no funds to continue our program. The program would be dissolved in September. We launched a desperate attempt to save the program through letters and telephone calls of

parent and professional support. Professional support was fairly easy
to obtain. Teachers, therapists, social workers, and others, both inside and outside of our school system, wrote to or called the school
board on behalf of the program.

I also asked teenage mothers, including those we had served
previously and those we were currently serving, to consider writing
a letter of support to prevent our program's closing. I provided paper and an envelope for each mother and asked only that they think
of what the program had offered them that they thought was worthwhile. Many of our teenage parents are school dropouts with reading and writing skills at a grade-school level. Even so, letters did
come back to us. Some were very well written, and some were barely
readable. Jessie's letter stood out among all of the others.

Dear Birth to Three Program,

This Program has really helped my children alot. When they got
there neither one of them was talking and they are really talking and
very good. And they home visits are very nice to. They come in and
teach they how to match thing and all kinds of thing. When they pick
them up Sara come to the door and gets them. The Birth to 3 Program
is one of the best Programs that I have heard of, and the teachers are
very nice and I know that I can trust them with anything and I really
think that it should say:

Thank You for Your Time,
Jessie

I read this letter in my empty classroom, and it brought tears
to my eyes. It was the most articulate parent letter we received and,
of all the letters people were so kind to write, this one said it all.
Jessie had written the perfect letter of support. She covered all of
the important points—how the program helps her children, the importance of our combined classroom and home visit approach, our
door-to-door transportation, and trust. Jessie had chosen to mention
trust, and it touched all of us who worked with her family.

I was equally impressed with the way she chose to end her
letter—with "Thank You for Your Time." Other parents had simply
signed their names, but Jessie had appreciated that someone on the
school board would take the time to read what a 15-year-old mother
of three would have to say about how the district's money should
be spent. We decided to put copies of Jessie's letter on the top of

the packets containing 45 other support letters. Every school board member and administrator received copies. Our letters, telephone calls, and other efforts finally paid off on June 26. The school board voted 8 to 1 in favor of continuing the funding of our program for 1 more year. We took Jessie and another mother out to lunch to celebrate our victory. It was a tangible way to express our appreciation for their support.

AN UNEXPECTED ENDING

If there is one thing that I have learned in my years of working with teenage mothers, it is to expect the unexpected. On a routine home visit to Jessie's house a few weeks ago, she interrupted my report about her sons' recent progress with, "In 5 days I'm going to be moving." I told her that would not be a problem because we had enough time to arrange for the bus to pick up Jerome and Lamont at their new address next week.

"No," she said, "we're moving to Oklahoma." I stared at her in disbelief, and she proceeded to explain that her mother was throwing her, the children, and Jessie's boyfriend out of the house. Jessie said things had gotten really bad. There were allegations of sexual assaults taking place in the home, public assistance checks being stolen, and other accusations being made. The situation sounded serious and too complex for my counseling abilities. Jessie had decided to move with her boyfriend to his family's home in Oklahoma. The bus tickets had been purchased already!

I didn't know what to say to Jessie. When I asked her if she had really thought out what such a drastic move would be like, she told me she had discussed the move with her social worker and that he had supported it. A telephone call to the social worker later confirmed that moving to Oklahoma was the best option—maybe the only option—for Jessie at this time. I told Jessie how much she and the children would be missed.

When I mentioned continuing the boys in some type of early intervention at their new home, Jessie again surprised me. She told me that she had talked to her boyfriend's mother, who had already telephoned the appropriate Oklahoma school district to find out how to enroll the boys in the local program.

I returned on the day of the big move to have Jessie sign a permission form to forward the boys' records. Her bag was packed and Jerome and Lamont sat expressionless on the front steps, not really understanding what was about to happen. Jessie told the boys to give me kisses for helping them to learn so much. Then I gave

Jessie a hug, and she said, "Thank you for caring about me and my kids."

What more could I say? Working with Jessie had been a challenge and I felt we both had benefited from the experiences we shared. I had learned some valuable strategies that I could apply to other challenging family situations. The time Jessie had spent with me would continue to be beneficial long after she was gone. And so, I turned to her and said, "Good luck, Jessie, and thank you for your time."

DISCUSSION QUESTIONS

1. What, if anything, did the early interventionist do that might have accounted for Jessie's receptiveness on the first visits to the home?

2. Was in-home assessment of the boys handled appropriately? Should it have been handled differently?

3. In this case, Jessie elected to enroll the boys in the program. What do you think contributed to her decision to do so? What would you have done if Jessie had decided not to enroll the boys?

4. Based on the information available, do you think that goal-setting for the boys was handled in the best way? How would you have proceeded in developing an individualized family service plan (IFSP) for this family?

5. The early interventionist's "camera trick" seemed to have the desired effect. What else might have been done to engage Jessie's interest in the boys' development? Was this even an appropriate objective for the early interventionist to try to achieve?

6. Should the early interventionist have done more to encourage Jessie to return to school? How would you have handled the issue?

7. Was it appropriate for the early interventionist to introduce the issue of birth control? How else might she have handled this rather sensitive issue?

8. The issue of "trust" is highlighted in this case. What did the early interventionist do to establish and maintain trust with this young mother?

9. It seems that the early interventionist chose to focus her interactions on Jessie and the two boys. Would you have done more to involve Jessie's mother (Maxine), her boyfriend, or other members of the household?

10. Jessie's social worker is only mentioned briefly in the story. Do you think it would have been important for the early inter-

ventionist to have ongoing contact with the social worker? What should the roles of the early interventionist and the social worker be? How would these decisions be made?

11. Not every program has both a home-based and a classroom-based component. What were the advantages of having each in this case? Would one be preferable in providing services to adolescent parents?

12. If you were responsible for evaluating the success of a program for teenage parents with at-risk children, what methods and measures would you use?

13. If you were a program administrator, what precautions would you take to ensure the safety of your staff members who work in potentially dangerous communities?

The First
Year Together

James M. Helm
and Linda H. Carothers

Born 10 weeks early, Evan spent the first weeks of his life in the intensive care nursery. It was a struggle for both him and his parents, Carolyn and Terry, but all survived and Evan went home. This case describes the emotional and physical stress that his mother faces in caring for her premature infant who has gastroesophageal reflux. The case also describes the efforts of a professional, Bonnie, who visited the family's home throughout the first year of Evan's life. Bonnie attempts to provide support as the family adjusts to the demands of an infant with special needs and, as Evan's need for special care subsides, she is supportive of Carolyn's attempts to recoup a part of her own life that had been temporarily abandoned.

Within a few days, Evan would be going home. Born 2½ months prematurely, he had stayed in the intensive care and intermediate care nurseries for weeks, and we were about to evaluate him with the Brazelton Neonatal Behavioral Assessment Scale. We, like others, find that the Brazelton NBAS is an excellent way to show parents the skills and behaviors of their baby, in addition to providing important clinical information. Although the Brazelton NBAS does not give us a score, it does yield a profile of the child's ability to manage the type of routine handling he or she will probably receive at home.

Evan's mother, Carolyn, was sitting by his crib as we began to administer the Brazelton NBAS. Carolyn was pleased that Evan would be going home soon. In addition to the emotional trauma of having a baby in the intensive care nursery, making the daily trips to the hospital and the nursery had been very tiring. Now Carolyn was quiet and appeared very interested in the exam. Later, we learned she was actually very nervous because "this was his first test and I wanted him to do well."

Evan showed us that, although he was quite competent in many respects, he was still at risk. Evan was competent in that he was able to bring himself to an alert state, focus on the examiner's face, and follow slow movements from side to side. He attempted to control interaction by looking away from the examiner's face for short periods, and he made efforts to console himself when he was upset by trying to slow his movements. Once he tried to get his hands together, and another time, he tried to grasp his face. These attempts were only temporarily effective, but showed us Evan's strategies for consoling himself. Knowing this, we were able to help him follow through with his own strategies by holding his hands for him. Evan also showed us that he was having difficulty making the transition from sleep to wakefulness. He needed help to do this as well. Evan tired quickly and needed a long break before he could complete the assessment. These behaviors, however, are typical of children born 2½ months prematurely. Overall, we were pleased that Evan was doing so well.

From our perspective, Evan's stay had been smooth. He needed the ventilator for only 10 days and, within 2 weeks, was breathing room air. A mild heart problem, which is typical in premature infants, responded well to medication, and he received 2 days of phototherapy for jaundice. Evan had some bleeding in his brain, also not unusual for a premature infant of 30 weeks gestation, but it had been very small, was resolved quickly, and was not likely to cause any developmental problems later. In addition, he had several spells in which he stopped breathing for short periods (i.e., apnea) and his heart rate slowed (i.e., bradycardia). Again, apnea and bradycardia are typical in premature infants. In sum, Evan had a very good prognosis and was fortunate to have parents with the means and motivation to offer an excellent environment for his growth and development.

It was time for Evan to go home. Carolyn and her husband, Terry, were happy and excited, and as Carolyn said later, "It was frightening at first to leave him behind, among hospital strangers, but as the weeks passed, it became more frightening to think of him ever coming home without a room full of machines to keep him alive."

A ROCKY START

Home life was not going to be as everyone anticipated. Evan developed gastroesophageal reflux (i.e., milk would not stay down), which tends to make babies uncomfortable and irritable. Evan spit up shortly after most of his feedings, and Carolyn was pumping breast milk to feed him from a bottle because he wasn't nursing well. Carolyn was troubled that Evan couldn't keep down her milk.

Evan was not thriving, and Carolyn and Terry were exhausted, frustrated, and feeling incompetent. After several visits to the pediatrician, Evan finally declared whose side he was on. This occurred when a nurse was feeding Evan, seeming to imply that all Carolyn needed to do was relax and feed Evan like she was. Suddenly, Evan spit up all over the nurse. Carolyn thinks that she concealed her pleasure fairly well. After the situation was fully assessed and it was confirmed that Evan was losing weight, he was sent to the hospital and admitted for failure to thrive. This was a blow to Carolyn's confidence. As she said later, "To me, that translated into being a bad mother."

Evan was only in the hospital a few days. Several tests were administered, and it was determined that reflux was the cause of the excessive vomiting and weight loss. As a result, medicine was prescribed and strategies were developed to assist Evan in accepting and retaining his feedings. Evan's parents learned the procedures, which seemed to have the desired effect, and Evan started to gain weight. Once again, Evan was ready to go home with his parents.

Before Evan was discharged, we talked with Carolyn and Terry about our home-based program called *First Years Together*. The program is a collaborative project between the hospital and the local school district and is designed to provide support to families while they make the transition from the intensive care nursery to home. Although Carolyn had been told about the project when Evan went home the first time, she didn't think she needed it or wanted it then. All that she had wanted was to take her son home and be a mother to him. Carolyn's feelings about the program had changed somewhat. Because she now believed that receiving support from people who were more familiar with premature infants might be a good idea, Carolyn gave permission for someone from the project to call her at home to explain the program in more detail and possibly set up a time for a visit. Eventually, arrangements were made for Bonnie, a project staff member, to visit Evan and his parents in their home.

A TIRED MOM

Bonnie's first visit took place 2 weeks after Evan's second discharge. Carolyn had requested an early afternoon visit because Evan would be napping and she could more easily talk with Bonnie. The family lived in an older, quiet neighborhood with heavily planted pine tree lots. Carolyn met Bonnie at the door and invited her through to the kitchen where she offered to make some coffee as she continued cleaning bottles from the morning.

"I'm sorry for the mess," apologized Carolyn. "I didn't get a chance to straighten this morning like I'd planned."

"Don't apologize," said Bonnie. "It just looks like a baby lives here." Carolyn laughed and they joked about how housekeeping standards dropped to a basic minimum with a baby in the house.

Bonnie warned, "It seems to me that, as my kids grew, their messes also grew." Bonnie was pleased that this seemed to break the ice and that Carolyn appeared so open and willing to talk.

Despite her pleasant manner, Carolyn looked exhausted. Her face and eyes were drawn and she sighed deeply between activities, as if she had little energy left. Carolyn seemed to have put herself on automatic pilot to make it through the day.

"I need to get these ready to go when Evan wakes up so I can manage him without having to prepare bottles," she said. "If I skip part of my routine, it seems that something always goes wrong." Carolyn's movements were slow and she was careful to lay out everything in preparation for the next feeding. As she described her schedule it was easy to understand why.

After Evan's reflux had been diagnosed, the doctors prescribed medicine and a number of feeding procedures. Carolyn, trying to be a "good mother," followed them precisely. She recited the routine as if being asked for the thousandth time: "I need to give Evan medicine 30 minutes before feeding, then I can only feed him 3 ounces. After he eats, I have to keep him quiet and hold him in an upright position for 30 minutes. After that, I can put him down, but I have to pump breast milk for the next round. During the day, I have to do this every 2 hours and, at night, every 4 hours unless he wakes up, which he usually does." She paused, stared out the window, and said in a lowered voice, "This sounded easy in the hospital."

Carolyn seemed to have hit a low point for energy and motivation. After 3 months of unsuccessful nursing, she had decided to give up breastfeeding because Evan would not accept milk directly from her. Nevertheless, she continued to pump her breast milk and feed it to him from a bottle. Every hour and minute of the day seemed to revolve around feeding Evan, who did not want to eat and often threw up what he did eat. Carolyn seemed to be nearing her limit.

As they talked, it seemed to Bonnie that Carolyn wanted to stop pumping breast milk, but felt guilty over the prospect of doing so. Bonnie wanted to grab Carolyn by the shoulders and tell her that she had gone above and beyond the call of duty. Evan would survive on formula but she might not survive if she continued pumping the breast milk. However, Bonnie knew that her role was to affirm and support Carolyn's decisions, not to direct them.

"Carolyn, I know that you've decided to stop nursing, but how do you feel about Evan getting breast milk?" she asked.

"It's difficult to set limits on how much care and devotion to give a sick child," answered Carolyn. "My heart says the care for my baby should be limitless, but your body knows better. Your body wins, but not until you exhaust yourself, your marriage, and your confidence."

"Do you think Evan needs the breast milk?" asked Bonnie.

"The pediatrician said we could try feeding him formula," answered Carolyn. "But all you ever read is how much better breast milk is for babies. I want to do everything I can for him." Carolyn's eyes reddened and teared up as she spoke.

"It looks to me as though you are doing everything you can— and then some," reassured Bonnie. "You look tired. Would you like to explore the possibility of formula feeding a little further?"

"Maybe," answered Carolyn, blotting her eyes with the towel that was slung over her shoulder. "I'm disappointed that I had to give up nursing Evan, but at this point, I just want some relief so I have energy left to be a mommy for him."

"That sounds like a good priority to me," said Bonnie. "Maybe you could talk further with your pediatrician about formula or, if you'd prefer, I would be happy to try to find out more about it at our office or at the hospital. There are also some other moms who have participated in our program who have gone through struggles similar to what you are experiencing. If you'd like to talk to one of them, I'm certain they'd be pleased."

They continued their conversation a while longer, discussing the various aspects of switching to formula, and Bonnie told a few stories about other mothers and babies she had worked with over the years. No decisions were reached, but some options were explored. Carolyn needed some time to think about what she wanted to do. The conversation gradually drifted toward Carolyn's experiences with Evan in the intensive care nursery, but this topic was soon interrupted by the sound of Evan stirring in the next room.

AN UNHAPPY BABY

Carolyn immediately left the room to get Evan. This was not a happy baby! He wrinkled his brow like a very old man. He rolled his head back, arched, and looked at everyone with huge, unhappy eyes. He seemed unusually stiff and uncomfortable. While waiting the 30 minutes between taking his medicine and being fed, Bonnie spent some time with Evan.

Through observation and questions, Carolyn and Bonnie began to try to figure out what did and did not work to increase Evan's comfort. Carolyn was a good observer and could identify a number of things that helped to comfort Evan. Offering him a pacifier, changing his position every few minutes, and using a rapid, rocking movement were all helpful in relaxing Evan, but no strategy had a lasting effect. Carolyn also pointed out that, although these strategies were somewhat effective when he was hungry, after feeding she needed different strategies because of the required upright position. For example, rocking after eating made the reflux worse.

Carolyn seemed pleased that she could offer suggestions and appreciated the positive comments about her skills. Helping Carolyn see both her own and Evan's strengths was a positive step toward rebuilding her confidence in herself as a parent. After all, the strengths were there; it was the confidence that was lacking.

REFLECTING ON THE PAST

Evan finished his bottle, but only after many fussy breaks during which Carolyn quickly lifted him to her shoulder, rocked him, and gently patted him on the back.

She explained, "I used to try to get him interested in the bottle again, hoping that he would drink a little more. But, now I know that it works better if I give him a break and help him calm down before I try the bottle again. If he stays mad for even a few minutes, the food usually comes right back up."

After the feeding, Evan was much more content and even dozed as he was held upright in Carolyn's arms for 30 minutes. Sitting outside on the patio, Bonnie asked a few questions about Evan's birth, and Carolyn described the events that took place as well as her feelings during Evan's first critical days.

"I was so scared going into the delivery room. I just knew that it was too early for the baby to survive," Carolyn reminisced. "But when they showed him to me, I looked into that little, pinched, wrinkled, blue-gray face and just had to smile. He looked like his dad." She paused for a moment to kiss Evan on the head and then continued. "He gave a single yelp as they carried him away to the intensive care nursery. You know, it's funny how important that little yelp was to me. While he was in the nursery, unable to make a sound because of the ventilator tube, I desperately tried to recall the sound of that one cry."

They talked a while longer, but soon it was time to put Evan to bed and Carolyn needed to pump milk in preparation for the next feeding. Bonnie helped clean up a little, and they arranged the next visit.

During the first visits, Carolyn and Bonnie often returned to a discussion of Evan's birth. One day in early spring, Bonnie complimented Carolyn on the beautiful gardens in their yard. "I did most of that when Evan was in the hospital," explained Carolyn. "I needed something to do that I could succeed at. I felt like such a failure as a mother." She went on to say, "Although I visited him every day, did all the caregiving tasks that the nurses would let me do, and kept on top of his medical progress, it was hard to feel like a good mother. Evan's life was in the hands of the doctors and nurses and $1,000-a-day hospital machines. I was just the visitor."

There were tears in Carolyn's eyes as she remembered the pain of those first few weeks. "When I was finally able to hold him," she continued, "my touch seemed to offer him little comfort among that tangle of tubes, wires, and needles."

THROUGHOUT THE YEAR

During the early visits, Bonnie and Carolyn talked about many issues related to Evan's care but also about him as a baby born prematurely. An important concept was that of adjusted age. It was important to remind Carolyn that to determine Evan's developmental age, she needed to calculate from the date he was due instead of the date he was born. Therefore, although Evan had been in this world for over 3 months, his adjusted age for prematurity was just 2 weeks. This helped Carolyn better understand why, for the 3 months that she had been caring and loving her baby, she had not received even one smile.

During one visit, Bonnie played with Evan while Carolyn prepared his bottle. Just as he began responding to Bonnie's smiling and talking, Carolyn came into the room. "He never does that with me," she said. She sat down beside Bonnie and they both talked and cooed to him. As he heard Carolyn's voice, he turned to look for her and gave her a sweet smile. Carolyn beamed and seemed surprised and thrilled when Bonnie pointed out that Evan turned to look for her voice when she entered the room. As Evan's health improved, Carolyn and Terry continued to reinforce and encourage his social skills. Evan became more responsive and social to his parents and others.

Although Carolyn claims that Bonnie showed her how to play with her son, the truth is that Carolyn had the ability all along. As Evan's initial difficulties dissipated, Carolyn used her skills and Evan responded to her interactions. Over time, there were fewer discussions of Evan's problems and the things he could not do. The focus of visits shifted toward Evan's progress and future. Carolyn always had questions, ranging from issues related to development to what kinds of toys to buy and when she should start feeding him solid foods.

GOING ON VACATION

As the year continued, Evan gradually outgrew the reflux and life became easier for his family. It was time for Carolyn to redefine her role. She was no longer the mother of a sick premature baby. Over the past year, Carolyn had done very little for herself. All of her activities had been related to caring for Evan. Now she was struggling with questions that many mothers face—when she should return to work, whether Evan should attend a preschool, and so forth—but answering these questions was particularly difficult for Carolyn. After watching her child cling to life, she couldn't help wanting to cling to him and make sure his life was never that hard again.

By this time, Bonnie was visiting less frequently but still calling on a regular basis. Bonnie was somewhat concerned about Carolyn because, although Carolyn seemed to want to spend some time apart from Evan, she didn't seem able to take action. Bonnie sent information on classes offered by their project and other programs in the community. They also discussed child care options and what Carolyn wanted for herself. Carolyn would plan to check out the various options they discussed, but never followed through. Although she said she wanted to find part-time child care, the applications were never filled out and returned.

Finally, Bonnie learned of an opening in a child care program that had a mother's day-out option. Bonnie knew the caregiver, someone she trusted implicitly. She called and told Carolyn that she "needed a vacation" and that she had plans for her to review. The vacation joke was a familiar one between them since Carolyn was always saying that she was going to take a vacation when she finally got Evan into child care. They laughed at Bonnie's travel agent role and visited the program together. Shortly afterward, Carolyn enrolled Evan. That year, he attended the program 2 mornings each week and the following year, he went 5 days a week. Carolyn then returned to work on a part-time basis.

Carolyn's concern about Evan's health and development continued for a long time after they left our program, but this was not unexpected. We did not intend to allay all of her concerns. Our goal was to provide support that would ease the added stresses that accompany caring for a premature infant. Through information-sharing and emotional support, we strived to enable this family to have the lifestyle they wanted to the greatest extent possible. This we felt we had achieved.

DISCUSSION QUESTIONS

1. This case does not provide detailed information how the *First Years Together* transition project was introduced to Carolyn and her husband. If you were in the position of offering the project's services to this family, how would you do it? How would you contact the parents? Where would you speak to them? Would you offer written information? What words would you use in explaining the project and offering services?

2. The first visit to a family's home is often uncomfortable for both the parent(s) and the professional. In this case, what did Bonnie do or say to reduce the tension and begin establishing rapport? What are some other strategies that you might use with families to establish rapport in such first encounters?

3. How well do you think Bonnie addressed the issue of Carolyn's continued pumping of breast milk for Evan? Would you have handled it differently?

4. Evidently Carolyn felt a need to talk about the events and feelings she experienced at Evan's birth and during his stay in the intensive care nursery. Was it appropriate for Bonnie to serve as her sounding board in these matters? Would it have been appropriate for Bonnie to suggest that Carolyn seek professional counseling?

5. Did Bonnie provide an appropriate level of support in finding child care for Evan so Carolyn could resume some of her own activities? Was Bonnie too directive or not directive enough?

6. List at least five specific things that Bonnie did or said that exemplify the concepts of "enablement" or "empowerment."

7. Suppose you want to initiate a neonatal intensive care unit (NICU) to home transition project in your own community. Write a brief proposal to submit to the town council or city hall. Your proposal should contain the following:
    *   A statement of the need for the project (i.e., rationale)
    *   A list of the proposed outcomes (i.e., objectives)
    *   An overview of the strategies to be used by the project staff (i.e., method)

- A statement of how the project will fit into the existing service delivery system (i.e., interagency coordination)

8. Suppose you are responsible for training and supervising staff for a project similar to *First Years Together*. In this position, one of your tasks is to develop a 3- to 5-page paper entitled, "Guidelines for Home Visitors." It will be used to introduce staff to the project's philosophy and some of the basic principles and strategies for conducting home visits.

An Orange Raincoat

Marilyn Espe-Sherwindt

*Pearl and her 9-month-old son, Robert, attend an infant de-
velopment program only to avoid Robert's removal from the
home. Pearl makes it obvious that she does not want to be
there and the staff feel dumped upon and unable to gain her
trust. Over time, the staff come to understand Pearl better and
find meaningful ways to provide assistance to the family. This
case describes the forging of a relationship between the program staff and this mother with mental retardation as they
work together to overcome barriers and establish a network of
support for Pearl and her family.*

Pearl never took off her orange raincoat—rain or shine, blizzard or
blistering heat. Pearl's coat was the subject of frequent discussion
at team meetings: What did it symbolize? Her lack of trust in us? A
signal that she might flee at any moment? A protective cloak against
us—because she saw us as one more potentially harmful group of
professionals in her life?

AT FIRST GLANCE

The referral was intimidating. "Both mother and baby are slow. The
baby's father lives out of state and has no contact with them." The
extended family was described in such terms as "questionable al-
cohol abuse," "history of mental illness," and "dual diagnosis."
Another source stated, "Mother does not know her own address
and telephone number. History difficult to obtain."

In person, Pearl was as intimidating as her referral. She was a
tall, sturdily built woman with an ageless face. She could have been
25 or 45 years old. Her responses to questions were curt and brief.

She never smiled or started a conversation with us or any of the other parents. Her 9-month-old son, Robert, was a fussy, irritable little boy with mild, yet obvious, delays. He was not yet babbling or sitting well. He smiled as seldom as his mother.

Pearl was in danger of losing custody of her baby. Agencies were concerned about her ability to care for Robert. There never seemed to be enough baby food in the apartment. Safety hazards abounded. We were told that Pearl often failed to respond to visitors' knocks on the door. It was also painfully clear that she did not want to be part of our program.

What were we supposed to do? We felt dumped on—early intervention to the rescue again because all other attempts to improve Pearl's caregiving skills had allegedly failed. We were the program of last resort.

TAKING A SECOND LOOK

It was hard to watch Pearl's unresponsiveness week after week. We greeted her warmly each day and told her how happy we were to see her and Robert, but she just stared at the floor. Conversations buzzed around her, but she rarely took part in them. And she never took off her orange raincoat.

We talked about Pearl and our frustrations at each team meeting. Our first attempt to complete an individualized family service plan failed. Although Pearl was receiving multiple services, it seemed that she viewed none of them as helpful. She regarded us with similar suspicion and would not identify any areas in which we could be of assistance to her or her baby. She came to us only because she had been ordered to come—or lose her baby.

We argued among ourselves as to the best strategy to take with Pearl. One person played the role of devil's advocate: "We are constantly getting more referrals. How can we justify keeping a slot open for a family that clearly doesn't want our services?" We finally decided that our job was to get Pearl to trust us and to come because she *wanted* to come. We realized it might take weeks—or even months—for that to happen.

So we waited; we welcomed; and we watched. We shared our surprise and pleasure with one another as some positive things began to happen. Although Pearl was not very talkative with Robert, she held him closely and stroked him. When staff members worked with him, Pearl followed every movement out of the corner of one eye. Her brief responses to questions suggested that she too was concerned that he was not yet sitting very well and was not a very good eater. It became easier to compliment Pearl. One day she almost smiled, although her hand came up to cover her mouth. But she never took off her orange raincoat.

OUR EYES ARE OPENED

One day Pearl did something that we talked about extensively in our team meeting. Robert, now more than 12 months old, was blowing soap bubbles with the speech-language pathologist. As usual, Pearl had been watching closely. Hoping to encourage some mother–child play, the speech-language pathologist had handed the bubble wand to Pearl. Pearl reluctantly took the bubble wand, held it for 30 seconds or so, briefly held it up to her lips without blowing, and then returned it to the speech-language pathologist. Was this yet another sign of resistance? After much discussion, we decided that Pearl probably didn't have the slightest idea how to pucker her lips and blow bubbles. Rather than fail in front of us, she had chosen not to participate. If we wanted Pearl to succeed, we had to plan activities that were attractive and made enough sense to her that she would be willing to take the risk of participating.

That strategy seemed to work. We began to see more changes. One day our log said:

> Pearl and Robert were more interactive today. Robert didn't like to look at or feel the porcupine squeaker. Pearl liked it and playfully teased him by putting it on his shoe or leg or on her own leg. She gently did hand-over-hand to get him to touch the porcupine. She didn't always pick up on his verbal cues, but the hand-over-hand movement was good.

A month later, after one of our regular "clothing swaps," we noted that Pearl was starting to talk to other parents in the group.

> Today Pearl talked to two of the parents while picking out some clothes for Robert. She commented on the difference in development between Robert and another child similar in age, "He [Robert] is even taller and cannot walk." So Pearl assisted Robert to pull to stand.

Pearl's own story emerged slowly and painfully. She had grown up in a rural community and dropped out of school in the third grade. Her babies had started arriving when she was a teenager. All of her babies had been taken from her at birth because someone had thought Pearl's mental retardation was too severe for her to care for them. Pearl saw Robert as her last chance—indeed her only chance—to raise a child herself.

The future did not look hopeful for Pearl to do that. She was not cooperating with the protective service agency involved with her. The safety hazards in her apartment were so significant that she had been asked to find a new place to live, but she had not done so. She often refused to let the agency's staff members come into her home. And now Pearl was pregnant again. Because we were seeing progress in our program, we talked repeatedly with the agency caseworker to advocate for more time for Pearl. The caseworker, however, was so overworked and overwhelmed she could not see any option other than to remove Pearl's son and place him in foster care.

THE MONTHS APART

Although living separately, Pearl and Robert continued to attend our program. Pearl would arrive early, in her orange raincoat, anxiously waiting for her little boy. Mother and son would smile broadly when they first caught sight of each other. Some weeks, it was clear that the pregnancy tired Pearl but she was trying very hard to interact with Robert during their time together.

As Pearl's body grew and changed shape, so did our relationship with her. She had been aware of our attempts to advocate on her behalf and indicated her gratefulness. Although she continued to wear her orange raincoat each week, it seemed less of a symbolic barrier between her and the rest of the group. One week we discovered that the reason she smiled so rarely was that she was embarrassed by the poor condition of her teeth. Another week, we wrote about her wry sense of humor:

> Pearl seemed very interested in a book of nursery rhymes and watched intently while Robert pointed to pictures and we named them for him. She looked at the cover of the book, which illustrated The Old Woman Who Lived in the Shoe, and commented, "Daggone! Look at all those kids!"

In our team meeting, we talked about how Robert had been placed in a unique foster home. The foster mother was willing to let Pearl visit in the foster home and went out of her way to make Pearl feel comfortable. Because Pearl spoke so highly of her, we began to view the foster mother as a sort of mentor to Pearl. Pearl's support network was expanding. Our staff, the foster mother, and the workers and drivers from the protective services agency were all part of the same trusted network, working with and on behalf of Pearl and her son.

Keeping in touch with the "network" took some time and effort on our part. Pearl knew how frequently we talked with the other people involved with her because we always asked for her permission. She became an increasingly active member of the communication loop and began to assume control in other ways as well. For example, when we talked with her about updating the IFSP, Pearl noted that Robert's walking and talking were behind. She knew that he was only using single words and stated, "I want to hear him say 'I want a bottle.' " Then Pearl added that she liked to meet the families here and got to know them more each time she came. But, she still wore her orange raincoat.

One day Pearl told her caseworker that she sometimes had problems understanding conversation. An audiological evaluation revealed that Pearl had a moderate to severe hearing loss in the right ear and normal hearing sloping to a mild hearing loss in the left ear. No wonder Pearl didn't respond to our attempts to engage her in conversation or to knocks on her door. The audiologist's recommendations, however, meant more appointments for Pearl. She was already visiting Robert, attending our program, keeping her obstetrical appointments, and looking for housing. Pearl's support network became even more important.

AND BABY MAKES THREE

After several months had passed, we learned from Robert's foster mother that Pearl had gone into labor shortly after our last meeting and had delivered a little girl. Because the baby had arrived a month early and was small, she had to stay in the hospital until she was feeding well and her weight reached 5 pounds. Apparently there was some question as to whether the baby would be going home to Pearl because even though progress had been made in other areas, Pearl still had not found a new place to live.

It was not that Pearl hadn't been trying. The problem was that the waiting list for subsidized public housing with enough bedrooms for Pearl and her two children was up to one year. Other housing options had fallen through because Pearl had not known how to complete the application forms or had not had enough money for deposits. As usual, Pearl was a topic of discussion at our team meeting. Even though we felt confident in our abilities to intervene with Pearl and her children, none of us felt very skilled in the intricacies required to obtain public housing. So, once again, we found ourselves on the telephone with Pearl's caseworker.

"We know you're very busy," we told her, "but we'd like to do what we can to help Pearl. We'd be happy to help her fill out the forms if you can put some pressure on the housing authorities." The caseworker agreed to our deal.

In the meantime, Pearl, in her orange raincoat, showed up at our program only 2 weeks after her baby was born. She smiled while telling us that she had figured out how to take the bus to the hospital when she was in labor. Her smile grew as she described her baby girl. She went on to say that she had talked to her doctor about getting her tubes tied, but that the doctor had refused to perform the procedure because Pearl was not capable of understanding and giving her consent.

Later, during our team meeting, we angrily discussed the doctor's refusal to grant Pearl's request for a tubal ligation. We had encountered this situation before with another mother with mental retardation. We were frustrated because some people did not understand that having mental retardation does not mean an inability to learn, generalize, or make wise decisions. We suggested that the caseworker find a psychologist who would talk with Pearl and evaluate her in a variety of ways, not just through intelligence testing. We recommended several names.

Eventually, the baby, named Maria, came home with Pearl. Every week Pearl and Maria arrived together and were reunited with Robert for the afternoon. Robert, who was almost 21 months old, enjoyed the visits. Our team was rather surprised by how well Pearl handled the simultaneous demands of two small children. Maria was doing beautifully. She was interactive, cooed, laughed, and was right on target for her corrected age. Pearl was absolutely delighted. One day our log read:

> Today Pearl chose to make a rattle bracelet for Maria. Then she played with Maria for a while, before placing her in her infant seat. Maria watched intently as Pearl talked and cuddled with Robert. Pearl's face still lights up when Maria attracts attention in the lobby or classroom. Pearl continues to be more talkative in group and able to discuss her difficulties with housing.

The housing problem had not been solved. Pearl and her caseworker kept us updated, but we were extremely frustrated. Pearl's hearing difficulties had not been resolved either. Maria's birth had interrupted Pearl's efforts to complete further diagnostic testing regarding her hearing loss. Pearl's next hurdle was a magnetic resonance imaging (MRI) appointment. Pearl had already refused to allow the MRI once because she was afraid of "that big black hole." When we asked her if she would like someone to accompany her and care for Maria while she was having the test, she agreed to keep the appointment.

One of us met Pearl at the hospital on the morning of her appointment. Pearl smiled broadly when she saw someone from our program, but reiterated how afraid she was about the test. However, that day, she successfully completed the MRI. Afterward, Pearl explained that, although she had been frightened, she knew we were waiting outside so she "just got it over with." In fact, she had refused a mild sedative so that she would be able to take Maria home immediately and care for her without feeling drowsy.

Pearl was also evaluated by one of the psychologists we had recommended. He found that she was quite capable of making informed decisions when information was described clearly and thoroughly to her. Pearl and the caseworker began to look for another gynecologist.

We thought we understood Pearl pretty well and felt confident in what we were accomplishing with her, but one day we found ourselves in a very humbling position. Pearl and the other parents had decided that they would like to make special gifts for their children for the holidays. The gift that Pearl had chosen required a significant amount of cutting around a complicated pattern. Pearl struggled and struggled, switching the scissors back and forth from hand to hand. Finally, after much perseverance, she completed the project. Much to our chagrin, someone who had been observing the session pointed out afterward that Pearl was left-handed and had been working with the right-handed scissors we had given her. We had unintentionally set her up for failure, but she had succeeded in spite of us.

OVERCOMING OUR HURDLES TOGETHER

During the next few months, Pearl found a new place to live, Robert came home, and Maria continued to thrive. Robert's foster mother purchased a housewarming present for Pearl—a special telephone with large numbers and an amplifier. Discussion at our team meetings focused on changes in Pearl's social interaction in our program. Our log read:

> Pearl continues to make more eye contact each time we see her. She takes pride in her appearance as well as her children's. While Robert was using the child-sized broom today, Pearl commented that he is probably taking after her because she's always sweeping to keep the floors clean for her babies.

We continued to admire Pearl's ability to attend to both of her children. Whether they were eating a snack, playing with a toy telephone, or playing with one of Maria's rattles, Pearl found a way to include both children. It was also clear that Pearl was no longer hesitant to try what she saw us doing with her children. One week's log read:

> When asked by the occupational therapist if she was picking up Maria each time she changed her diaper on the floor, Pearl replied that no, she was helping Maria roll onto her stomach by rotating her opposite knee to the floor—"just like you showed me."

Our strategy to do whatever was necessary to respond to Pearl's immediate needs was working. Pearl had even stopped wearing her orange raincoat. During another IFSP update, Pearl identified the following goals: 1) to change her children's pediatric clinic days so that the appointments will better fit the family's schedule, 2) to learn to read so that she can keep track of Robert's and Maria's appointments, and 3) to make toys for Robert and Maria "so that they will have a better life." Pearl was feeling empowered.

However, our role as Pearl's advocate had not ended. Due to continued delay in his expressive language, Robert had begun attending a toddler play-language group at a nearby center. Pearl expressed some reluctance about Robert continuing in the play group because "it's not doing anything—he's not talking yet." Our speech-language pathologist talked to the center's staff by telephone and set up a time for Pearl to talk to them. Not only didn't Pearl understand the goals for Robert in the play group, but the center also had no idea that Pearl had a hearing impairment and was unable to read. Their previous attempts to communicate with Pearl had been by letters or telephone calls. In many ways, their perceptions of Pearl resembled ours when we first met her. It was important for them to hear how Pearl could change if the professionals working with her could change along with her.

MOVING ON

We had known Pearl for more than 2 years, and it was becoming more difficult for her to attend our program. Her new apartment was not on a bus line convenient to us, and the demands of two children and their activities and appointments kept her busy. Once again, Pearl was the main topic of discussion at our team meeting. We knew that transition had to be planned carefully in order to help Pearl continue to succeed. Some issues were still unresolved—the hearing aids, the tubal ligation—but the caseworker was willing to assist Pearl with those. Pearl had moved to an apartment complex that contained a Head Start program, and Robert would be eligible for services in the fall. When we talked to Pearl, she appreciated our concern and was excited about a "school" for Robert. "No one in my family ever went to school that young," she said. There was also an adult literacy program down the street from her new apartment. We offered to help, but Pearl chose to do it on her own. She made the telephone calls, kept the appointments, and asked for help in completing forms when necessary. Then Pearl, Robert, and Maria moved on with their lives.

Two of our staff were visiting in Pearl's neighborhood about a year later and dropped in to see her and the children. Pearl had just finished giving both children baths. Robert and Maria soon dropped their shyness and were laughing and playing while the adults talked. Pearl had made friends in the neighborhood, and Robert was attending Head Start. Pearl still had not gotten her hearing aids or tubal ligation, but she had managed to care for her children and keep them healthy and happy. "Please come back and visit me any time," Pearl said as she closed the door.

At the next team meeting, we described the visit with Pearl. Some of our staff were relatively new and had not known her. We talked at length about her orange raincoat. For us, it had come to symbolize the barriers between a parent with mental retardation and the professionals and systems serving her. In many ways, we had all been wearing orange raincoats. Pearl had taught us to leave them at home.

DISCUSSION QUESTIONS

1. The staff's strategy for gaining Pearl's trust is summarized by the statement, "We waited; we welcomed; and we watched." Was this the best strategy to employ? Could or should a more active approach have been taken in getting Pearl to be more open?

2. Although not completely satisfied, the staff seemed content with the progress that Pearl and her family made. Could they have been as successful: 1) if the program did not include active participation by parents in the classroom, or 2) if the program provided home-based services only?

3. Pearl's network of services and support is mentioned throughout this case study. The network and communication among its members, however, appears to have been rather loosely structured. Should more structure have been imposed upon this system?

4. The staff obviously took on more roles and responsibilities in assisting Pearl than would be typically expected. Did they overstep their bounds? If so, who should have been responsible? What role should the program staff have taken in facilitating action by others? If not, could the efforts of these staff members be replicated in other classroom-based programs?

5. Were there any aspects of this case that you feel could have been handled more effectively or sensitively? What alternative strategies would you propose?

6. How should we measure success in programs involving parents with mental retardation? Are these measures different from those appropriate for other early intervention programs?

7. What stereotypes exist in society regarding parents with mental retardation? How might those stereotypes become barriers to family-centered early intervention?

8. What other "systems" should early interventionists become familiar with in order to develop support networks for parents with mental retardation?

9. How would you develop an individualized family service plan (IFSP) for families such as Pearl's? What formats would you use? What strategies would you employ in gaining parent involvement in the process? How would your strategies differ from those you might use with parents who do not have mental retardation?

10. Both Pearl and Robert have been identified as having disabilities or being at risk for disabilities. In such cases should each identified family member have a separate service coordinator? If this is the case, how might early interventionists separate or coordinate the roles of each?

Kindergarten's Not for Another 2 Years

Mary Frances Hanline

Maureen and Jerry had been very pleased with the services they and their son, Marcus, had received for more than 2 years at the Geary Street Infant Development Program. The private program had been extremely supportive of the family through some very difficult times including Marcus's diagnosis of agenesis of the corpus callosum. Soon, Marcus would be 3 years old, and it was time for him to make the transition from the infant program to the community's school-based pre-school services. Andi has been assigned to work with the family to plan Marcus's transition. Theirs is the first family she has worked with in her new job. This case describes the anxiety experienced by both Maureen and Andi as they take on the challenge of ensuring a smooth transition and quality services for Marcus.

Andi glanced around the coffee shop. It was attractive and comfortable with a restful blue decor. Although hesitant to have a first meeting with a parent in so informal a setting, this looked as though it might work. It was a quiet and cozy atmosphere with the smell of pastries permeating the air. "Besides," Andi thought, "this was the mother's choice and, if I get too nervous, I can always keep eating!"

Andi was anxious because this was her first real "transition family." The school district in which she had been a preschool special education teacher for the past 5 years was implementing new procedures to facilitate transitions into preschool special education programs. The procedures had been developed by the local inter-

agency coordinating council. Written policies, agency responsibilities, timelines, and lines of communication were all established.
Andi's job was to provide support for families, help teachers develop curriculum strategies to ensure continuity in the children's
programs, and evaluate the transition services. Andi had recently
attended a meeting for families who would soon be making transitions from the privately funded Geary Street Infant Development
Program to public preschool programs. During the meeting, families
were able to talk with several preschool teachers, representatives
from the intake IEP committee, and parents who had successfully
made the transition with their children. It was at the meeting that
Andi met Maureen and Jerry, the parents of a 30-month-old toddler.

A PAINFUL PAST

Maureen walked into the coffee shop a few minutes after Andi arrived. Spotting Andi, she headed directly to the table without a
smile or wave of greeting. Andi thought, "This is it—my first transition family. And she sure looks intense!"

The two women greeted each other and made small talk until
their order of tea and croissants arrived. Immediately, Maureen said,
"Let me tell you about Marcus. He's now 2½. Although he seemed
quite normal at birth, we slowly discovered that our son has some
special needs. He had a detached retina that was re-attached, and
he was developing unevenly on his sides. I felt we needed to do
something, and I decided—literally after watching a movie about
babies with visual impairments in a theater—to take Marcus to
something like Geary Street just as a precaution, because something
could be going on with him besides vision. We went to Geary Street
for about a year before we learned more about his condition. I felt
somewhat self-conscious about being in the program because I
thought Marcus's problems were so much more minor than the other
children. Boy, was I wrong!"

Maureen continued to talk, and Andi listened carefully as she
occupied her hands with her cup of tea. "In the beginning we thought
it was very minor. He was just about 2 years old when the full
diagnosis was made. Marcus has no neurological fibers connecting
the two hemispheres of his brain, and he has a smaller left hemi-
sphere. He has agenesis of the corpus callosum, which is extraor-
dinarily rare. It was a tremendous shock to us to get this news because I was 6 months pregnant at the time. My focus had been on
preparing for our new baby. Suddenly, I was struck with the real-

ization that Marcus was probably going to have a more severe disability than I had ever imagined."

Maureen paused a moment and, looking thoughtfully into her tea cup, began again. "A footnote that I have to share is that I lost the pregnancy 3 weeks after we found out about Marcus's brain. Jerry and I were both in absolute shock. We decided that we needed to carefully plan out the rest of the year for Marcus, especially what needed to be done within the school system. So, here we are now." Maureen stopped speaking, sighed deeply, and dramatically took a bite of her croissant.

Andi could see that Maureen was deeply troubled. She sympathized, "You've certainly been through a lot in the past year. I'm sorry. I guess it hasn't been easy for you or your family, and now you've got this new transition." Andi paused, but Maureen did not respond. "Have you and Jerry thought about how you were going to plan the transition?" continued Andi.

"What do you mean?" Maureen asked.

"Well," Andi replied, "the staff at Geary Street can help you. And I can help you. The meeting the other night was one way we are trying to assist families to make the change you will be making—by giving you information about the transition. We also have written information that I can share with you. I can connect you with other parents. We can spend time talking. Whatever you would like."

At that moment, the waitress reappeared. Both women requested more tea. Maureen began speaking again, almost as though she had not heard Andi. "You know, Geary Street was wonderfully supportive for us. It was the group that gave me the chance to be with other parents and get used to the idea of what it was that went into helping children with disabilities. And it gave me a place to take my own feelings, because as we got this news, I suddenly needed to have people who would understand what was happening. And I felt very comfortable. But just as I got the diagnosis and began to express my frustration and grief, now we have to go the next step of planning an IEP to get him into public school."

Maureen continued to talk about her worries about the upcoming transition, her fears of leaving the Geary Street program, the pain of Marcus's diagnosis, and the loss of her pregnancy. She needed little prompting from Andi. Andi glanced at her watch after the waitress came to deliver the check. She was horrified to see that she and Maureen had been talking for 2 hours. Andi realized that she had to get back to the office to meet her other obligations, but she didn't like the thought of leaving before determining how she could assist Maureen.

When Maureen next paused, Andi interrupted, "I don't want to cut you short, Maureen. I've enjoyed talking with you today, and meeting here at this coffee shop was a great idea. But, I have another meeting in a few minutes and need to leave. Would you like to meet again?"

Maureen said that she would and asked about the possibility of getting together the following week. Andi thought that would work and suggested that they meet at the Geary Street program so she would have a chance to meet Marcus and they could both talk to the staff there. The two women agreed on the following Thursday morning, paid their bill, and left. Parting outside the door of the coffee shop, Andi said, "I'll see you Thursday then—and perhaps Jerry could come, too, if he has the time."

Walking to her car, Andi thought, "Whew, I wish I had a degree in counseling!" She pondered approaching the issue of counseling with Maureen.

PLANNING FOR SUCCESS

The following Thursday, Andi met Marcus. He was a delightful youngster with curly, blond hair and a ready smile. He remained in the classroom, playing enthusiastically with several other children and the physical therapist while Andi, Maureen, Jerry, and the early interventionist, Romaine, left to talk privately. As she walked to the meeting room, Andi thought, "Boy, would I love to have had that child in my class! He's wonderful and has a lot of potential for growth. I wonder if I made the right decision to leave the classroom."

During the meeting, Maureen and Jerry received a booklet that described in detail the IEP process for the public school system. The process was discussed and Maureen's and Jerry's questions were answered. Then Maureen spoke up, "You've demystified the process for us, and I think it sounds great. We like things planned out and you know we've been putting a lot of energy into planning for Marcus lately. But, it sounds frightening. What if we don't get exactly what Marcus needs on the IEP? It almost sounds as though we're playing God." Jerry nodded in agreement with his wife.

"It's not as frightening as it may seem," answered Romaine. "It will work, but it's going to take some advance planning."

At this point, Jerry interjected, "You said the first step was to refer Marcus to the school system. I'll do that. Then the assessment—right? Then the IEP meeting? Let's get started on that planning. I want to get the best preschool for my son. We've been Marcus's primary educators up to this point. If we're handing the job over to someone else, we want to make sure they do a good job."

"Of course you want the best for Marcus," Andi reiterated. "There are some wonderful preschool programs in the school district that will be very appropriate for Marcus. Would you like to visit some of them?"

"That sounds wonderful," Maureen said. "Since Jerry's going to take care of the referral, I'll visit programs. I'm not working, so that will be easier for me."

During the remainder of the meeting, it was decided that Jerry and Maureen would continue to read the information that had been provided to them and would assume responsibility for asking any questions that arose. Although offered, they preferred not to talk with other parents. Romaine would assist Jerry and Maureen in updating the information in Marcus's file and establishing and prioritizing goals and objectives for the upcoming school year. Andi would assist in setting up visits to preschools and in defining the type of environment that seemed most appropriate for Marcus.

As they were leaving, Maureen approached Andi. "Could we meet and talk again? Our breakfast the other day was wonderful." Andi and Maureen agreed on a home visit the following week.

During the home visit, Andi listened to Maureen repeat much of the conversation that had occurred over breakfast 2 weeks earlier. She was feeling more uncomfortable as she was convinced that Maureen might benefit from professional counseling. Andi did not feel capable of helping Maureen resolve some of her difficulties and felt that encouraging Maureen to talk with friends and family might not be the best solution.

At an appropriate time in the conversation, Andi said gently, "You seem to be in a lot of pain about Marcus's disability and the loss of your daughter. You've been through a lot. Maybe you would feel better if you could talk to someone who could help you resolve some of the pain. I know a wonderful counselor who has helped a lot of parents of children with disabilities. Would you like to call her?"

Maureen sat back in her chair, took a deep breath, and said, "I suppose so. It might help . . ."

As Andi wrote down the name and telephone number of the counselor, Maureen abruptly switched the topic of conversation. "I want to visit every preschool program in the district. I want to find a healthy environment for my child—one in which children like

Marcus are perceived as growing children with potential. I'd like him to have a chance to be around regular kids, knocking around on the playground. Is that possible?"

Andi assured Maureen that good inclusive preschools were located throughout the city. She gave Maureen a list of the sites, as well as contact persons and visitation policies at each site. Maureen agreed to arrange the visits herself. Andi attended the first two visits with Maureen. After that, Maureen felt comfortable going alone.

APPROACHING THE SCHOOL SYSTEM

Although they had brief telephone conversations, the next time Andi saw Maureen was at Marcus's IEP meeting, which was approximately 2 months later.

Maureen stopped Andi before they entered the meeting room and said, "I want you to know—we decided to go into this meeting armed with every gun we have. We brought as many specialists as we could, we read all of our reports, and we did our preparation sheet."

Andi smiled in response and thought, "Marcus is certainly lucky. His parents will settle for nothing but the best."

The IEP meeting lasted more than 3 hours—much to the chagrin of some of the school personnel.

In a follow-up home visit, Maureen told Andi, "I loved the whole IEP, partly because Marcus has begun to make some nice strides. Specialists at the school district were very pleased with what he could do. I had the sense that we had nothing but allies at the IEP meeting. The social worker who led the meeting never once left us with a doubt that she was interested in every bit of input we had about Marcus. I didn't expect my input to be welcomed on such an equal footing."

"I'm glad it worked out so well for you," said Andi.

"You know," Maureen continued, "the IEP turned out to be a really felicitous occasion. All of these people were sitting around this table, madly keen on the progress that our son was making. They actually used most of the meeting to tell all of the things that Marcus can do. We came away with a very satisfactory IEP, and I couldn't be happier with Marcus's placement."

Maureen looked at her watch. "Oops, I have to go. We'll be away on vacation all summer, so Marcus won't start preschool until the fall. Thanks for all of your help. You helped make the transition easier, and I'm looking forward to getting my life back in September. I've decided to look for a part-time job, and I might even start painting again. I haven't called that counselor yet, but I'll do it in September.''

Andi replied that she was glad she had been helpful, wished Maureen and her family a happy summer, and said that she would be available in the fall if Maureen needed anything.

DISAPPOINTING RESULTS

School had been in session for almost 5 weeks. Andi had not heard from Maureen, so she assumed everything was going smoothly. Marcus's teacher was one of the best in the school district and collaborated well with families. Andi mailed Maureen and Jerry a form to evaluate the transition services they received, smugly expecting a satisfactory report. The following week, Andi received a telephone call from Maureen.

With little introduction, Maureen stated angrily, "I want you to know, I had no trouble sending Marcus off to school this fall. I was only too excited. I desperately needed time to myself. But things certainly haven't gone as we planned. Jerry says I'm perched like a hawk over everyone at the preschool. But, I don't care! I'm still waiting to see when they're going to take that all-powerful IEP and translate it into meaningful things in the classroom." Maureen took a deep breath, and continued with increasing agitation, "Well, I haven't even discussed his IEP with his teacher. We need to go over that IEP so that we can chart out the goals and things Marcus can do. No one has even looked at it! If this is one of the better preschools, I'd hate to see the others!"

Struggling to remain calm, Andi asked, "Have you talked with Marcus's teacher about your concerns?"

"Of course I have," Maureen replied tersely. "Romaine told me to do the same thing, but the teacher says she has other children, too. She says she'll get around to Marcus soon. I've been going to school every day with Marcus so I can help his teacher, and she still can't find time for me!"

"I'm sorry things aren't going as you would like them, Maureen," Andi sympathized. Andi was trying to choose her words carefully and be fair to everyone. "But I'm afraid I'm going to give you the same advice as Romaine—try to work out your disagreements with the teacher. It really is a tremendously busy time of year for teachers. Marcus's teacher has 10 other children to get to know. I can understand your frustration about the IEP, but I'm sure Marcus has made progress over the past few weeks. Why, just being in school every day is a new accomplishment for him. Sometimes it takes a while to understand and recognize the structure in a classroom and to realize that children are learning."

Andi paused. When Maureen did not respond, she continued, "Maybe you should let it go for a little while—take some of the time while Marcus is in school to do the things you talked about doing for yourself. If things haven't improved in a few more weeks, you could take some action then." Maureen continued to express her anger and disappointment, but agreed to be patient and give the teacher a bit more time.

A CELEBRATION OF TIME

Six weeks later the situation was much improved. Maureen invited Andi to observe Marcus's classroom. After the observation, the two women revisited the coffee shop where they had first talked. Since this was a celebration, they ordered chocolate eclairs and French Roast coffee instead of croissants and tea.

Maureen began the conversation, "I want you to know that I was really angry with you when I called to complain about the beginning of school, but I took your advice anyway and simply sent Marcus to school. After 2 weeks, I began to spend just one morning a week volunteering and I fell madly in love with just being there and getting to know the children. I began to appreciate far more the subtlety of what constitutes good preschool education. Marcus is in a wonderful setting. The class meets the criteria Jerry and I had hoped for in terms of curriculum and the way the classroom is set up. And the way the teachers and assistants talk to Marcus and his little peers is no different from the way I hear regular preschool teachers talking. I'm grateful that Marcus is in an environment like this. And, guess what? I'm in charge of the parent group! We have our first meeting in 2 weeks."

Andi refrained from saying, "I told you so," and simply expressed her happiness that Marcus was doing well. She had been worried that her advice to Maureen had been too directive—and Maureen's comment let her know that she probably had been.

Maureen smiled wisely as she placed her empty cup in its saucer. "The process that I thought was going to be so difficult was much less frightening in retrospect. You know, I've learned to enjoy Marcus much more. I've learned to trust him, and I've learned to trust the integrity of the people who are providing services. I realize that they're there because they care. For me, the process had to do with letting a bigger group of people care about my child. I have a feeling that now I'm healed to a certain extent and I can help other people accept my child, rather than the other way around. I know I can really appreciate my son, and I think there is probably no greater gift than to appreciate the child you've been struggling so hard with."

Andi again expressed pleasure that everything had turned out well. She thanked Maureen for sharing her thoughts and feelings so openly. "I always learn so much from parents who are as articulate as you and as willing to talk," Andi added.

The two women left the coffee shop together. Andi thought, "My first transition family—sure hope I did the right thing. I wonder if Maureen ever got counseling."

As the women parted, Maureen looked back over her shoulder and said with a twinkle in her eye, "Kindergarten's not for another 2 years—right?"

DISCUSSION QUESTIONS

1. Did Andi interact with Maureen and provide services in a way that empowered and enabled Maureen to handle the transition effectively? Did she respond to Maureen's feelings, as well as Maureen's desire for information, appropriately and sensitively?

2. Was it appropriate for Andi to suggest that Maureen seek counseling for herself?

3. Should Andi have encouraged Jerry to participate more actively in the transition process?

4. A goal of transition support services in the early years is to help prepare parents for future transitions. Were services provided to Maureen with this goal in mind?

5. The transition support services described in this case are not available in all communities. What are the benefits of having a separate program to assist families in making transitions? Could the benefits of this program be realized in other communities without adding a separate program or increasing the number of staff members in existing programs?

6. The transition support services offered to the family in this case appeared to be successful. How might the process be adapted for families who are less well-educated or who have less time to commit than Marcus's parents?

7. Some communities do not have a separation of services for infants (i.e., birth to 3 years) and preschoolers (i.e., 3–5 years). What are the advantages and disadvantages of having separate services for infants and preschoolers? What are the advantages and disadvantages of having continuous services from birth to 5 years of age?

8. Write a transition plan for Marcus and his family based on the information available in this case study. Choose any format you think would be best. Be sure to include: 1) family priorities (i.e., goals and objectives), 2) strategies for achieving goals, and 3) who would be responsible for each activity.

No Place
To Call Home

Roy Grant

*Jessica, Eric, and Joseline are toddlers with developmental de-
lays and, although they have lived under similar circumstances, they are not related. All three were former residents
of welfare hotels in New York City which were designed to
provide temporary housing for homeless families. This case
describes a child care program for children living in this once
famous hotel. The issues the staff members faced are told
through the stories of their work with these three young children and their families. The dismal environment surrounding
the classroom and the challenges the children present pale in
comparison to the difficulties the parents have encountered
and their tentative futures.*

The 1980s saw an enormous rise in poverty and an equally dramatic decline in the quality of life for the poor. As more families
competed for fewer affordable housing options, the number of
homeless people grew and, for the first time since the Great Depression, there was a dramatic increase in homelessness among families
with children. In New York City, approximately 200,000 children
are doubled up in overcrowded community housing. Families who
do not have this option find themselves in the homeless shelter
system. In 1987, at the peak of the crisis, most of New York City's
homeless families were living in welfare hotels. The most notorious
welfare hotel in New York was the Hotel Martinique.

The Hotel Martinique Day Care Center and All Children's House were spon-
sored by the Association to Benefit Children. Funding was provided by New York
City (i.e., Agency for Child Development), New York State (i.e., Department of Social
Services and Office of Mental Health), and private sources (e.g., Kaplan Foundation,
Eisman Foundation for Children).

THE HOTEL MARTINIQUE

The Hotel Martinique was once a grand place. Signs of its former splendor were still visible, despite the heavy steel doors and security checkpoint. The high ceiling was in ornate beaux arts style, but its majesty no longer created the sense of spaciousness and elegance of the past. Instead, it caused reverberations that endlessly magnified the loud sounds of the hotel and intensified the atmosphere of imminent violence. A basement cabaret was once an important off-Broadway showcase. During the 1960s, the Martinique was home to the Theater of the Ridiculous. How ironic this seems in light of its revealed destiny.

After the noise level, the odor was the most overwhelming characteristic of the Martinique. It was an unfamiliar and pungent smell that instantly identified this very special place. The odor clung to your clothes and many of the child care staff had clothing they wore only to work for this reason.

The residential rooms were very small, with barely enough room for the dilapidated beds, cribs, and dressers they held. On average, there was one bed for every two occupants of a room. Infants and toddlers had no floor space on which to crawl and school-age children had nowhere to do homework. Nearly all of the children were without toys or books.

There were no kitchens and, although hot plates were strictly forbidden, nearly everyone used one. Sometimes security guards demanded sexual favors from the women in the hotel to keep from reporting their use of hot plates to the management. This would be grounds for eviction—possibly into the street.

About 440 large families lived in this hotel, more than 1,000 of the residents being children. Nearly half of the children were 5 years of age or younger. More than 200 were infants and toddlers, for whom there were no programs at all.

AN OASIS

On the first floor of this once-grand hotel, we created a day care center for 32 children between 2½ and 5 years of age—a safe space in the midst of near chaos. The hotel residents soon started calling it *The Oasis*.

The first child who entered the day care center did so while the renovations were still underway. The 2½-year-old boy happened upon the open doorway and wandered in with his mother in close pursuit. The day care center was about 1,100 square feet with an extremely high ceiling. At this time, it was completely empty. There were two sheds being built for overnight storage of play materials. One shed would double as a play house when the center was in operation, and the other was a tiny shared office for the director and social worker.

The boy took one look at this vast space and ran as fast as he could, crashing hard into the roll-down steel gate protecting one of the sheds. He fell backward, hitting the floor very hard. Much to our surprise, both he and his mother laughed delightedly at the incident. My first thought was how disturbed this behavior was, but then I realized how starved for physical movement a child this age might be at the Hotel Martinique. Behavior that seemed bizarre in another context may be perfectly normal in the abnormal environment of a homeless shelter.

There is a misconception in some administrative circles that homeless parents do not want to be separated from their children. This is often used as a justification for not providing day care services at shelters. Much to the contrary, we found that parents were very happy to have their children included in our day care center after they got to know us. Homeless parents do not always trust the services they are offered and, like all good parents, they want to be sure that their children are safe and well supervised. In a shelter, this usually means you have to keep your children with you.

As is true in any child care, the first day was difficult for many of the children. They cried and clung to their mothers when they tried to leave. For those children who were particularly fearful, we invited the mothers to stay and some of them seemed to enjoy playing with the toys as much as the children did. After the children felt comfortable being left in day care, the mothers welcomed the respite from some of their child care responsibilities. Some children just walked away from their mothers and did not look back. This behavior left more of an impression on the staff than the tearful separations.

Most parents readily answered all of our questions about their children. They were nearly overwhelmed with gratitude when we asked, "What can we do to help you?" It was as if that offer had never before been made.

JESSICA AGUERA

Jessica Aguera was among the first group of children to attend the Hotel Martinique Day Care Center. Jessica, almost 3 years old, was the older of Mr. and Mrs. Aguera's two children. The family was evicted from substandard city-owned housing for nonpayment of rent. They were placed in more than seven shelters in less than a year, including several congregate shelters and small welfare hotels.

Congregate shelters are generally converted armories. A huge room is lined with hundreds of cots side by side. There is no privacy, with bathrooms being shared among many. These facilities were designed for homeless single adults but were also used— sometimes illegally—for families with infants and children.

Jessica had been identified by a pediatrician as having developmental delays and was diagnosed as having a hearing impairment before the family became homeless. When Jessica began child care at the hotel, she did not speak at all. She also had serious motor delays. Her balance was poor, and she could not run or hold a pencil or crayon firmly. Chewing was also difficult, and food would drip from Jessica's mouth when she ate. All in all, Jessica appeared to be a child with brain injury and possibly mental retardation.

At first, Jessica made no friends. Although she was receptive to attention from the teachers and volunteers, she would not seek out adults or other children independently. At circle time, Jessica did not participate and did not appear to understand any of the activities. Her attention span was extremely limited, being less than a minute in length. The other children generally ignored Jessica. If no adult specifically sought her out, Jessica would spend her days sitting by herself at a table and staring at the group. As we spent more time working individually with Jessica, she blossomed in ways that we never expected. She began to speak, using progressively longer sentences. After nearly 5 months with us, Jessica was saying things like, "I want to play with this. Will you help me?" She was one of the very few children in the day care center who could use dolls dramatically and narrate her play.

Jessica learned to enjoy the company of the adults in the day care center and requested their attention, but she remained isolated from other children. Given more time, coaxing, and encouragement, Jessica eventually developed a friendship with an electively mute girl in her class. In fact, it was only through overhearing her friend whisper to Jessica that we learned she could talk. After about 6 months of day care, Jessica began to play with the other children and, for the first time, we heard her laugh. Although completely nonverbal when she first arrived, her expressive language skills were now at age level. She remained clumsy and hypotonic and had trouble chewing.

It was only after Jessica made notable progress that Mr. Aguera began to keep appointments with our social worker, who tried to gather birth and health histories. Mr. Aguera answered all questions with, "I don't remember. You'll have to ask my wife." This would have been fine except Mrs. Aguera did not keep any appointments we made with her. We knew that she had just had another baby, Lisa, and that she was overwhelmed by her responsibilities. It was only later that we learned she was suffering from postpartum depression.

The little history we could gather revealed that Jessica had been a full-term baby, with a normal birth weight. She was delivered by Cesarean section because of breech presentation and spent 2 weeks in a neonatal intensive care unit with jaundice and a dislocated hip. An allegation of child abuse made against her parents resulted in Jessica's placement in foster care for a short time. We could only speculate that Mrs. Aguera might have been seriously depressed when Jessica was an infant as well. However, it is also possible that her depression may have developed only after the family lost their housing and began being moved from one shelter to another.

When Mrs. Aguera finally began to keep appointments with us, she brought Lisa. At 9 months of age, Lisa did not make any spontaneous sounds. She did not move her head in the direction of sound or appear able to track objects with her eyes. Lisa could not sit up on her own and looked extremely floppy when strapped in a stroller. Many of our meetings with the family focused on their need for housing.

Mr. Aguera said, "I'll never accept housing from New York City. That's how I got homeless in the first place. The next time I'm homeless, I may not be lucky enough to be in a hotel as good as the Martinique."

It took months to develop a trusting relationship with the Agueras but, in the end, they agreed to follow through with our suggestion to take Jessica to a local hospital for a more complete evaluation. Mrs. Aguera even agreed to have Lisa evaluated, acknowledging for the first time that, "She isn't doing what babies her age are supposed to do." We were hopeful that the two little girls would get the services they needed to grow and develop.

Soon after the family agreed to the evaluations, Jessica was absent for several consecutive days. Because her attendance at child care had been excellent, we felt the need to investigate. We went to the family's room, but no one was there. The room was empty. We asked around and were told by neighbors that the family had moved to Florida to live with Mr. Aguera's parents. They left no message for us, no address, and no telephone number—not even the name of the city or town to which they had moved.

ERIC JOHNSON

Eric Johnson was also in the first group of children at the day care center. He and Jessica were classmates for about 5 months, but the two children never interacted. Eric did not appear to notice that Jessica no longer attended the classroom.

Ms. Johnson was a single mother from a middle class economic background. She had run away from home as a teenager to escape a very strict and abusive mother and an "uninvolved" father. Shortly after running away, she married.

"Things were great at first," Ms. Johnson told us. "Then he started using more and more crack and beating me all the time. I went to court and got a protection order against him. Well, a lot of good that did me. . . . He attacked me in the street, and the cops wouldn't do anything. I locked him out and changed the key, but he just knocked down the door. Then I called the police, but they didn't come. I was afraid he'd kill the kids, so I took them with me and moved in with my mother." Eric had just turned 2 years old and his sister, Nichole, was 6 years old at that time.

Eric had already been showing signs of hyperactivity. The household was tense and tempers flared. Finally, Ms. Johnson's mother told her that Eric couldn't stay with her because he was too active and difficult. The family was separated. Ms. Johnson and Eric entered the homeless shelter system, and Nichole remained with her grandmother. Once homeless, Eric and his mother first slept in city offices because all of the homeless shelters were full. They spent 3 weeks in a huge congregate shelter. Eric developed a sleep disturbance, which continued for as long as we knew him. He was calmer in a small welfare hotel in the Times Square area, but 4 weeks after being placed there, the family was moved to another congregate shelter. There, Eric's activity level increased to the point that he was "out of control."

When the family was transferred to the Martinique, Eric was so wild that another hotel resident told Ms. Johnson, "You better get him to a special school." She even recommended an appropriate therapeutic preschool. Ms. Johnson looked into this program and Eric was accepted and enrolled. Unfortunately, it was a 3-hour program that required more than 1 hour of bus transportation each way.

"I couldn't do anything with my life when he was in the school,"

Ms. Johnson explained. "I would have had to drop out of the job training program I'm in, and then I wouldn't be able to get a job and afford rent so I can get out of here."

Eric was very difficult to manage when he started day care at the Martinique. He ran around the room aimlessly and threw objects without regard for whether children might be hit. Many of the homeless children we served ran around aimlessly their first week of day care. Similar to the toddler who happened into our center during renovations, the children were often overwhelmed by the contrast between this colorful and stimulating place and their usual surroundings. Most children gradually learned to follow the class routine and to accept structure. Eric did not.

Eric could not sit still long enough to eat his lunch. He would put food in his mouth while he was standing and then run around the room as he chewed. When a teacher attempted to limit Eric, he would have a tantrum, banging his head repeatedly on the floor.

Eric breathed through his mouth and frequently drooled. One eye watered incessantly. He could not follow simple spoken directions or answer simple questions. His speech was difficult to understand.

Naptime was initially a very difficult time for most of the children. Some were just unable to sleep, others screamed in fear as soon as the lights were turned off. Unlike most of the other children, however, Eric did not gradually calm down and try to nap. He would run around the room, tapping the other children, who would shout in protest. Eric had to be removed from the room at naptime.

We hired an additional teacher assistant to work one-to-one with Eric. Otherwise, the other children would not be safe. It was impossible for one teacher assistant to keep up with Eric throughout an entire day, so we put the day care staff on rotation, taking turns working individually with him for an hour.

Before he began day care, Eric had been given a physical examination at a community clinic near his former address. The physician recorded that Eric was the product of a full-term pregnancy, with a normal birth weight. He wrote that Eric was "in fine health," his development was "within normal limits," and that "Eric could tell a story." We took our own history from Ms. Johnson who reported that Eric had been a low birth weight baby (3 pounds, 11 ounces), born 2 months premature, and had spent nearly a month in a neonatal intensive care unit.

Ms. Johnson said, "Eric was a difficult baby. He never slept well, and he cried all the time." His development was normal until he started walking. "Then he never stopped running around!" Eric did not begin toilet training until he started day care when he was 3½ years old.

When Eric started day care, he could say only very short phrases such as, "Want this," "Gimme," and "I go there." Like so many other homeless children, his language improved dramatically within a few months of entering day care. Even so, he remained difficult to understand.

Eric's activity level was very high in the tiny hotel room. Ms. Johnson told us that we "better do something for him because he will get hurt jumping around the crowded little room." He once bumped his head on a dresser while jumping up and down, trampoline style, on the bed. Neighbors of Ms. Johnson told us that they frequently heard her yelling and threatening Eric. "She's gonna hurt him if you don't do something for him," they warned us.

We asked Ms. Johnson about this and she told us, "I'm not an abusive mother, but I don't know how to control him. Sometimes I feel like I have to hit him to get him to stop. But then I'm afraid, if I hit him, I won't be able to stop myself."

We referred Eric for a neurological evaluation at a voluntary teaching hospital, which was arranged on an emergency basis because of the likelihood of injury at the hotel. Eric was diagnosed with attention deficit hyperactivity disorder and Ritalin was prescribed. Unfortunately, there was a 3-week delay in filling the prescription. First, the neurology resident who wrote the prescription used the wrong form for a controlled substance. When we corrected this, no pharmacy would fill a prescription for a controlled substance for a family living at the Hotel Martinique. We had to transfer Eric's care to a hospital with an outpatient pharmacy, where the prescription was finally filled. The hospital has since closed their outpatient pharmacy because of a budget gap.

Eric also was diagnosed as having emotional disturbances because of his preoccupation with guns and killing. "You also be a ghostbuster. We kill all the ghosts," Eric would say. After playing out a gruesome killing, Eric would say, "I'm a baby. Take care of me. Give me my bottle."

Ms. Johnson dropped out of her job training program so she could spend more time looking for housing. She eventually found an apartment near her mother, moved in, and her daughter, Nichole, rejoined the family. We could not find a therapeutic nursery for Eric. The only preschool near the family's new home was a half-day Head Start program.

We offered follow-up services for the family, but Ms. Johnson asked us not to pursue this. "I've got to put being homeless behind me. I've got to make it on my own now—with no help from anyone but my mother," she told us.

JOSELINE VASQUEZ

Joseline Vasquez attended All Children's House, which integrated homeless children with neighborhood children. Joseline and her mother lived in a small welfare hotel. Their room was tiny, and they shared a bathroom in the hallway with six other families. When she began child care at 3 years of age, Joseline could not run, jump, or climb. Her balance was very poor, and she sometimes bumped into things or tripped while walking. Joseline could not follow spoken directions, and her speech was incomprehensible. Her longest utterances were two-word phrases.

We met with Ms. Vasquez to find out more about Joseline and to arrange a hospital-based developmental evaluation. Ms. Vasquez could not focus on Joseline's needs because of the intensity of her own. "I was an abused child," she told us. "My brother and I were placed in foster care when I was 2 because my mother was a drug addict. When my father remarried, they made me live with him and his new wife. When I was 4, they gave my mother visitation rights and that was the beginning of the end. She introduced me to drugs. My mother beat me all the time. My stepmother beat me, too. When I was 5, I started growing up in the streets.

"I had to start working when I was 10. My stepmother charged me rent. I had to pay for my brother's clothes or else he couldn't go to school. I also had to clean the house. If I didn't do a good job, my stepmother beat me and kicked me. To this day, I cry hysterically whenever I hear on the news about a child being abused. Every abused child—that's me.

"The day my brother was old enough, he joined the Army. I was going to join, too, but I met George and fell in love. Joseline was a planned baby, you know. We wanted her very much. In fact, just as soon as I realized I was pregnant, I stopped using angel dust."

Joseline was born full term, and the family of three moved in with George's mother and his siblings. Ms. Vasquez said that she could not stay there because the place was always a mess and people were always coming and going. She implied that there was a lot of drug use in the apartment and possibly drug dealing. Ms. Vasquez and Joseline, who was then 2 months old, moved in with her only friend. The friend was homeless and lived in a small welfare hotel. Ms. Vasquez and Joseline doubled up in that hotel room until they received their own first shelter placement.

Five months later they were moved to another small welfare hotel that was infested with mice. Two months after that, they were switched to another, and the following month to a hotel where they stayed only 1 week. At this point, Joseline was 10 months old. For the next 3 months, the family was moved back and forth between small welfare hotels and large congregate shelters. During this period, Joseline was frequently ill because of the unsanitary conditions at the shelters. She had many infections and still has recurrent ear infections.

"I had to do something to protect her health," Ms. Vasquez explained. "These places are dangerous. You don't know who's sleeping next to you. You can't let your kid go to the bathroom without you because you don't know who's in there. I kept Joseline in a crib the whole time and strapped her in a stroller and wheeled her around because I was afraid to let her out of my sight. Joseline started crawling when she was 6 months old, but I had to force her to try to walk. Joseline would fall so hard that I sometimes had to take her to the hospital. I was always afraid they would think she got the bruises because I abused her."

We had seen many homeless children with motor delays who caught up just from being in a normal setting where they could run and play. But Joseline's delays seemed far more serious than usual. Her movement had been severely restricted and we did not know the extent or reversibility of the damage that had been done. Ms. Vasquez reluctantly agreed to a hospital-based developmental evaluation. Less than a week later, the family got permanent housing and, despite our best efforts, we were unable to find out where they lived.

EPILOGUE

The events described above took place in 1987. New York City's annual budget for sheltering homeless families that year was $125 million. The three families described here were among more than 5,000 families with more than 10,000 children living in New York City welfare hotels. The average age of these children was 6 years, and more than 2,000 were infants and toddlers. Of the children of day care age, barely 1 in 10 ever attended a program. Those that did go to child care rarely stayed longer than 3 months. Once the families were rehoused, the program staff were rarely given addresses so that follow-up services could be provided.

The abrupt departures of the children and families were not only disruptive to the children's progress, but also disheartening for staff members. Just as a staff member developed a trusting relationship with a parent and the child was making progress, they were suddenly gone without a trace. One day care director at another large welfare hotel once revealed her secret for guarding against the depressing effects of these departures. Basically, she said that staff members should do what they can in one day, without making great plans for the future, and hope that what is done will make a difference. As she put it, "Every month is September and every day is Monday." The director of All Children's House had another strategy. All of the homeless children at this center made "good-bye books" during their first week. This helped them to be more prepared to leave when the time came.

Now, 5 years later, there are still more than 5,000 homeless families in New York City shelters, with more than 10,000 of the occupants being children. Most of the large welfare hotels and their day care centers, however, are now closed. The Hotel Martinique was the first welfare hotel that New York City closed when the crisis of family homelessness appeared to have ended. This crisis has not ended. Homeless families and children are more likely than ever to be placed in congregate shelters, which are the most damaging of all shelters. Here, the children are least likely to receive early intervention services.

DISCUSSION QUESTIONS

1. Given the limited amount of time that these three children spent in day care, as well as the environment in which they lived, do you think their participation in this program had any sustained impact on their development?

2. What impact, if any, do you think the program had on the children's families?

3. What do you think were among the most important aspects of the program described in the case study?

4. Suppose you were responsible for setting up early intervention services for homeless children and their families in a large city. Develop a draft proposal of your project that includes:
   - Project objectives: what you anticipate your project will accomplish
   - Project methods: the types of services you would make available for children and their families as well as a brief rationale for your decisions
   - Project evaluation: how you would measure or otherwise determine the effectiveness of your project

The Disney Connection

David E. Jones

Tommy Minh Pham was born with Larsen syndrome, a rare genetic syndrome that made him particularly vulnerable to the typical bumps and bruises of early childhood. When Tommy was 3 years old, that vulnerability was realized when he became paralyzed and completely dependent on a ventilator. This case is about the efforts of a home-based preschool teacher, Isabel Morris, to have Tommy integrated in the district's regular education program. It describes the enormous effort necessary and barriers encountered in coordinating the many people and agencies involved in making such a goal a reality. It also describes Isabel's attempts to ensure that Tommy's parents are actively involved in the decisionmaking that takes place, which is made somewhat difficult because Mr. and Mrs. Pham do not speak English.

Isabel's frustration about Tommy's educational placement caught Principal Mark Rawlings off-guard. As Tommy Minh Pham's home-based preschool teacher for the past year, Isabel Morris had played a key role in planning Tommy's transition to a school setting.

Mark motioned Isabel to a seat in his office. "What's going on?" he asked.

"I'm upset because I think we've stopped short of what's best for Tommy," Isabel answered. "Mark, we're allowing fears about his serious medical condition to keep us from giving him the learning environment he really needs."

As she spoke, Mark recalled last week's meeting in which he had expressed his pleasure that things seemed on track for Tommy

The author gratefully acknowledges the helpful input of Dr. Patricia Barber, Deborah Dale, and Freda Noller in the preparation of this chapter.

to enroll in school at Claremont in 5 weeks. At that meeting, Mark had thanked the group members for their work in thinking through the issues they would face in having Tommy, a child who was chronically ill and dependent on a ventilator, in their school. As he listened, Mark became more aware of just how deeply Isabel felt about Tommy's transition to school.

Without a doubt, the issues surrounding Tommy's school placement were among the most complex Mark had faced in his 10 years as principal of Claremont Special Education Center. Many concerns and obstacles had surfaced as the family, educators, and medical professionals worked together to make it possible for Tommy to attend school. No one person had the full perspective necessary to ensure that Tommy's school placement would occur. A critical ingredient was that everyone—family members, teachers, doctors, nurses, and Tommy—had to be ready to move forward at the same time. It had taken months for everyone to become comfortable with Tommy's transition to school.

Isabel served as the coordinator for Tommy's transition planning group. Mark knew that she was Tommy's greatest advocate and that last fall she had provided the impetus that had brought Tommy's family and the educational and medical professionals together to talk about Tommy attending school. For nearly 7 months, she had been involved in coordinating plans. It was clear that she was dissatisfied with the pace of the process.

Isabel paused a moment to gather her thoughts before she spoke again, "I'm not blaming anyone. We've all worked hard, but we stopped short. Tommy has normal intelligence. You and I know that to have Tommy here in a special education school is one of the most inappropriate placements we could make."

A HOSPITAL VISIT

Isabel first met Tommy when his discharge planning team invited her to the hospital. His year-long hospital stay was nearing its end. Earlier in the summer, a hospital social worker had contacted the school district about Tommy's need for home-based early intervention services. Within a short time, Isabel was assigned as Tommy's preschool teacher. The purpose of the hospital visit was for her to get acquainted with Tommy and to receive a brief orientation to his medical care. Isabel welcomed the opportunity to meet Tommy, but, in the back of her mind, she was also aware of how much she wanted simply to allay her own fears.

"- Hi -," said Tommy as he was introduced to Isabel. His voice came out in a slow, breathy tone because of the tracheotomy tube.

"I'm glad to meet you, Tommy," replied Isabel. "I think we're going to have a good year together." She felt a pang of embarrassment as she realized she had spoken to him more loudly than she had intended.

Isabel was immediately taken with Tommy's eyes. There was merriment in his expression that she had not expected. As she stood beside his bed, Tommy's nurse described his medical condition, "Tommy, I'm going to tell Ms. Morris about you, is that okay?" Tommy winked his approval and the nurse laughed. "As you can see, he's got a sense of humor." Tommy grinned. Isabel smiled and felt a sense of relief. The nurse then began her description with an overview of his medical history.

Tommy was born with a fragile bone structure from a genetic condition known as Larsen syndrome. He was paralyzed from his neck down at 3 years of age as the result of a fall. Since the accident, he has been dependent on the ventilator for breathing.

"Come take a look at the ventilator and I'll tell you more about it," said the nurse. "Tommy's ventilator is the positive pressure type, which means that air is forced into his lungs via the tracheotomy tube. Because this type of ventilation can harm his circulation and antidiuretic hormone balance, we have to take frequent readings of his vital signs. He will have round-the-clock nursing care. We feed him through a button gastrostomy. He now weighs about 32 pounds." The nurse gave Isabel a chance to ask questions and then continued.

"When Tommy's home, he'll have a custom-fitted ventilator on the back of his wheelchair. He wears this body jacket to provide support and stability for his neck. As you can see, it extends from his neck to his waist. When he's in bed, the jacket is worn somewhat loosely, but when he's moved it's tightened for maximum support."

Tommy didn't pay much attention as the nurse spoke about him. A television program about sharks had captured his interest. For her part, Isabel felt overwhelmed by all of the new information. She was simply taken aback by the complexity of Tommy's medical needs. She thought, "I know there's a little boy beyond all those tubes. I just can't see him yet."

The nurse sensed Isabel's discomfort and said with a smile, "If you have trouble with the equipment, Tommy can help you." Tommy turned from the television program and grinned at the nurse and Isabel. Isabel understood that she needed to give herself time to get used to being with Tommy. Toward the end of her visit, one of Tommy's ventilator alarms sounded. Isabel tried to hide the panic she felt as the nurse moved toward the machine. Tommy calmly said to his new teacher, "I'm—okay."

SUPPORT FROM A COLLEAGUE

Isabel was scheduled to work with Tommy for an hour and a half 2 days a week. The second week of Tommy's home-based instruction proved as difficult as the first week. This week, Tommy's lessons were interrupted by medical procedures three times. One of those times was to control a severe spasm in his right leg. Isabel felt exhausted at the end of the lesson.

"I didn't think teaching Tommy at home would be this hard for me," Isabel confided to Laura Anderson, Claremont's school psychologist. Isabel had asked Laura to meet with her in the teacher's lounge. "After I met with the nurses and doctors in the hospital, I thought to myself, 'I can handle this. It's going to be okay.'" Isabel took a deep breath and continued, "But now that he's home, we're in this little room in the far corner of the house. Even though there's a nurse right there, I can't help but worry about what I'm going to do if his ventilator stops."

Laura poured Isabel a cup of coffee and motioned for Isabel to continue. "Laura, I know he sees me startle every time one of his alarms rings. What does it do to a child to think his teacher is afraid to be around him?"

Laura replied, "Hey, didn't you tell me last week that you had to give yourself time to get used to being around him? From what you've told me before, Tommy's a pretty accommodating child."

"Well, I guess you're right," Isabel said. She was silent for a moment and then continued, "I can't help but wonder what his parents think of all this. You know they came to this country as refugees in the late '70s. Neither of them speak much English. What must it be like for them to have people in and out of their house at all hours? Tommy's been out of their home for a year, and we bring him home and say, 'Isn't this wonderful?'" She took a sip from her cup and then continued, "I know I shouldn't let it bother me, but the 'whoosh' of that ventilator sometimes gets to me . . . and so does the medicinal smell. For the most part, as soon as we get into our lessons, I don't mind. I guess I'm only bothered when the medical procedures get in our way. The home care nurses and I are trying to arrange our schedules so that his routine care doesn't have to interfere with my instruction time." Isabel brightened a bit as she remembered how hard Tommy had tried during that morning's session. "Laura, do you think you could schedule some time in the next week or so to do some assessments of Tommy's abilities?"

Laura paused and replied, "I'd be happy to go with you. I'll need to do an evaluation on him anyway. A preliminary home visit will help me decide which instruments to use later. You know, I've never tested someone with a tracheotomy before. I wonder how his expressive language is affected by that tube? From your description though, he seems to be pretty verbal. He must have learned a lot of English while he was in the hospital."

"I can't guarantee that he'll have enough stamina for any extensive testing," cautioned Isabel. "We may have to split the testing over several days."

"You're probably right," said Laura, a little hesitant to commit so much time.

"I think the place to start is for you to spend some time just getting to know him," suggested Isabel.

A WORD OF CAUTION

Isabel couldn't wait to get back to Claremont to talk with Laura. As she drove into the school parking lot, Isabel laughed to herself about what Tommy had said that morning. She also realized that her comfort and confidence in working with Tommy were increasing each day. Once in the building, Isabel went straight to Laura's office.

When Laura looked up from her papers, she grinned at the mirth in Isabel's eyes. "I have to tell you what Tommy said to me about your testing yesterday," Isabel chuckled. "He said, 'You tell her I'm mad because she didn't keep going. I know a lot more letters!' "

Isabel's tone turned more serious. "Laura, I know you haven't had time to put together all of the results from your assessments, but you've spent time with Tommy now. Do you think there's any reason for me not to push for a school placement?"

Laura saw the earnest look on Isabel's face and measured her reply, "I think he could benefit from school and the other kids could learn from him as well. But it's going to be a tough road. We've served lots of kids with complex needs, but never anyone like Tommy. Maybe we should take things slowly."

Isabel replied, "I can appreciate what you're saying, but Tommy can't spend the rest of his life in his room. Someone has to take the initiative to get him into school. He has the right to be integrated."

Laura paused for a moment and then said, "I think you're doing a great job with Tommy. I just don't want you to underestimate what you're up against with this. On the one hand, it looks like he can benefit from school. But, on the other hand, his safety is a big issue. I'm afraid there isn't going to be one right way for us to do things in his case."

"You're probably right about that," said Isabel. "By this time I usually have a good idea about what the family wants for their child. But language problems make ongoing communication so difficult in this case. I'm going to have to find a translator so I can find out how they feel about Tommy going to school."

A HALLOWEEN FRIGHT

"Mark, I sure appreciate you going to bat for me about Tommy," said Isabel to Claremont's principal as she passed him in the hall. "I think Tommy is going to be ecstatic when he hears that he can come to Claremont's Halloween party."

Mark responded, "All I've been hearing from you is Tommy did this or Tommy said that. I can't wait to meet the little guy. It sounds like it's going to be a major operation just to get him to school though."

Isabel nodded and let out a long breath, "You wouldn't believe it. It's been an eye-opening experience for me just to arrange the consent forms, not to mention the logistics of getting him here. I had to contact the district office for a translator in order to talk with his parents and get their okay. Then I had three extensive conversations with his home care nurse and two more with his pediatrician."

Isabel took a deep breath and continued, "Now the pediatrician wants to send over an orthopedic specialist to check Tommy's body jacket before he'll sign the doctor's release. Once that's done, I'll call transportation to make arrangements to get him here. I won't even tell you about the checklist of supplies we're supposed to bring. The doctor even wants to have two back-up ventilators on hand— just in case!"

Isabel worked hard to make all of the arrangements for Tommy to attend the Halloween party. He arrived in costume and make-up just like the other children, and his eyes drank in the sights of gala decorations and the children's merriment.

For better or worse, Tommy's attendance at the party hadn't gone exactly as Isabel had imagined it.

"Now that was a memorable way to end a Halloween party,"

declared Claremont teacher Sally Campbell. The mischief in her voice was not lost on any of the other school staff who were helping to clean up after the party.

"Memorable is not the word for it. I think my pulse is still racing," said Laura Anderson.

"Hey, we survived," chimed in Mark Rawlings. "I don't think I ever saw any of us move as fast as when Tommy's ventilator alarm went off. All things considered, we did a good job of keeping our heads."

"Keeping our heads?" asked Sally incredulously. "It was pure panic when we wheeled Tommy out of the gym down the hall to his back-up ventilator. Of course that thing stopped just as we were ready to load the kids on the buses."

"We must have been a sight!" exclaimed Isabel. "With two of us pushing his wheelchair, the nurse using the handbag to give him air, and Mark in his clown suit directing traffic all the way down the hall! Of course, the most amazing thing is that while we're rushing around, Tommy is laughing so hard that tears are streaming down his face. His costume make-up was rolling down his cheeks in rivers."

Sally Campbell quipped, "Yeah, we're all thinking, 'Dear God, don't let him die' and he's thinking, 'Wow, I hope they push me faster.' He was having the time of his life as we went speeding around the corner."

Isabel nodded in agreement and said, "You know when I'm with him I'm struck by the differences in our perceptions. He's had medical emergencies numerous times. He knows someone will be there to help him. He just doesn't react to his situation the way I expect. It's hard to believe, but I'm sure I think about that ventilator more than he does. Did you see how much he enjoyed having the other kids around him?"

SEEKING APPROVAL

Mr. Pham, Tommy's father, listened attentively as the translator relayed Isabel's words to him. Tommy's mother, with an ear to the translator, moved quietly around the table making sure that everyone had plenty of snacks and tea. Isabel had asked them about their goals for Tommy. Mr. Pham spoke briefly to his wife and then through the translator said, "It's hard to know what to think. Through our doctor, I have heard about many new opportunities for children like Tommy. Right now, I want him to learn more of our language. Beyond that, I just want him to keep learning and doing better."

Isabel smiled and said, "I enjoy working with Tommy and he seems to be doing very well." She then asked Tommy's parents what they thought about Tommy attending school. As the translator talked with Tommy's parents, Isabel mused about the challenge of bridging language and cultural barriers to explain educational rights and school policies. During the past month, Isabel had been impressed by the Phams' care of Tommy, particularly their knowledge of his medical needs. On more than one occasion, Isabel had seen Tommy's parents show a nurse how to adjust Tommy's equipment.

After several minutes of conferring, Mr. Pham's response was spoken by the translator, "For Tommy to go to school would be happy news for us. But there are many things to consider about his health. We need to talk with his doctor about this plan." Isabel and Tommy's parents went on to discuss Tommy's progress and what school might be like for him. At the close of the visit, Mr. and Mrs. Pham gave Isabel permission to speak with their pediatrician about school for Tommy.

Dr. Kenji Nakamura had been Tommy's pediatrician since Tommy's birth. Tommy had always had a special place in the doctor's heart. In the anxious days immediately after Tommy's accident, Dr. Nakamura had led the fight to save Tommy's life. Even when Tommy's family began to give up hope, Dr. Nakamura persisted in his belief that Tommy would live. Countless hours of intense medical procedures, experimentation, and collaboration paid off as Tommy stabilized 4 weeks after the accident. Dr. Nakamura understood better than anyone that the commitment to saving Tommy was also a commitment to maintaining a high level of care for the rest of Tommy's life. He also knew the difficulty of maintaining a balance between Tommy's quality of life and medical precautions. Since Tommy had come home, Dr. Nakamura had visited him twice.

Isabel had spoken with Dr. Nakamura several times during the fall to get recommendations about educational activities for Tommy. Now that discussions were underway about Tommy attending school, she wanted to make sure Dr. Nakamura was behind the plan.

"Hello, Dr. Nakamura. It's great to speak with you again," began Isabel. "I'm calling as a follow-up to the letter I sent you about Tommy Pham going to school."

"Yes, Ms. Morris, I read your letter, and I think you made some good points about the benefits of school for him, but I think it's overly ambitious to talk about Tommy attending school in January."

Isabel had expected such words of caution from him, but she

was encouraged that Dr. Nakamura seemed somewhat receptive to the idea.

Dr. Nakamura continued, "I agree that one of the key issues is Tommy's quality of life. As his doctor, I think a lot about whether being on the ventilator without social or school activities is best for him."

Isabel took advantage of his pause, "As I think about it, it's not only the academics, but it's also the opportunity to be with other children. I remember when he was in the hospital, he enjoyed it so much when the neighborhood preschool asked him to judge the coloring contest."

Dr. Nakamura listened and replied, "I don't think there is any doubt that it would benefit Tommy to be around other children, but transporting him safely is a big obstacle. The neurosurgeon says it's best not to move him around at all. The orthopedic surgeon says that Tommy's bones are so weak that there is no anchoring point to attach a steel plate to stabilize his neck. The body jacket is our best solution, but it's not perfect. An outing here or there may not be a problem, but transporting him every day increases our risks greatly. We must also think about his stamina and ability to concentrate for 5 or 6 hours a day. Before I approve any plan, it will have to be very flexible to accommodate his medical condition."

They talked a few more minutes about the transition plan. At the close of the conversation, Isabel asked if Dr. Nakamura would be able to attend the planning meeting for Tommy the first week of December.

"I'll mark it down in my calendar and do my best to be there," replied Dr. Nakamura.

A DECISION IS MADE

Claremont's conference room was nearly full. As she looked around the room, Isabel reflected on the amount of time she had spent over the past month to make sure the other school staff would be ready for the meeting. While she continued to hope that a placement could be made in Tommy's neighborhood school, Isabel knew that she had to cover her bases with the Claremont staff. She thought to herself that this was the biggest staffing she had ever seen. Claremont was represented by Isabel, Mark Rawlings, Laura Anderson, Susan Sheridan (the school nurse), Sally Campbell, and the school's occupational therapist and physical therapist. A representative from the district's special education office sat next to Mark. Tommy's parents were present and were seated next to a translator provided by the school. Dr. Nakamura and two of Tommy's home care nurses were also on hand.

After a round of introductions, Mark Rawlings provided a brief overview of the agenda. In their turn, the education professionals provided summary information about their assessments of Tommy. They also outlined ways they thought a school environment would benefit him. Occasionally, the translator would raise her hand for someone to slow down or to give her time to clarify points with Tommy's parents. For the most part, Tommy's parents seemed well-informed about the placement process. From her conversations with them earlier in the fall, Isabel sensed that they would be happy if Tommy were able to go to school. When the education team was finished, the home care nurses and school nurse discussed their opinions about Tommy's medical care while in school. Although liability issues weighed heavily on people's minds, the general consensus was that a school environment would be beneficial for Tommy.

Finally, Mark asked Dr. Nakamura to give his recommendation about Tommy's school placement. Dr. Nakamura summarized his understanding of the educators' recommendations. He then offered his opinion that continued home-based education with occasional school activities would be the wisest course to pursue. Isabel felt her stomach tighten as the physician spoke. Clearly, the momentum toward school placement had stalled. What seemed so possible just minutes before, now looked out of reach. Dr. Nakamura had spoken against the transition plan.

The one last hope lay with Tommy's parents. Isabel felt herself tense as she heard Mark ask Tommy's parents what they thought. Via the translator, Tommy's father said he felt he knew his son better than anyone else. Even so, it soon became clear that he was hesitant to take any action without the doctor's approval. Home-based instruction would continue.

Isabel sat stunned as she watched her plans unravel before her eyes. All we needed, she thought, was for Tommy's parents to say, "Yes, we want Tommy to go to school." Despite her efforts to make things clear to Tommy's parents, they did not feel they had the right to make the final decision. They had trusted the doctor to save Tommy's life, she thought, and we put them in the position of having to go against that trust. Shortly after Mr. Pham spoke, Mark adjourned the meeting.

After the meeting, Isabel spoke about her disappointment with Laura Anderson. "Laura, everything went wrong," she said. "I thought I made it clear to Tommy's parents that they have the final decision about Tommy's placement."

Laura gently responded, "Isabel, do you hear what you're saying?"

"What do you mean?" asked Isabel.

"You make it sound like Tommy's parents didn't make any decision at all," said Laura. "I know you're disappointed. Many of us are. But Tommy's parents did make the final decision—they agreed with the doctor's recommendation. It may not have been what you wanted to hear, but you know they acted in Tommy's best interest."

This wasn't what Isabel wanted to hear either. She still thought the right decision was for Tommy to go to school. However, Laura had made a good point and she would have to consider it as she recovered from her disappointment.

A DISNEY ADVENTURE

About a month after the planning meeting, Dr. Nakamura called Isabel, "Ms. Morris, I'm calling with some good news. We just received word from Wishes, Inc., that Tommy has received a grant to go to Walt Disney World in February."

"You've got to be kidding," laughed Isabel. "That's great! He's going to be so tickled."

"I can't believe it myself," replied the pediatrician, "but I have the tickets right here in my hand to prove it. I called you so you could, perhaps, use some of your sessions to help prepare him for the experience. I'm working on the logistics of getting him to Florida. We're trying to ensure the stability of his neck while he travels. You can't imagine what an experience this has been for me to arrange the consent forms with his family, the hospital, the airline, and the folks at Walt Disney World. The list of supplies we're going to have to put together for this trip is amazing. It's going to be an unbelievable process to get him there."

Tommy, his parents, and one of the home care nurses made their trip to Disney World a month later. A few problems were encountered, but, in general, the trip was a big success. Tommy returned home safely with a smile on his face, stories to tell over and over again, and a pair of Mouseketeer ears that didn't come off his head for at least 2 weeks.

Two weeks after Tommy's return, Dr. Nakamura was having lunch with several pediatric residents. He had just seen Tommy the day before and was telling the residents about Wishes, Inc. and the family's trip to Walt Disney World. He said, "I've been thinking about what this trip has meant for Tommy and his parents. There isn't any doubt that it has been a real boost to his confidence. I've also been thinking that if we could make arrangements for him to fly 1,000 miles to go to Walt Disney World, we may be able to make arrangements for him to go a few miles to school. Actually, it was his parents who brought up the idea after they returned from Walt Disney World."

After he thought a moment, Dr. Nakamura decided to turn Tommy's situation into a teaching experience for the residents. He looked at one of the young physicians and said, "These children require an ongoing commitment not only to medical care, but also to quality of life. Tell me, Dr. Markham, how would you balance the issues of cognitive and social development with medical risk?"

GETTING THE GO AHEAD

Isabel was elated when Dr. Nakamura called in March to say that he would support a school placement for Tommy on a trial basis. She immediately reported her conversation with the pediatrician to Mark Rawlings. By the middle of March, the paperwork was at the special education office. Fortunately, most of the plan was known by the district because of the earlier transition planning meeting. On this day, Mark received a call from the district's assistant director of special education.

"Mark, this is Mike Peterson from the special education office. How are you doing? I'm calling to give you an update about the plans to have Tommy Pham in school. I've had our people take a close look at the transportation, liability, and medical issues. It looks like we'll be able to do it. Between me and you though, this is going to cost a lot of money."

"I hear you," replied Mark. "This has been a difficult case for us to consider, but all in all I think the people at Claremont are looking forward to having Tommy here. I think we're up to the challenge."

"That teacher, Isabel Morris, did her homework on this one. It made our decision a lot easier," said Mike Peterson. "You know, I heard that Sonya Michaels may get a kid who needs a ventilator in her school next year? I think we're going to see more kids using technology in the future. We'd appreciate it if your team would consult with Sonya and her staff about the transition process."

Mark considered his response for a few moments and said, "I think our people would be happy to consult with Sonya's staff. In my view, the first thing is for Sonya to begin now. Our experience is that the process doesn't flow out of any IEP. There simply aren't any clear-cut policies on how to handle issues such as emergency care, liability, and transportation. It all needs to be worked out. Isabel's been working on the transition plan in one way or another for months.

Mike Peterson then questioned Mark about the collaboration process for the school. Mark replied, "No question. This was a team effort all the way through. The school staff and the medical people had to work together. The parents were the final decisionmakers though. They're the ones who had to weigh all of the risks and benefits. I have to tell you though, it was something to do all this work through a translator!"

As the conversation concluded, Mark offered, "This situation seems to be working out okay for us. We feel reasonably prepared, but we don't have any clear idea of how this is all going to work. We're going to try to stay flexible and take it a day at a time. I guess that's the best we can do."

MAKING COMPROMISES

Mark Rawlings waited a moment before responding to Isabel's statement about the "inappropriateness" of a school placement for Tommy at Claremont. "Isabel," said Mark, "I can understand how you might feel this isn't the best place for Tommy, but I don't think it would deny him his rights that much if he had to make some concessions to his medical condition."

There was a silence and then Mark continued, "Personally, I think Tommy would probably do quite well in a regular school classroom. I don't see that as impossible at some later time. He's a lot higher-functioning than I expected. But we're talking about a process here. We're going to have some good kids here at Claremont this fall. I don't see that it's going to be punitive for him to be here. After all, Claremont does have resources that the regular schools don't have and I don't think the district wants to risk the liability of having him in a setting without fully trained professionals. Who knows, Isabel, if things go well maybe we will be setting the stage for him to be integrated next year."

Isabel shook her head, "It took a virtual miracle for us to get to this point. If the trip to Walt Disney World hadn't occurred, we wouldn't be talking about Tommy's schooling today. The trip had nothing to do with education. The medical people put the trip together. I'm afraid that this district is going to get complacent and want to keep Tommy here at Claremont just because they're afraid of a lawsuit. Is it going to take another miracle to move him to a regular classroom? Time is an issue in his life. He deserves a chance to be treated like a typical kid."

"We'll take the next logical step in due time," responded Mark. "I think Claremont is going to be a great experience for him. Besides, what are you going to say if his parents like Claremont so much that they want to keep him here next year?"

DISCUSSION QUESTIONS

1. Mark Rawlings stated, that it would not deny Tommy his rights if he had to "make some concessions to his medical condition." Do you agree? What do you believe is the least restrictive environment for Tommy?

2. What were the benefits of Dr. Nakamura's active involvement in educational planning for Tommy? In general, how can educators facilitate collaboration between schools and medical teams? Should other team members share this responsibility?

3. List specific instances in which Isabel demonstrated adherence to a family-centered approach? What principles of family-centered practice are represented by each of these actions? Did any of Isabel's action violate family-centered principles?

4. To what extent do you think cultural differences or language barriers may have affected services provided to the Pham family or the decisions that were reached? Were issues of cultural diversity dealt with appropriately?

5. Was it appropriate for Isabel to advocate so strongly for Tommy's placement in a classroom setting? Should she continue to advocate for Tommy's inclusion in his local elementary school?

6. The content and nature of Isabel's home-based instruction with Tommy is unclear. What approach would you take if you were responsible for providing home-based early intervention services to Tommy and his family?

7. Imagine that you have been asked to consult with a preschool early intervention project that is attempting to make the transition of a child who is ventilator-assisted into a school-based program? What suggestions would you make to assist the team in planning and implementing this transition?

8. Decisions about Tommy's educational placement required members of the planning team to balance quality-of-life considerations with those of medical risk and safety. These dual concerns may also affect decisions about Tommy's participation in daily classroom activities. How should such decisions be made?

9. What are the legal responsibilities of the educational system for providing medical services to students with special health care needs? Do these children have a legal right to inclusion in a regular education setting? What are the responsibilities of educators or related services personnel for performing routine medical procedures in the school setting?

Peter and the Watermelon Seeds

Virginia E. Bishop

Peter loves to play with blocks, swing with his friends, and slide down the sliding board. While not remarkable for most 4-year-olds, his ability to enjoy these activities along with the other children in his preschool is a real accomplishment for Peter. Peter is blind. At 1 year of age, he was diagnosed with retinoblastoma—tumors in both eyes. Chemotherapy was unsuccessful and both of Peter's eyes were surgically removed by the time he was 2 years old. This case study describes a rather typical day for Peter at preschool. On this particular day, Miss Murray, the consultant for children with visual disabilities, is visiting the classroom. She has worked along with the regular preschool teacher to make the adaptations necessary for Peter's full inclusion. These adaptations are described in the case as well as other helpful hints for enabling children like Peter to handle the challenges of everyday activities independently and with confidence.

"**H**ow come you don't have any eyes?" asked 4-year-old Peter's friend, as they sat on the floor in the block corner of their preschool classroom.

" 'Cause my eyes got sick and the doctor had to take them out," answered Peter matter-of-factly.

"I'm gonna build a house for my cars," announced Peter's friend.

"Not me," replied Peter. "I'm gonna build a big, big house—up in the sky!" He began to stack his blocks one upon the other, never losing contact with the top block as he added one more. Suddenly, the tower of blocks buckled in the middle and came tumbling down.

Peter's delighted grin told how much he enjoyed building and letting his towers fall, listening to the delicious sound of blocks crashing in front of him. The boys' teacher rang her little bell to tell the children that it was time for the next activity. The boys gathered up their blocks and threw them into the box. Peter swept his hands across the floor around him to be sure he'd found all of his blocks and put them away.

"When you have put away your toys, you can line up at the door to go outside," announced the teacher. "Peter, there's one more block near your hand. Put it in the box and then line up behind Sam." Peter found the stray block, dropped it noisily into the box, and walked quickly along the wall to the classroom door where the other children were already lining up.[1] He touched each child lightly on the arm to see where the line began and ended, and stepped behind the last child. As the line of children moved out into the hall, Peter rested his hand on the shoulder of the child in front of him to maintain his position in line. The line broke up as the children entered the playground, and they scattered toward their favorite equipment. Peter paused a moment, listened, and ran toward the swings.

COURAGE AND SAFETY

The itinerant teacher of children with visual impairments, Miss Murray, arrived just as the class came outdoors to play. She approached Peter and said, "Hi, Peter. How's it going?"

Peter acknowledged her by turning around and giving her a hug around the legs. "Hi, Miss Murray. I'm gonna swing today." Miss Murray took Peter's hand and they walked to the swings.

"Remember what we said about swings?" asked Miss Murray. "You have to take turns and they're all full right now. But we can wait for a turn if we walk *around* the swings and wait on the bench. Be sure to listen to the kids' voices and the squeaks of the swings or you might get too close and get knocked over. If you're not sure there's an empty swing, just call out and ask." Peter soon got a turn on the swings and Miss Murray took the opportunity to speak to Peter's teacher. "Hi, Vicky. How's Peter doing?"

"No problems so far," answered Vicky Jenkins. "He gets along pretty well with most of the kids, but I do have to watch a few of the girls who want to mother him. Then again, Peter usually walks away from them himself when he's had enough hugging."

---

[1] Peter's early vision may be responsible for his excellent orientation in space and above-average mobility skills compared to other children with blindness.

"How is playtime outdoors working?" asked Miss Murray. "I remember you were concerned about the swing safety."

"I think Peter has gotten the idea of a wide turn around the swings. He did have a close call once—got nudged with someone's feet. He didn't fall, but he was startled," said Vicky.

"No harm done," said Miss Murray. "Peter has to learn how to handle himself on his own. Don't feel a need to intervene unless you feel that there's a real danger. Try to do it verbally first, providing there's time. And try not to yank him away without a warning or explanation if it can be helped. Peter needs to know why things are happening."

"Yes," agreed Vicky, "I've noticed he asks a lot of whys and what ifs lately. I try my best to let him feel whatever we're talking about. The other day he asked where the water went in the sink, so we let him put his fingers in the drain hole. Then we let him play with a funnel to show how water went in one side and out the little hole at the bottom."

"Very creative idea!" said Miss Murray. "That's just the kind of practical, concrete experience Peter needs. What he can't see he has to learn by touch or sound."

The two teachers strolled toward the sliding board, following Peter as he ran in that direction. Vicky paused to settle a squabble at the slide and then continued, "I noticed that Peter doesn't like the seesaw. He refuses to even try it. Why do you suppose that is?"

"I've noticed that with other children who are blind. I think it may be that when the seesaw lifts the child into the air, all contact with the ground is lost. The feeling of being suspended in space may be frightening. They also don't know when the seesaw is coming back down again and how fast. If you can't anticipate that bump by seeing it coming, it might be too scary to be any fun," Miss Murray speculated. "It's hard for sighted people to understand what it's like to be blind. Try to imagine an experience like an elevator or an escalator if you had no sight and you had never seen one before. What would that be like?"

Peter was squealing with delight as he slid down the sliding board and bounced off the end on his feet. What an accomplishment! Miss Murray remembered Peter's first encounter with the slide, how he ran his hands over the structure and how he had to gauge the height by following its slant with his fingers. She remembered how terribly afraid he was to climb the ladder to the top, but how desperately he wanted to do what he heard the other children having fun doing. With some verbal coaxing, holding his hand as he slid down the first time, and catching him at the bottom, he finally mastered his fear. Within a relatively short time he was able to push away help assertively and say, "Don't touch me. I can do it myself!" Soon after, he was climbing the ladder and sliding down in a variety of positions, landing safely in the sand at the bottom. Watching Peter, Miss Murray believed that he could do just about anything he wanted with a little preparation and experience.

Returning to the classroom, Peter again found his place in line and walked with his hand on a child's shoulder. This time, Peter lost contact with the child in front of him several times, but he walked quickly and regained his position in line.

EXPECTATIONS AND ADAPTATIONS

Back in the classroom, Peter found his seat at the table while some of the children used the bathroom. The bathroom door had a sign hanging on it. The children turned the sign to the "NO" side as they entered and back to the "YES" side when they exited. There was a sandpaper dot on the upper righthand corner of the "NO" side so Peter could use the bathroom signal card too.

During snacktime, Peter opened his own milk carton by feeling for the place to put his thumbs and then pressing it open. Instead of drinking his milk, Peter raised and lowered his straw in the milk to make "empty" noises. The little boy beside him started to giggle and did the same with his own carton. Before long, the table broke out into an entire chorus of squeaking milk cartons and straws. A plate of cookies put an end to the noise and Peter chose a chocolate chip one by smelling several and choosing the "chocolatey" one.

Toward the end of snacktime, Peter intentionally poured about a teaspoon of milk through his fingers and onto the table. He set the carton down and felt the wet spot with his other hand. The teacher was about to wipe up the spill with a sponge when Miss Murray signaled for her to wait by holding up her hand. Miss Murray approached Peter and said, "Well Peter, I guess you'll have to clean that up before the movie." She placed the sponge in one of Peter's hands and guided his other hand to find the spill. When the sponge had absorbed the milk, Miss Murray said, "It's all dry now— good. Now put the sponge in the sink and hurry on over for the movie."

While Peter was putting the sponge in the sink, Miss Murray whispered to Vicky, "It's probably a good idea not to let him get away with doing things that you wouldn't let the other children get away with. It's not that spilling the milk was really bad. It's just that he should be held responsible for what he does, whenever possible. If he decides to pour milk on the table, he should be the one to wipe it up. He can handle that."

The children were settling in for a videotaped movie and a little boy offered Peter the empty chair beside his own. The teacher leaned down to Peter to give him a quick introduction to what the movie was about and reminded him that he needed to listen to find out what was happening. The movie started and the children quieted. Peter's thumb went into his mouth and his index finger into his eye socket, as he usually did when he was listening intently to something—or when he was bored. Miss Murray put a stuffed teddy bear in Peter's lap and whispered, "You need to hold onto Mr. Bear and don't let him get away until the story is over. Help him listen too, by holding him in your lap with both hands." Peter held Mr. Bear in a death grip with both arms. The little boy who had offered Peter the chair asked if he could have an animal and Miss Murray pulled one out of the basket on the shelf. The movie was *Jack and the Beanstalk,* a favorite of many of the children. The two boys held their stuffed animals and echoed the giant's, "Fee, fie, foe, fum" in their best and deepest "giant" voices.

When the giant met his fate and the movie was over, the children moved back to the tables where the coloring pages and crayons were ready for use. The teacher looked quizzically at Miss Murray, as if to ask, "How can Peter color, too?" Miss Murray went to a large box in one corner of the room. The box was labeled "Peter's stuff." She took out a screenboard, which was a 12″ × 18″ rectangle of window screening with masking tape on all four edges to prevent scratches. She quickly attached a sheet of newspaper-weight paper to the screenboard with paper clamps and placed it in front of Peter. With a wax crayon, she drew five circles, spaced well apart on the paper. Peter's fingers eagerly searched the paper for the raised-line "balls" and found all five. Miss Murray showed Peter how to color one of the balls with a crayon. She then asked what color he wanted to make the next ball and Peter decided on red. Peter did the rest of the balls by himself. Although he didn't stay in the lines very well, he was able to fill in enough of the spaces within the circles to feel the "balls" he had colored by himself. He was proud when the other children got stickers on their papers and he did too. His was a "sniffy sticker" (scratch 'n sniff sticker). This was definitely a piece of artwork for the refrigerator at home!

After completing his coloring page, Peter asked to use the bathroom. He followed the wall with his hand, found the bathroom door, checked the sign, and turned it over to the "NO" side before entering.

The teacher took advantage of Peter's absence to ask a question, "I noticed that you asked Peter what color he wanted to use. Colors are a big topic for children this age. We're always talking about what color things are. To tell you the truth, it makes me feel awkward to talk about colors in front of Peter. It almost seems rude."

"I know what you mean," acknowledged Miss Murray. "I suppose I asked Peter what color he wanted more to give him a choice—some control—than anything else. Color is a part of our world, and Peter will hear about it his whole life. There's no sense in pretending it doesn't exist. If you think it confuses him, perhaps you could use some scented markers for his coloring for now. But don't avoid talking about what color things are. He'll need to know what color the grass is, the color of water, the sky, a banana . . . even if he will never see them himself."

The conversation was interrupted by sounds from the bathroom. Peter was singing to himself—short tunes with pauses every few seconds. Miss Murray smiled and the teacher asked, "And that singing—does that have anything to do with being blind? He does it every time he goes into the bathroom."

Miss Murray explained that Peter could be experimenting with echoes and how they bounce off the walls and objects. "Some blind children do this to help orient themselves within closed areas," she said. "It's relatively unconscious behavior and it can actually be quite useful in some situations, if it doesn't disturb others. It can be discouraged after a particular area, like the bathroom, has been explored thoroughly. Just give him a simple reminder such as, 'We heard your singing all the way out here in the classroom! Can you please keep it quieter next time? It won't bother anyone that way.' "

Peter returned from the bathroom and headed over to a corner where he heard a group of children playing with cars and trucks. It was time for free play and the children busied themselves with assorted toys and make-believe play. The teachers continued to talk while they monitored the children's play. Vicky asked why Peter kept his head down so often, especially when he wasn't really involved in an activity.

Miss Murray explained, "When a child is blind, like Peter, there isn't any real reason to hold up his head. There's nothing to see. The child has to learn to hold his head up just because it's the way other people do it and because it looks nice. Peter will probably need reminders to hold his head up and additional motivation like, 'Let me see that handsome face of yours' to help Peter develop the habit of holding his head erect." Miss Murray continued to explain that children who have some vision do just the opposite. They gaze at any strong light source and have to be reminded to look away. Children may also shake their heads from side to side as a means of stimulation or as a way of orienting to sound.

"Every child is different," concluded Miss Murray, "and it's probably best to try and figure out what the child is getting out of an unusual behavior before trying to modify it."

A NEW EXPERIENCE

The last activity of the day was a watermelon party. The class went out on the grass near the classroom door to begin the festivities. The teacher placed the watermelon in the middle of the circle of children and they all admired it and talked about how it grew. The teacher encouraged the children to touch it and allowed them to try and pick up the "monster melon."

Peter was fascinated, "Boy, this is real, real, big!" he exclaimed, trying to lift up one end of the melon. "I bet my Dad could pick it up though. He's real strong." He ran his hands along the sides and ends of the melon and then commented, "It's like a ball . . . but not really . . . just sorta like a ball."

The teacher made the first cut, lengthwise, and then she and Miss Murray each took a group of children to cut the two halves into smaller pieces. One at a time, the children were allowed to help cut their own slice of watermelon. When Peter's turn came, Miss Murray guided his hands so that he could feel the knife cutting into the wet, slippery watermelon. The children were soon busy biting, chewing, spitting seeds, and enjoying the sloppy affair. But Peter stood immobile. He was holding his watermelon in front of him with the pink juice running down his arms. He looked forlorn and helpless, seeming not to know what to do with the slice of watermelon. It then dawned on Miss Murray that Peter may have never experienced watermelon before or perhaps he couldn't relate this cold slab of wetness to the neat chunks he may have been given at home.

She took Peter's index finger and poked it into the pink part of the melon and then into the firmer rind. She explained that the soft part was for eating, but there were small, hard bits called "seeds" all mixed up in it. She helped Peter find a seed and feel how hard and slippery it was. She then encouraged him to take a bite and asked him if his teeth or tongue had found any seeds yet. Perplexed, he nodded his head "yes," but he didn't know how to spit them out. They just slid down his chin. Miss Murray coaxed Peter to blow the seeds out, but he was only minimally successful. Even so, he managed to get a few seeds into the air instead of on his chin. From the look on Peter's face, it was safe to say that he did not especially enjoy this new experience. This was confirmed when Peter announced sheepishly, "I like my mom's watermelon better—hers doesn't have seeds."

The buckets of water available for clean up were the source of as much fun as the watermelon itself. The splashing of water and giggling that accompanied it were much more to Peter's liking. In the midst of the fun, a taller version of Peter strode into view and said, "Hey there, Buddy. . . whatcha doin'?"

Peter turned and hugged his dad's knees. "Guess what, Dad? We had watermelon today, and guess what? Their watermelon has a lot of seeds. And guess what? I know how to spit now! I can show you how to spit. Wanna see me spit? I can show Mommy how to spit too. What d'ya think of that, huh?"

Peter's father smiled, patted his son on the back, and said, "Okay, Buddy, we'll go home and show Mommy how to spit. Find my pocket and let's go." Peter put his fingers in his dad's back pocket and followed him toward the gate.

DISCUSSION QUESTIONS

1. Is the method of consultation employed by Miss Murray overly directive or not directive enough?

2. Miss Murray has obviously chosen to provide some level of direct intervention with Peter. Do you think that this is important in developing Peter's skills? Should she provide more hands-on intervention with Peter?

3. How did Miss Murray handle the questions posed by Peter's regular classroom teacher? If you were the consultant, would you have responded to the teacher any differently?

4. Do you think that Miss Murray's methods of consultation will enable the teacher (Vicky Jenkins) to handle new situations with Peter as they arise? Is the teacher learning how to identify appropriate goals and develop interventions for Peter?

5. Miss Murray has obviously chosen to work on functional skills within the normally occurring routines of Peter's child care setting. Will this be enough to prepare Peter for inclusion in a regular kindergarten setting when he is 5 years old? If not, what else is needed?

6. What format would you use if you were responsible for developing a written intervention plan (individualized education program or individualized family service plan) for Peter? Based on the events described in the case study, develop a rough draft of an intervention plan for him.

7. Very little is said about Peter's parents in this case. How important is it that they are informed about what is going on in the classroom? What options for communication with them might be employed?

8. What should the respective roles of the consultant and regular teacher be in communicating with the family or providing suggestions for helping Peter at home?

Only Time Will Tell

Jean Lowe _____

> *Jonah was born bearing the burden of his mother's history of drug abuse. The mother, Karen, had succeeded in freeing herself of her addiction to heroin but the methadone that had helped her for so long was now a source of bondage for her newborn son. This is a story about the struggle of the newborn, Jonah, as he goes through withdrawal from methadone. It is also the story of Janet Cruz, a professional who provides support to Karen throughout this traumatic ordeal and who tries to ensure a smooth transition from hospital to home when Jonah is discharged.*

The baby is lying on a warming table, his arm shaking uncontrollably as he cries. A medical student watches as the nurse washes the baby, who was born only a few minutes ago. The baby's cry is unusually high-pitched. He has little ability to self-calm. Each time he tries to place his hand near his mouth, he is unsuccessful and seems to get more frustrated. The baby's father anxiously waits in the corner, not sure of the activity around him. Concern is worn on all of the faces surrounding the crying and tremulous newborn.

DAY TWO

A few days have passed and much information has been gathered about the baby, who has been named Jonah. Jonah's toxicology screen was positive for both methadone and cocaine. Jonah's mother, Karen, had been taking methadone during the pregnancy.

I met Karen 3 weeks ago. She was one of a group of mothers on methadone with whom I was asked to talk. The mothers-to-be wanted more information about the effects of methadone on newborns and what it would be like for their babies to go through drug withdrawal. Karen was quiet during the video I showed of a new-born withdrawing. After many of the women left, Karen expressed interest in learning the infant massage techniques we were using to calm babies. She also told me how she had become addicted to pain medications 10 years ago after a back injury and was later turned on to heroin by a boyfriend. The use of heroin led to her eventual addiction. Although Karen had not been on heroin dur-ing this pregnancy, she was taking methadone, a legal substitute for heroin. She greatly feared the birth of her baby and did not know what to expect. Her 5-year-old son had previously been removed from her custody because she was unable to care for him. I remem-ber her telling me that her new boyfriend, who was also on metha-done maintenance, was excited about the arrival of his first child.

Jonah was in obvious withdrawal shortly after birth. His jittery movements and crying persisted for 2 days, and there was little anyone could do to console him. He scratched his face trying to get his hands to his mouth. His knees and elbows were rubbed raw from his agitated movements, and the muscles in his tiny legs were so stiff that it was difficult to straighten his legs to diaper him. Jonah was given low doses of methadone to help him through with-drawal.

Karen was still hospitalized because Jonah was delivered by Cesarean section. I went to visit her and found her awake and on the telephone. She hung up when she saw me, but she didn't seem to remember me.

"Karen, my name is Janet Cruz. I met you a few weeks ago. I've seen your baby, Jonah, in the newborn nursery and wanted to con-gratulate you and see how you are doing."

"Oh, now I remember you," Karen replied. "I'm still in a lot of pain from the C-section and not thinking clearly. How is my baby doing? Do you know when he can go home with me?"

Karen began to get teary and seemed somewhat groggy from the pain medication. She had been told by the physician that her baby would be in the hospital for at least 2 weeks and possibly as long as 6 weeks.

"Karen, it must be hard to think of going home without your baby," I sympathized. "As I explained before, it will help Jonah if he can be weaned slowly from the methadone. I would like to work with you and show you the infant massage strokes so you can help calm and comfort Jonah during his withdrawal."

Karen agreed to meet with me but was not sure how she would

be getting to and from the hospital. Her mother usually provided her with rides, but she was out of town. She said she didn't think she had the energy to walk to the bus from her home, but she would try to come by the nursery before being discharged the next day.

DAY FIVE

Karen and her boyfriend, Pete, were in the newborn nursery tending their baby. Pete held Jonah as Karen tried to cut the baby's fingernails. She was absorbed in her task, insistent on cutting Jonah's nails short so he would no longer claw at his face. The baby was sedated due to his agitated state. I approached the family to talk to them.

"Karen, I am so glad to see you again. How are you feeling?"

Karen introduced me to Pete. She was still in pain and again seemed sad and teary-eyed while holding the baby. Jonah was still irritable and having some difficulty feeding. He seemed to know his mother's voice and quieted as she talked to him. I tried to provide some comfort to Karen, "It seems like Jonah really knows your voice. He's calmer with you around."

As I talked to Karen, Pete faded into the background as though he wished not to get involved. He was quiet and seemed particularly shy and nervous around the nurses. I asked Karen and Pete if they would like to videotape Jonah and learn infant massage. Karen said that she was in pain from her C-section and had another appointment. Another time was scheduled to work with the baby. In the meantime, the parents were encouraged to visit the nursery at any time of day and to contact the developmental specialist if they had questions.

DAY SIX

Jonah was weaning slowly from the methadone and beginning to have some calmer wakeful periods during the day. While caring for Jonah, a nurse noticed sudden jerky movements. Jonah appeared to be having a seizure. A developmental specialist was equally suspicious of seizure activity. When the tremors were noted again later in the day, a neurology consultation was ordered and seizures were confirmed. Jonah was transferred to the neonatal intensive care unit because his seizures were difficult to control and the physician wanted him to be monitored closely.

DAY SEVEN

Karen was called regarding Jonah's seizures. She came to the NICU
and appeared to be very scared. This time her mother was with her.
The physician discussed Jonah's new problem and the need for him
to take phenobarbital three times a day to control the seizures. Later
in the day, the neurologist also told Karen that her drug use may
have contributed to Jonah's seizure disorder. Obviously upset, Karen
withdrew to her baby and cried quietly. Her mother also appeared
to be shaken by the news, but she directed her efforts to comforting
Karen.

DAY TEN

During medical rounds, it was noted that Karen had not been visiting Jonah regularly, although she called once or twice a day. Jonah
remained unstable and his seizures continued to be uncontrolled.
He was weaning from the methadone and only receiving it two times
a day. His primary nurse was becoming very attached to him. She
put a mobile on his crib and she held and played with him when
she was on duty in the nursery. Various team members discussed
what seemed to be an unstable home situation; however, no one
had actually been to Karen's home. A home visit by the social worker
or home health nurse was scheduled.

Karen called the nursery, and I asked to talk to her. I empha-
sized the importance of her visits to the nursery, explaining that
these visits are especially important for a mother with a history of
substance abuse. I also scheduled a time to meet her in the nursery
to instruct her in infant massage.

DAY TWELVE

Karen kept her appointment in the nursery and looked good when
she arrived. Her mother, who had been providing her with rides to
the hospital, accompanied her. Karen said that Pete is reluctant to
visit the hospital because he doesn't feel welcome in this environment.

I videotaped Jonah and Karen with the infant massage therapist. Karen was shown basic massage strokes with emphasis placed
on reading Jonah's cues. Karen quickly picked up what was shown
and interacted nicely with Jonah. I reinforced the fact that Jonah
seemed to know Karen's voice and reacted well to her touch. He is
clearly calmer when Karen is around. I encouraged her to visit as

often as possible because her calming influence may help him with-draw more quickly.

Karen talked more freely as she massaged her baby, mentioning that she felt uncomfortable coming to the NICU because it seemed as though everyone was watching her. She felt labeled as a "drug mom" and talked about how guilty she felt about Jonah's seizures. Karen admitted to having used cocaine the night she went into labor.

"I was terrified about going into labor," Karen said, "and heard all these stories about the nurses in the labor room. My friend told me the nurses are mean to mothers on drugs and don't give them medicine during delivery. I was so scared about the pain that I used the coke to relax."

Karen's mother listened, but said nothing. Later, in private, she told me that she felt guilty about not being there for Karen when the baby was born. She wanted to help Jonah and Karen but was not sure what would be best.

After talking to Karen and her mother, I asked them if they would be willing to meet with the doctors and nurses to try to prepare for Jonah's discharge. This would be a way to get the staff together to have them talk to Karen at one time. I promised Karen that I would be present and advocate for her.

DAY THIRTEEN

During medical rounds the next day, the staff discussed Jonah's mother again, berating her for not visiting him more often. Jonah was taking methadone once a day and doing well. His seizures were under control with phenobarbital and he was expected to be ready to go home in a week providing his mother had discharge training.

I told the staff that I met with Karen and her mother the preceding day and described the positive interaction Karen had with her baby. I also mentioned that Karen had difficulty coming to the hospital due to transportation problems and that she felt alienated by the medical staff. I discussed the possibility of a care conference, so the treatment team could meet and talk with Jonah's family. One of the nurses remarked that Karen made many excuses about why she could not visit and they were not sure she was invested in the baby. They agreed that a care conference would be helpful since the plan was to send Jonah home.

A care conference was planned for the next day. The treatment team, which included the neonatalogist, neurologist, pediatric resident, primary nurse, social worker, discharge planning nurse, and developmental specialist, would meet for 20 minutes prior to meeting with the family. The goal of the staffing would be for the team to share information and suggestions in working toward a discharge plan. Selected members of the team would meet with Karen to discuss important medical and developmental issues as well as important goals to help in Jonah's transition to home.

DAY FOURTEEN

The care conference was scheduled to take place in the afternoon, but Karen came to the hospital earlier to be with Jonah. Pete was still reluctant to come to the hospital and chose not to attend the meeting. Karen's mother, however, said she would go to the meeting with her daughter.

Karen was obviously anxious about the afternoon conference. I tried to explain what to expect and told her that the staff would meet together first so they could discuss what was needed prior to discharge. I asked Karen to write down her questions regarding Jonah's home care. I also encouraged her to ask questions, especially if she did not understand what people were asking or telling her.

During the staffing prior to the care conference, it was clear that certain team members did not think Jonah should go home. The primary nurse was especially upset at the prospect of Jonah going home with Karen. She worried about Karen having a relapse and the impact this would have on Jonah. The social worker informed the team that there was not enough evidence or reason to make a referral to Child Protective Services. The neurologist felt that Jonah was ready to go home since he had been seizure-free for a week. The plan was for Jonah to be completely weaned from the methadone the next day. Then he was to remain methadone-free for 3 days before going home. Karen was to spend a night in the nursery with Jonah prior to discharge. A final recommendation was for the parents to be trained in cardiopulmonary resuscitation because infants who have been exposed to drugs have a higher risk of sudden infant death syndrome.

Karen and her mother joined the pediatric resident, neurologist, and myself. They were informed about the plan to send Jonah home within the week. This was clearly good news to Karen, and she began to ask questions regarding his seizures and medicine. It was recommended that, at least for the first month at home, Jonah be seen twice a week by a home health care nurse and every other week in the pediatric clinic by the pediatric resident who cared for him in the NICU. Developmental follow-up was to be coordinated with the nurse's home visit or Jonah's pediatric clinic appointment. Karen agreed with the plan and was relieved to have a nurse coming to her home. She was very willing to bring Jonah to medical appointments at the hospital, although transportation continued to be a problem. I let Karen know that we could arrange to have Jonah's Medicaid pay for a taxi to bring him to medical appointments.

Karen planned to spend the next night in the nursery and both she and her mother were scheduled for CPR classes. Karen was encouraged to have Pete receive CPR training as well. A developmental follow-up was planned to take place in Karen's home a week after discharge. Another meeting with the infant massage therapist was scheduled prior to discharge. Karen was encouraged to use the massage, especially before feeding Jonah since it had been helping him with gas. Jonah ate quickly and was generally frantic around feeding time, causing him to swallow a lot of air. His primary nurse also agreed to work with Karen to show her ways to calm Jonah.

DAY NINETEEN

On Jonah's 19th day, he went home. Karen spent the night and, according to the nurses on the night shift, did well. Karen had been coming to visit her son more consistently after the care conference in which she learned of Jonah's discharge. Pete came to a CPR class, as did Karen and her mother. Jonah was successfully weaned off methadone and, although he still had some jittery movements and stiffness in his legs, there had been great improvements. Jonah was able to remain awake and alert for longer time periods and appeared to enjoy interactions with his parents. Even so, Jonah was still easily overaroused and liked to be wrapped tightly in a blanket. Karen was able to calm him with massage, and a pacifier often helped to keep him contented.

It is difficult to know what will happen with Jonah in the future. Karen has been a drug addict for 10 years, and Pete has a history of using a variety of illegal drugs. Although they seem committed to working with Jonah and trying to avoid using all drugs except methadone, only time will tell. The treatment team hopes that the support Karen and Pete were given in the nursery and the ongoing follow-up appointments scheduled to occur at home will help them to remain motivated to provide a supportive environment for their young son's development. Perhaps Jonah will make a difference in their lives.

DISCUSSION QUESTIONS

1. Karen's infrequent visits to the hospital contributed to some of the criticism she received from the staff. Should more have been done to encourage Karen to visit more often? Should more have been done to encourage Pete?

2. Overall, the interventionist in this case study did not question Karen's decisions or actions. Should a more directive approach have been taken?

3. The neurologist made it clear that Karen's addiction may have contributed to Jonah's seizure disorder. Was his honesty the best approach to take with this family?

4. With time, it became obvious that some of the staff members did not have positive impressions of Karen and Pete. Did the interventionist do anything to try to change their impressions? What else might she have done to make the hospital atmosphere more encouraging for Karen and her family?

5. Was the decision to send Jonah home with his mother a wise one? Was enough done to ensure his health, safety, and an environment that is supportive of his development?

6. Suppose you were assigned the responsibility of making home visits to Jonah and his family twice a month. What would you try to accomplish? Where would you start? What strategies would you employ?

7. What are the potential barriers to Karen's and Pete's successful parenting of Jonah? What services and resources are important for a community to have if it wants to assist parents like Karen and Pete in rearing their children after they leave the hospital?

The Blooming of Rose

Eileen Ziesler

Rose was limited in many respects, but not in all. Viewed from the right perspective and under circumstances that provided opportunities, Rose's strengths shone through. This case describes the support provided to Rose and her family by a primarily center-based preschool program. In particular, it is the story of one professional's repeated contacts with the family during a 7-year period as she provided services to two of Rose's three children. Rose's limitations, multiple family crises, and the transition of the children into new services pose challenges for this professional and others in the community.

I have a passion for growing roses, although the success rate for wintering-over roses in our northern climate is very poor. To improve my chances, my husband has constructed a greenhouse, and I sit now in the early morning warmth and contemplate one of my roses. I have planted it in this protective environment, and I faithfully monitor its well-being. The yellowed, tall, new growth is fragile and spindly. Too much moisture, sun, or fertilizer will kill it; too little and it will not have the strength to grow and bloom. I do not want this rose to die. It was a gift from a special friend.

A DUBIOUS BEGINNING

I met Rose on a cold February afternoon 8 years ago. I was 32 years old and well into my profession as a teacher of young children with disabilities. I was going to her home to begin an assessment of her little boy, Ronald, who was almost 3 years old and not yet talking.

I knocked on the outer porch door and, not caring to wait in the below-zero temperature, let myself into the enclosed porch. A path to the inner door had been created by a border of unused chairs, broken appliances, toys, and bundles of clothing. This type of clutter is a common product of our community's economy, which necessitates the philosophy, "Some day we might need it, but for now just put it over there." Having grown up in this same community, I understand the philosophy. To this day, I spend too much of my time tottering between "save it" and "throw it out." This family wasted no time contemplating such a choice. I doubted they had ever thrown away anything in their lives.

Rose opened the door and my lungs filled with 90-degree, wood-heated air. My next breath took in the combined smells of spilled milk, soiled diapers, and other human and animal odors. I offered my best smile as an initial greeting, followed by a brief introduction of who I was. I then squatted down to be face-to-face with a smiley, bright-eyed child who was clad only in a diaper. He was dirty and the remains of his last meal adhered to his little body, filling me with intense desire to draw a bath and wash him with warm soapy water before proceeding further with the evaluation.

He smiled a sweet smile, grunted, and gestured toward my basket of intriguing objects. I glanced around the room wondering where to put my purse and coat and where to set up the testing for this child. Rose offered no suggestions. She filled the recliner she sat in, beads of perspiration on her brow and upper lip. She was a heavy woman and was sweating profusely, though she wore only a sleeveless cotton dress. I was suddenly aware of how moist I was feeling myself in my turtleneck and wool sweater. Rose stared at the television.

The adjacent room offered no better place, so I perched on the edge of a low chair. Ronald squatted in front of me and we proceeded with the assessment. When we were finished, I gave Ronald one of his favorite items from the assessment to keep—a red and blue ball. I tried to share some positive impressions I had of his development with Rose, but her eyes remained glued somewhere inside the television. I then asked Rose some questions about Ronald's personal, social, and adaptive skills. All I got were a few half-hearted answers of "yeah" or "nah" and a seemingly more intense focus on the television. I felt I knew why Ronald wasn't talking— he had never heard the human voice! I felt like giving up.

Ronald was distracted by something in the front hall. He dropped the ball and eagerly headed toward the door. Heavy footfalls upon the porch flooring gave a clue, followed by the appearance of a large, shadowy figure on the opposite side of the smudged window. The man opening the door had the darkest, biggest, and hairiest face I had ever encountered. The experience was comparable to meeting a grizzly bear at close range in the woods—alone. Now my desire was to be safe inside my own, tidy, middle-class home. I offered my best smile for the second time, introduced myself, and stated the purpose of my presence. Ronald had completely lost interest in me and my toys. He rushed toward the bear and latched onto its lower legs, whereupon he was lifted up and tossed to the ceiling. Ronald squealed with joy. My heartbeat resumed. It was not a ferocious grizzly bear I had just met, but a large, timid man named Harold. This was Ronald's father. I gave a sheepish smile to Harold and Rose and said my good-byes.

Our speech-language clinician is a rather fragile woman, careful and meticulous, a well-dressed professional, a working mother, a caring and genuine person. Carrie is very responsible when it comes to the families she serves. In the 10 years I have known her, I have never seen her give less than her best. She tries to do everything right. Everything right in this case included going on a home visit with me to meet the family in their own environment. I offered some of my impressions of Ronald and his family based on my first visit, but nothing could really prepare her for the experience. The number of joint visits Carrie and I make together to families has decreased considerably since this adventure. Nevertheless, Carrie was a great help in understanding the nature and causes of Ronald's language delays. In addition to assessing Ronald, Carrie was able to draw Rose out a little, and we discovered that she stuttered quite badly. We also learned that Ronald had a 10-month-old sister, Tina.

We completed our assessment, and I prepared to receive Ronald into my classroom. I worried before he arrived: Did he have any real clothes? Would he be bathed? How would the other children and parents respond to him? Would he even arrive? I discussed my concerns with Jody, my classroom assistant. Jody and I have grown quite close over years of developing the program together and overcoming many obstacles. We worried together, but our worries were unnecessary. Ronald arrived promptly on his first day of school with a fresh-scrubbed look, long pants, a buttoned-to-the-neck shirt, a matching vest, new shoes, and a just-combed curl in his hair.

SUCCESS, CHANGE, AND SETBACKS

Jody, Carrie, and I found Ronald to be an eager learner and better behaved than your average 3-year-old. His progress in language was immediate and gratifying, but his progress in articulation was negligible. Rose's and Harold's participation in the program was only short of miraculous. Rose gave me detailed reasons for absences 3 months in advance. The whole family attended all of the family program activities, consistently dressed in their best. Rose sent special treats and snacks to school for Ronald to share with his friends.

Home visits were another story. During visits to their home, I tried to offer Rose a few strategies to improve Ronald's vocabulary. My intent for these visits was not to teach the child, but to provide ideas and model strategies that might be used at home. Rose continued her intent focus on the television, despite the fact that the television was often not turned on! During successive visits, I noticed that Rose would occasionally glance in my direction as I spoke. Her glances became more frequent and more sustained with each visit. She began to watch Tina and Ronald at play, and I began to talk less and watch the children more, limiting my discussion to the here and now of what the children were doing and saying. Rose showed me some mail order books that she had purchased for the children through a book club. These books were written on a fifth-grade level, but I did my best to use the pictures in the books to model teaching strategies. In this manner, we struggled together for 3 years, and Rose made slow but steady progress in understanding child development. As time passed, I began to see suggestions of smiles upon Rose's face and hear faint chuckles of amusement as she allowed herself to enjoy the antics of her children. Tina grew alongside Ronald, her speech developing without the numerous omissions and substitutions of Ronald's speech. She seemed quicker than Ronald, but Rose was concerned and asked that she be assessed by the school. We found Tina to be of average ability.

In the spring of Ronald's second year with us, Rose experienced ongoing trouble with menstruation and we began to worry about her health. A strong odor accompanied this change in her health. The gains Rose had made began to deteriorate and the smiles faded from her face. I felt her slipping away and I didn't know how to hold on to her. She did not reach out to me.

Surprisingly, Ronald, now 4½ years old, continued to thrive. One day he was playing with plastic magnetic letters. "E-er!," he called out, "Urse, urse, E-er!" Although he only spoke in two- or three-word phrases, he could correctly spell many words he had seen. When I asked him where he learned "nurse," he bubbled, "E-V, E-V." That television had served a purpose after all!

In Ronald's last year with us, a new family development occurred. Rose was pregnant. Her health returned and, with it, her social skills. Although her pregnancy did not show until the last trimester because of her excess weight, it weighed heavy on my mind. I fretted about a third child in this family as I thought about the difficulties I experienced in raising my own three children who were in their primary and later elementary years.

Rose's third child was born in December, and she named her Anna. I saw little of Anna in Ronald's last semester with us, but what I did see was troubling. When Anna was 4 months old, I gently shared my concerns with Rose. Anna's eyes were crossed badly and her weight gain would have put her over the 99th percentile for her height and age. She was a flaccid baby, hypotonic with minimal head control, and absolutely no motivation to move about, play with toys, or make sounds. Much to my amazement, Rose and Harold had already sought medical help for Anna through our county's early intervention program for infants. Anna was scheduled for eye surgery and occupational therapy. A chapter was closing for me with Ronald's family, but I knew I would pick up the book again.

LETTING GO

Ronald began kindergarten, but he continued in Carrie's speech-language program. The emphasis on phonics in kindergarten was a challenge for Ronald, whose articulation showed little progress. I tried to speak with Ronald's new teacher, but she was not receptive. It was not an easy year. Rose hovered about, creating tension for the teacher, and Ronald became a scapegoat in the classroom. He could not process auditory directions or do seatwork at the rate the other children could, but there were a few moments where his own resiliency and strength shone through.

During one of my visits to the kindergarten, the children were about to begin a music listening game with the actions of a song about colors coming from the recordplayer. "Red stand up, blue stand up, yellow and green stand up. Blue sit down, green sit down . . ." I sat rigidly in my chair as the first group of eight children attempted to perform the series of listening directions. It was apparent that only the brightest were succeeding. The others didn't have a chance and looked forlornly to each other for clues—but there were none. I was sure that Ronald would be among the second group. He gripped his piece of yellow construction paper in one hand and waved at me with the other from his place between Miss Red and Mr. Blue. I plastered an encouraging smile on my face and the music began.

To my amazement, Ronald not only stood on the correct cues, but also helped the distraught Miss Red and Mr. Blue to perform the correct motions for their colors. Unable to face another round of the color song, I winked good-bye to Ronald and left.

A NEW CHAPTER

I had little contact with Rose for a year and a half. Anna was receiving outpatient therapies, and Ronald began first grade. Then a bombshell hit the family. The early intervention staff shared with me the terrible news that Anna's therapy wasn't covered by the family's insurance. The family had assumed the charges were covered in some way by the early intervention program and innocently allowed the bill to climb to almost $2,500. No one and everyone was to blame. Little by little, the family chipped away at the bill with monthly payments of $10 and $20, and some external support was found to cover a portion of future costs. Even so, the family terminated Anna's therapy.

Soon after the beginning of the next school year, we began our multidisciplinary team assessment of Anna. She was approaching her third birthday. Anna wore strong corrective glasses, had numerous ear infections, and had speech-language patterns similar to Ronald's. In addition to severe language delays, Anna showed significant delays in motor skills, particularly gross motor skills. She didn't begin to walk until she was 2 years old. One major change from our first assessment with the family 4 years ago was the amount of information provided by Rose. We used the Minnesota Child Development Inventory, a 320-item parent questionnaire. Rose and Harold answered more than 300 questions without help and asked me for clarification on the remaining queries. Their responses indicated the same degree of delay as the information obtained from the Battelle Developmental Inventory (BDI). I felt proud of their effort to assist in our evaluation and humbled by the accuracy of their responses. Anna became a student in my classroom when she turned 3 years old.

Rose lived across the street from the elementary school where our program operated. She brought Anna to school every day, stood near the door, and she stayed. Subtle hints did not dissuade Rose from her position at the door. She couldn't be encouraged to join in the children's play, nor would she accept offers of a chair. Little Anna stood with Rose each morning until Rose would finally tell her, "Go play." In my mind, I nicknamed her, "Stand-Around Rose." While I practiced serenity in accepting the things I could not change, my teammates tried to instill in me the courage to change the things they felt I should change.

I felt very alone in this dilemma. My firm belief in parent involvement supported Rose's constant presence in the classroom. Needless to say, I won no popularity votes for my decision to leave Rose alone. Anna's second school year began with Rose as permanent a fixture as the doorway in which she stood.

A NEW ROSE

Then small changes began to take place. Our Parent–Teacher Association instituted a parent volunteer program, and Rose agreed to a few specific times to help in other areas of the school for an hour or so. She also volunteered to be a Girl Scout leader assistant and put in a great deal of time preparing for weekly meetings. By October of Anna's second year, Rose was staying 5 or 10 minutes by the door and then explaining to me for another 5 or 10 minutes why she couldn't stay longer that day. Real progress, and it wasn't even in the IEP! We breathed a sigh of relief for ourselves and felt happy for Rose's newfound pride.

Rose's activities in the parent volunteer program and the Girl Scouts also opened my eyes to some social realities I would have preferred not to see. As Rose became a more visible and responsible person in the school, her naivety and limitations were out in the open for everyone to see and comment upon. I learned that the intolerance, scapegoating, and sense of superiority inflicted upon Ronald by the children in his kindergarten class were, in all likelihood, learned from the adults in their lives. Those of us who had grown to love and appreciate Rose were stunned at the insensitive behavior displayed by some of the adults in the school, and we rallied around Rose as her cheerleaders. The cheering section included our immediate early childhood staff, parents of children in the same session as Anna, and a few select staff members from other areas of the school.

Something else happened in that school that changed the dynamics of our relationship with Rose. Soon after Christmas, a new little boy joined our class. He had autism, displayed aggressive behaviors, and was generally difficult to control. He was particularly enchanted by the slamming of doors. Cabinet doors, classroom doors, toaster oven doors—any door at all would be opened and slammed continuously if left unchecked. When we interfered with his door slamming, he screamed and kicked. In fact, any transition set off a tantrum. Although we had one staff member assigned to work exclusively with this child, two or more staff members were often needed when he was out of control.

Rose became indispensable for helping the other children with the activity in progress or otherwise seeing to their needs. For example, if we were getting ready for snack and our new little boy objected, Rose would help children wash hands, find their places, and get their dishes. I often wondered what Rose thought about how we handled these situations, but her presence at these times indicated her unspoken support. Her ability to fit into place in our room when she was so needed was a gift to us. It never occurred to me at that time how naturally, capably, and confidently she stepped in and kept the classroom going.

Anna had a successful second year in the classroom. Her speech and language progressed, although these skills continued to lag behind her overall development. She loved to play in the housekeeping corner with the other children and readily engaged in pretend play with the kitchen toys, dress-up clothes, and baby dolls. Anna was content to follow the lead of the other children, but she was definitely not a leader. She was, however, the apple of her mother's eye. Rose dressed her in stylish little sweat suits, dresses and tights, and leggings and bulky tops. Rose sewed and decorated these outfits, often relying upon used clothing from the clothing center and offers of clothing from other mothers. She also delighted in fixing Anna's long, thick hair. In some ways, it seemed Anna was a little doll that Rose dressed up.

NEW TROUBLES

Despite her many and varied accomplishments, some things about Rose stayed the same. She still stood in the doorway to watch when she brought Anna. She continued to provide lengthy and detailed explanations of any change in her schedule. She watched Anna with the same look of unconditional love. But through the smiles and chuckles, there was often a look of sadness in her eyes. When those eyes remained sad for a long time, I ventured to ask her how she felt—Was she getting sick? Was there something bothering her?

"It's Ronald," she said one day. Ronald, now a third grader, was fighting a lot. The other children continued to pick on him and he was falling behind academically. Rose had been trying her best to keep things on an even keel by closely monitoring his homework and keeping her eye on the playground activities. Her close supervision of Ronald was a constant source of complaint by his classroom teacher.

A re-evaluation was eventually conducted and Ronald was found eligible for additional services. He began a new education program that involved spending a portion of his day in a self-contained class and the remaining time in closely supervised activities in an inclusive setting. As the year passed, Rose began to identify with that program. She developed a closeness with the teacher and a foster grandparent who worked in the program.

We moved into Anna's and Rose's final year with a spirit of, "nothing can go wrong" and, "You've come a long way, baby." As a fourth grader, Ronald was doing well with the joint programming of regular and special education. Tina, now a first grader, was doing well, and Anna continued to do well in my classroom. Halloween came, and we all dressed up in costumes. Even Rose came dressed in a clown costume she sewed—complete with nose, wig, and funny shoes. The school staff didn't recognize her, and it was interesting to sense the slight shift of attitude toward this clown of unknown personage. We were all the same, a bunch of teachers enjoying the fun of Halloween with our students.

So it was that somewhere along the way, amid this spirit of optimism and progress, Rose stopped smiling again. The touches of make-up upon her face, the style of her hair, and her smiles and chuckles were the first to leave. These niceties were replaced with increased body odor, ill-kept clothing, blotchy skin, and red eyes. I asked what was wrong and hugged her. She gave no response. It was in Ronald's classroom, with the teacher and the foster grandparent, that Rose shared her secret. Harold had been beating her in front of Ronald. Rose expressed concern that this was having an effect upon Ronald's behavior. She didn't seem to be aware of her own plight. With the support of the foster grandparent and teacher, she made the decision to move to a shelter for abused women. Rose came to us to let us know of her decision. She cried a little and then said with fierce determination, "I gotta do something!" In the next few hours, Rose made all the necessary arrangements.

We all worried about how this experience would affect Rose, who had no job skills, had never been on public assistance, and had a strong sense of a family being "Dick, Jane, Sally, Mother, and Father." I expected her situation to deteriorate before it improved. I also expected Rose to disappear from the school grounds until this issue came to some resolution. I was wrong on both counts. Rose was back at work in her volunteer job, having arranged transportation for herself and Anna. Anna talked about meeting other children at the shelter. Rose's make-up returned, and she adopted a new hairstyle. Rose basked in the care of the shelter, and in less than a week, a stronger Rose returned to Harold. "He's a good man if he don't beat me," was her explanation. We never heard another word.

CLOSING THE BOOK

The school year ended. The team found no reason for Anna to remain in preschool, so she was registered for kindergarten with high expectations for success. Her family took full responsibility for watching over her eyes and glasses. Another surgery would be scheduled in a year. Carrie would continue to monitor her hearing and conduct speech-language therapy. Anna had grown to a new level of assertiveness and self-confidence without losing her sweet and gentle nature.

And so, Rose's youngest child, Anna, left my classroom this year. As usual, we had an awards ceremony and ice cream party—a rather teary affair of hugs, certificates, and good-byes. We finished our awards, and I invited the families to move over to the tables for our ice cream sundae party.

"Not yet," announced the usually quiet Rose. She and Anna left the group to retrieve some mysterious gift. Rose had told me 3 weeks earlier that she already bought me a gift but couldn't decide what to buy for Jody. Jody graciously received a potted geranium, and I received a rose. The roots were bound in a plastic covering with a picture predicting a magnificent yellow bloom. I hugged Rose, gave her a kiss, and looked at her closely. I remember Rose 7 years ago, sweating in her chair, and also remember her smiling face as she presented me with my rose. Her sincere and open enjoyment of that moment filled my classroom like the fragrance of a rose in full bloom fills the air.

DISCUSSION QUESTIONS

1. Was there anything this early interventionist could have done differently to make the early home visits with Rose and her family more comfortable for all involved?

2. What were the strategies used by this interventionist and other program staff that contributed to Rose's "blooming"?

3. To what degree do you think Rose learned new skills and knowledge from her children's and her own participation in the preschool program? In other words, which of Rose's newly displayed competencies were a function of new learning and which were a result of providing opportunities for the performance of existing abilities?

4. Assume for a moment that you were Anna's preschool teacher (i.e., the early interventionist featured in this case study). Write a letter of introduction about Rose that you will forward to Anna's new kindergarten teacher. In this letter, be sure to describe Rose's strengths as they relate to facilitating Anna's development.

5. The early interventionist's positive perceptions of Rose and her children were not always shared by other professionals; nor were her ideas about strategies for working with Rose. How were such situations handled by the early interventionist? Would you have done anything differently?

6. Was there anything this early interventionist could have done to circumvent some of the difficulties that arose between Rose and Ronald's teacher when he entered public school?

7. The multiple and changing needs of Rose's family resulted in the involvement of a number of agencies and professionals. Would it have been desirable to have more communication and coordination among those involved with the family? If not, why? If so, who should have been involved? How would this coordination have been ideally organized? Would it have needed to change over time?

8. Anna is now entering kindergarten and the preschool will no longer have ongoing involvement in the family's life. How do you think this family will fare over the next 2–5 years? What would you hope the school system or other community agencies could provide to increase the probability that Rose and her family will continue to "bloom"?

The Eye
of the Beholder

Sandra Petersen
and Hal C. Lewis

*Jessica's disabilities were the result of her encounter with cy-
tomegalovirus while still in her mother's womb. Now, almost
3 years old, she still was fed through a gastrostomy tube and
required a ventilator to breathe. Looking beyond the obvious
challenges she faced, Jessica was a curious and delightful toddler. A desire to provide their daughter with an opportunity
to be with other children led Jessica's parents, Sharon and
Douglas, to enroll her in an inclusive model preschool at the
university. Jessica, however, had far more severe disabilities
than the other children who attended the model classroom.
This case describes the difficulties encountered in attempting
to integrate Jessica into the daily activities of the program and
the program director's efforts to help the child care staff overcome their anxiety and reluctance. This case also touches on
the more general issue of forging alliances between child care
staff and professional support staff.*

"Those eyes! Your eyes are beautiful, Jessica!" said Maria, the special educator, as she knelt beside the little girl's chair. Jessica's eyes
were indeed beautiful—dark brown, framed by long black lashes,
naturally large and then magnified by thick glasses. Jessica was sitting in an armchair that seemed cavernous for her small frame, with
toys arrayed in front of her. Although she tried to conceal her interest, Jessica was intrigued by her two visitors. The ventilator that

assisted her breathing made a rhythmic background noise in the living room of the quiet apartment.

"We've talked so often on the telephone that I feel as though I know you," said Anne, the nursing coordinator, as she extended her hand to Jessica's mother, Sharon. Sharon introduced both women to her husband, Douglas.

Jessica sat very still, listening to her parents talk. Occasionally, she raised a small toy with her thin arms, moved it to where she could focus on it briefly, and then threw it on the floor.

"We'd like to tell you about our child care center and answer any questions you might have tonight, but we'd also like to learn about Jessica," said Maria. She waited a moment and then added, "Where would you like to start?"

Sharon settled on the floor next to Jessica's chair, absent-mindedly picking up the toys and returning them to Jessica, who immediately threw them down again. "Well, she's almost 3 years old," began Sharon, "but she doesn't crawl. She won't eat anything by mouth. In fact, she got an ulcer when one therapist had us withhold her gastrostomy feedings to get her to eat. I hated that. She signs a little, but mostly uses signs she's made up. She's been in the hospital—a lot." Sharon sighed heavily.

Jessica gestured to her parents as she slumped down into the big chair; it was hard to keep herself upright, much as she tried. Her father came over and helped her to the floor. She lifted her hands to about cheek-level and opened and closed her fingers. "You want your puppets?" asked Douglas.

"She loves playing with her dad," Sharon said.

Maria and Anne joined the family on the floor as Jessica drew them into the play by offering them a toy and then accepting its return. "She's really a charmer," Anne beamed at her.

Sharon gave a sad smile and responded, "We didn't know what she'd be like at first. They told us she'd been exposed to a virus in the womb—cytomegalovirus, or CMV. I must have picked it up at work. She was so sick when she was born. She couldn't breathe and couldn't eat. She was in the hospital for months. She still gets pretty sick from colds and viruses in winter, but I know she wants to be with other children. When she can be off the ventilator for a little while, we take her to the park. She gets so excited watching the kids!"

"We certainly have lots of kids for Jessica to play with," said Anne. "Maybe this is a good time to tell you about our program."

The teacher and the nurse told Jessica's parents about their child care center at the university. "This is a new program we're really excited about," began Maria. "Our first goal is to provide quality child care that is accessible to everyone. Our next goal is to teach other child care providers to work with the infants and toddlers who have complex medical needs—children like Jessica. We believe that being attached to machines doesn't take away a child's needs to play and explore and to enjoy other children."

"And it sure doesn't take away a family's need for child care arrangements that they're comfortable with," added Anne. "By the way, we're open every day from 7 A.M. to 6 P.M."

"But you don't actually mix in children like Jessica, do you? Or do all of the children have disabilities?" asked Douglas.

Maria explained, "Most of our kids are typical children. Some have special needs, although not quite like Jessica's. One child has lots of delays, but no diagnosis. One little boy has Down syndrome. Another has a genetic problem that has kept his weight very low, and his low energy makes it hard for him to keep up developmentally. We have come to think of children as being on a wide continuum of abilities, with every one of them somewhere on that continuum. Take Jessica, for example. She's really engaging. She wouldn't let us sit on the sofa and talk to you, ignoring her. She's pretty strong in connecting with people and is creative in communicating. But her muscles aren't very strong, and her development there isn't as good. Each child needs something different from us, but they all need nurturing caregivers, interesting things to explore, and the chance to be with other kids their age."

SECOND THOUGHTS

Maria encouraged Jessica's parents to try the child care center, but did not voice her concerns about the program. The center had opened as part of a training program for child care providers to learn about including children with special needs. In order to establish a replicable personnel preparation program, the project team had chosen to hire care providers who met basic state requirements, who could be representative of the staff employed at any community-based center. As a group, those hired had some education in child development and many years of experience working in child care. They had little prior learning or experience, however, in the special needs of children with disabilities.

During the first several months, efforts had been focused on establishing consistent, developmentally appropriate child care for all children. Maintaining the quality of that care while gradually introducing children with special needs was more stressful than

Maria had anticipated. The first children with special needs to enroll had relatively mild conditions compared to Jessica's. Although the staff were eager to serve children with disabilities, there were difficulties in putting that eagerness into skilled practice. The children often gave confusing cues, and the staff tended to keep children with special needs separate "to protect them" from the other toddlers. Staff members were ambivalent about applying the extra training they were being offered in typical and atypical child development. Sometimes they hinted that the training sessions were "too academic" and not about the "real world" of child care. Most frustrating to Maria and the project team was the staff's hesitance to use the team's consultation suggestions for blending specialized techniques into daily routines.

Maria discussed these concerns with Anne during the drive home. She wondered aloud whether the staff were prepared to fully include a child with needs as complex as Jessica's. Anne shared her unease and raised another concern of her own. "We need to find out if Jessica is still shedding the virus and whether that poses a health threat to the other children, their parents, or our care providers," she said.

Anne began a thorough study of CMV the next day. She found that all of the published health guidelines concurred—there is no reason to exclude a child with CMV. The literature indicated that staff must be trained in correct handwashing and other infection control procedures and must use them scrupulously. Anywhere from 40% to 75% of the children attending any child care center carry this virus. Jessica posed no more of a threat than these children. Anne and Maria were relieved that Jessica could be safely enrolled.

Resolving this issue had taken time and Jessica's mother, her interest piqued, was becoming impatient. "Are you going to take my daughter or not?" she pressed during a telephone call. "We certainly want her," Maria reassured Sharon. "Please come and visit our program and let's decide how best to get started."

Sharon came to see the child care center. The rooms were bright and cheerful. The children were busy playing, and it was not readily apparent which children had special needs.

In Maria's office, they had an enrollment interview. The toddler room's head teacher, Penny, was present to answer questions about her classroom. As the meeting proceeded, Sharon became more enthusiastic.

"This is really exciting—the idea of Jessica going to school here. All she ever does is go to Gramma's house or the hospital. Sometimes she can be off the ventilator for a little while and we can take her to the park. She loves to watch the kids. She has a sign for 'kids.' " Sharon eagerly showed them the sign and then her smile suddenly faded. After a brief pause she continued, "It's so different with a child like her. I'm always taking her someplace medical— getting fitted for braces or seeing another specialist. But for me, going to the therapist is not like other mothers who take their little girls to ballet lessons."

"No, it's not," Maria agreed.

The head teacher was more positive, "This will be different. She'll be here just like all of the other children. You'll be surprised."

ON THE OUTSIDE LOOKING IN

Penny's optimism reflected how she and the other care providers believed they had included children with disabling conditions. However, the project's inclusion efforts had met with only partial success so far. Maria had attempted to be the conduit for information between the care providers and the professional support team, but the messages coming both ways often seemed to get lost. For example, after consulting with the project's physical therapist, Maria presented some positioning ideas to help a child with Down syndrome increase her muscle tone, but staff often seemed too busy or too forgetful to implement these suggestions. The speech-language therapist had suggested that a "sign of the week" be posted to encourage the use of an alternative communication system, but again the care providers seemed unable to incorporate it. Furthermore, they did not document the carefully measured feedings or provide the quiet, one-to-one interactions that Maria, after consultation with the project nurse, felt were so important for a toddler with failure-to-thrive. The project team was repeatedly surprised by the care providers' skepticism toward therapeutic interventions.

Despite the inconsistent delivery of special services, Maria saw that Penny and the other care providers loved all of the children. They hugged them and talked to them, and the children with special needs were treated no differently in this respect. The warmth and good intentions of the care providers combined with the chance to be with peers whose activities were so fascinating, was irreplaceable. Maria continued to counsel the staff about the benefits of therapeutic interventions, but for now, their simple eagerness to include children with special needs and their basic caring attitude were of fundamental importance. Maria still worried about whether Jessica's complex needs would be too taxing for the program, but she and the transdisciplinary team were increasingly impressed by the healthy effects of the staff's positive, caring attitude. As head teacher, Penny confidently reassured both Maria and Sharon that Jessica would thrive because, "She just needs to be with the other kids."

Jessica started attending the child care center. The care providers, who had taken other disabling conditions in stride, found this child frightening. Jessica didn't help matters out when she pulled apart the ventilator tubing, setting off the alarm. This met with their immediate and undivided attention. Jessica couldn't make any sounds and for days would only sign "naughty nurse." She seemed fragile and thin and not nearly strong enough to play with toys or participate in activities. There was worry that they might inadvertently harm her, so the care providers subtly drew a circle around themselves and the other children, leaving Jessica on the outside. If Jessica was ready for a tube feeding, the other children's lunches were delayed and they were kept outside until Jessica was finished. Jessica's cot was set up in an alcove, away from the other children, so that, "she could rest undisturbed." She was rarely touched by the other children or interacted with playfully.

"This is not inclusion!" Anne complained to Maria. "Jessica isn't getting anything out of this that she wouldn't have gotten at home. In fact, this is worse because she's being made to feel different here."

"I know," agreed Maria. "She's been here for 3 weeks, and I've been trying to let everyone get comfortable. I'm meeting with Penny and the rest of the staff today. I believe we can work it out."

At the meeting that afternoon, the care providers assured Maria that they loved having Jessica in their room, saying, "She's no bother at all."

"Maybe that's what I'm having trouble with," said Maria. "Perhaps you should be seeing her needs as problems to solve. Let me explain. You know that we wanted to bring Jessica into our child care center because of all the good things she can learn here. What she really needs to learn is that she is just like other children in many ways. She'll only learn that if we let her really be with the other children."

Maria went on, "For example, I've noticed that you never let the children eat at the same time that Jessica is being fed. But you know that all of the children enjoy the social aspects of sharing a meal."

They thought about that. "I guess that's true," said one care provider, "I don't think we meant to keep her away, though."

A CHANGE OF VIEW

The care providers were surprised and sobered as they realized the many ways in which they were sabotaging their own efforts toward inclusion with Jessica. First, they began to understand how frightened they were of her alarms and machinery. Over several weeks of talking and consulting with the professional team, they began to believe that she would not "break" as they helped her settle into a well-supported position. Jessica even surprised Penny by signing "eat" to her one day as she began to receive her tube feeding seated at the low table, next to other toddlers eating their lunches.

Jessica was interested in the changes starting to take place, but she was still not very responsive. The more she was included, the more closely she watched the care providers and the other children, but she made few attempts to actively join in the activities. Meanwhile, those huge brown eyes drank in everything.

The impact on Jessica was revealed at home first. Sharon would bring her to the center each morning bubbling with news. "She signed to us last night to sing your songs, 'Twinkle, Twinkle, Little Star' and 'The Itsy, Bitsy Spider.' We sang them over and over. It was great!" One day she reported, "Jessica pulled herself up to stand last night! I couldn't believe it!" Another morning she announced, "We went to Gramma's on Sunday, and Jess signed 'No, I want school!' "

As the care providers realized how much their program meant to Jessica, they began to look for more ways to include her in all of the activities. They requested advice from the transdisciplinary team. Maria worked with each professional and conveyed their information back to the care providers. Penny learned to support Jessica's back during music time so she could sit up and be more alert. Jessica fought her at first, but then stopped struggling and happily joined in the fingerplays. The care providers requested a class in sign language from the speech-language therapist and began to sign with Jessica. When Jessica showed interest in an activity, they helped her to do the activity herself. Jessica began to think of herself as one of the children. When the children put on their jackets, Jessica insistently signed "outside" to the care providers. Jessica brought her own puppets from home to use at circle time. Jessica was able to put stickers on paper to make pictures. To build on this skill, Penny bought clear contact paper for the base of a leaf collage. Jessica was delighted. After watching her friends for a while, she even worked on gluing papers together. Despite receiving her food through a gastrostomy tube, Jessica handled crackers and cups of juice at snacktime—just like her peers. A couple of times she even brought food to her mouth, which was a big step forward. She began to play with toys and puzzles near the other children, and she tried to take toys away from them and fought to protect her own.

Late one afternoon, Maria and Anne sat in the staff office and marvelled at Jessica's growth as well as that of Penny and the other care providers. They had learned to combine good intentions with the ability to use transdisciplinary consultation. As they returned to the classroom to see Jessica playing intently with the others, Maria commented, "Those beautiful eyes! Boy, do they shine!"

DISCUSSION QUESTIONS

1. Although we only have glimpses of the actual conversations between parents and professionals in this case, how well were these handled by the project staff? Did they exemplify the principles of family-centered care? Would you have taken a different approach in any of the conversations?

2. This program's approach to enrolling new children was to conduct an initial home visit followed by the family making a visit to the classroom. How important were each of these steps and could they have been conducted in a different order? Which staff members should be involved in the various stages of the enrollment process?

3. How important do you think the daily communication with the mother was when she brought Jessica into the classroom each morning? If the center provided transportation, how might the staff maintain ongoing communication with Jessica's parents?

4. Jessica's story does not describe efforts to prepare the other children and their parents for the enrollment of a child who has complex medical needs and is dependent upon mechanical life support. Is this important? If so, how would you go about this?

5. Anne and Maria determined that there was no reason to exclude a child with CMV from their classroom program. Even so, who has the right to know if Jessica is shedding the CMV virus? Would the situation be changed if Jessica were HIV-positive, had AIDS, or was infected with herpesvirus?

6. How effectively do you think Maria and Anne handled the difficulties they encountered in getting the care providers to incorporate therapeutic interventions into the daily routines and to fully include the children with disabilities?

7. This case describes a program that used a transdisciplinary consultation model for developing and implementing therapeutic interventions. What other methods or models might be used? What would the advantages and disadvantages of each be?

8. Which elements of early intervention must be in place to make a child care center an acceptable placement for a child with disabilities? What level of technical support and supervision is necessary?

9. What policy, funding, legal, or ethical issues are raised in considering typical child care centers as intervention sites for children with disabilities?

Shaping
Ben's Future

Karen E. Diamond
and Phyllis Spiegel-McGill _____

It is seldom easy to go against established practices. Sam and Amy learned this firsthand when they decided that they wanted their son, Ben, enrolled in a regular kindergarten class in their local elementary school. In their community, children with disabilities routinely went to a separate school designed to meet the special needs of these students. This was not what Sam and Amy wanted, and they were willing to fight the system on behalf of their son. The staff of the local elementary school are up in arms at the prospect of Ben's placement there and not satisfied that Ben's best interests have been considered. This case focuses on the decisions and actions of Ben's current preschool teacher, Kate, as well as those of Jackie, the director of the preschool, in handling the tense situation. They, too, are uncertain of what is best for Ben and must come to terms with their torn allegiance to the parents and the educational system of which they are a part.

Sam and Amy arrived at the preschool promptly for their morning meeting to talk with Kate about school programs for their son, Ben. The couple sat side by side in the chairs opposite Kate. Although Amy was ordinarily a little shy in formal meetings, she appeared unusually nervous this time. Sam looked quite serious, and he was the first to speak.

"We've been thinking hard about kindergarten for Ben next year," Sam began. "We know he has disabilities, and we see all the things he can't do. He can't walk, he doesn't have much language, and he still wears diapers. But we also see how much he's gotten out of being in a class with regular 4-year-olds this year. Ben knows how to get somebody's attention to play, how to take turns at snack-time, and how to stick up for himself when somebody's giving him a hard time." Sam paused and turned toward Amy, who nodded in agreement. Then he turned to face Kate again.

"He sure seems to understand what's going on when the other kids are talking to him. I wish he'd do that well when I ask him a question," Kate added with a laugh.

Kate was Ben's teacher and had known him and his parents since Ben was 4 months old. Ben was born almost 3 months prematurely and had spent the first 3 months of his life in the hospital. He had been enrolled in early intervention programs from the time he was well enough to go home. Now 4½ years old, Ben has moderate to severe cerebral palsy and takes several medications to control seizures. Although the physical therapists and his parents worked to teach Ben to walk, it was so difficult for him that he now uses a wheelchair. This seems to suit Ben. He likes being wheeled around by his teachers and peers rather than working so hard to walk. Later, he might get a chair with a motor that he can steer—when he can do it safely. Ben currently attends a preschool program that integrates children with disabilities with typical children. This past year, Ben has been trying to improve his communication with the other children in his preschool class. He loves being with the other children and really wants to play with them, but it is hard work. He cannot get around the classroom the way they can; they talk too fast and their games are very confusing for him. In fact, it is much easier for Ben to play with 2-year-olds, but he doesn't think it is nearly as much fun.

"We've been coming to the parent meetings here at Ben's preschool for a while," said Amy in a soft voice, "and we've listened to lots of people talk about what's happened when their children entered kindergarten." She glanced quickly at Sam, and he returned a nod of support. "We know that there are some kids with disabilities like Ben's who have been integrated into regular school programs," she continued, "but not in our district. And we've listened to parents who are really happy with their children's placements in special classes. You never know how things are going to work out, but Ben's done so well here this year and he gets so much out of being with typical kids his own age that we think we should see if he can go to a regular kindergarten next year. We don't know what it will be like. We're sure it won't be easy, but we want to try."

"I agree that a regular kindergarten class is something to think about for him," said Kate, "but you know the therapists he sees here usually do therapy in the classroom. That would probably be a lot harder to arrange in kindergarten. He gets occupational and physical therapy four times a week and speech-language therapy every day. It's hard to know how the school staff at a regular kindergarten will feel about having him there. Around here, most of the children with disabilities like Ben's are in self-contained classes at the Cooperative. The Co-op schools only serve children with identified disabilities, so they have all the resources that children like Ben need right at the school. The folks at Crestland Elementary probably won't know what to think if you bring up the idea of having him in a regular kindergarten."

"I guess you're right," said Amy, "but we'll never know what would have happened unless we try. It's what we think would be best for him."

"He's going to have to learn to cope in this world when he gets older," added Sam, "and other kids are going to have to figure out how to get along with him. It seems to us that school is the place to start."

A SUPPORTIVE VOICE

"You know, the school district's psychologist, Bill Frank, is going to be really surprised when he hears that Ben's parents want him to go to kindergarten next year," said Kate. "He just finished his evaluation of Ben, and he's already talking about enrolling Ben in a class at the Co-op Center. He won't know what to think when he hears that Sam and Amy want to enroll Ben at Crestland." Kate was meeting with Jackie, the director of the preschool, to decide what to do about her conversation with Ben's parents that morning.

"On the one hand, I agree with what Ben's folks have said about him," continued Kate. "Ben does enjoy being with his peers, and he has made a lot of progress this year. He's very social, and I do think that some of his progress has been from watching and playing with nondisabled children his own age. He certainly gets a lot of reinforcement for using his communication skills with them. On the other hand, Ben has so many medical and therapy needs that it's hard enough for us to coordinate all of them—and we've had lots of practice. It'll be really hard in a regular kindergarten with

25 other kids, even if he could get an aide for part of the day. And we're trying to maintain a good relationship with Bill Frank and the other folks at Crestland Elementary . . . Well, I just don't know what we should do. I'm not at all sure that they're ready to think about having a kid like Ben in a regular class."

"I don't know what the answer is," replied Jackie, "but I do know that we've always tried to give parents enough support and information to come up with a plan that would meet their family's needs and their child's, too. Ben's folks have always been support-ive of him, and it couldn't have been easy for them. Did you know that their older son, Jake, is in first grade at Crestland? They must know something about what they're getting themselves into."

"At least the building's fairly new, and all of the classrooms are on one floor," added Kate. "Amy said she was going to return Bill Frank's call this afternoon. He wants to review the results of his evaluation with her and Sam and start thinking about a place-ment for next year. Boy, he's going to be surprised when he hears about kindergarten!"

"Did you tell Amy that we'll be happy to be there when she and Sam meet with the folks from Crestland?" asked Jackie. "You know, if this is what they really want, we should see if we can't help figure out a way to make it work."

"I'm so glad to hear you say that!" replied Kate.

MEETING OBSTACLES

"Jackie, what is going on here? I thought we had come up with a reasonable plan for Ben, but his parents aren't being realistic!" ex-claimed Bill Frank over the telephone. He had obviously heard the news. "I've talked with the staff here at Crestland," he continued, "and we all agree that we might be able to compromise and try having Ben in our self-contained class here. He could be main-streamed with the kindergarteners twice a week for art. But his folks want him in kindergarten full-time!"

"Yes," said Jackie, "I just heard about that myself, and I thought. . . ."

"I don't know how we could possibly have him in a kindergar-ten class," interrupted Bill. "We have nowhere near the number of staff we'll need and the teachers will be up in arms! It's hard enough finding physical therapists and occupational therapists for kids in classes at the Co-op Center. I just don't see how we could come close to providing the therapy he'll need if he goes to school here. Honestly, I can't imagine what his parents think Ben's going to learn in a regular kindergarten. The kids in those classes are working on letter sounds and learning to read. Let's be realistic. Ben can only say about 15 words. Oh, I know his parents say they don't care if he learns the alphabet, that their goals for him are to learn the routines, be as independent as possible, and get along with the other kids. But that's not what school is for. He needs to start learning the pre-academics he'll need to cope in the world, and that's what they work on in the Co-op classes. He'll learn something there! You've got to talk with them, Jackie. They won't listen to me!" Bill finally stopped his tirade and waited for a reply.

Jackie knew what Bill wanted her to say, but she also considered her allegiance to the family. She took a deep breath and began, "Bill, I'm not sure how this would work. I know the kids in the Co-op classes learn a lot. The problem is, nobody around here has ever tried integrating a child like Ben into kindergarten. People at other places say that it can work well to have kids with disabilities, like Ben, in regular classes if you provide the right kinds of support for the classroom teachers."

"Yeah, but that's a big 'if,' " said Bill. "Our budget's at the limit right now, and other parents won't like the idea of Ben getting all of those services, even if it doesn't cost us any more than sending him to Co-op. You know, when kids are at the Cooperative, nobody sees the number of teachers or therapists providing services to the children. But when there's a kid like Ben at Crestland, everybody will see what's happening. There are lots of folks who might not like the fact that we're spending all this money on him while we're cutting a gym teacher!"

"I know it's a problem," agreed Jackie, "but it's one that we're all going to have to face sooner or later with a lot of kids. You know that Amy and Sam have been thinking about Ben attending a regular kindergarten class for a long time. They know he's not an easy kid. If we don't deal with this issue now, it'll keep coming up. What do you think, Bill? Can we get together with Ben's parents and Kate, his teacher, and at least talk about this?"

There was an uncomfortable silence followed by a long sigh on Bill's end of the line. "All right," said Bill, "I suppose we can talk about it. Let me know when you can set up something. I'd like to get this straightened out and come to some sort of agreement before it's time for his committee on special education meeting and annual review. There's nothing worse than involving a whole school committee in a conflict over a placement for a kid. Why don't we meet at the preschool?"

"Thanks, Bill. I'll arrange something right away."

"I'm sure they'll think I'm awful because I think Ben needs a special education class," Bill added. "It's just that I know a regular kindergarten class is not what would be best for Ben. If they could only be made to understand. . . ."

MEETING THE OPPOSITION

"You know what's going to happen, don't you? Amy and Sam are really convinced that kindergarten is the best place for Ben," said Kate. She and Jackie were discussing their roles in the upcoming meeting with Ben's parents and the Crestland staff. "They're even willing to take care of some of his PT and OT privately so that Ben will have time to be with the other kindergarteners."

"That might help," replied Jackie. "Did you know that Emily Pike, Crestland's special services coordinator, is coming to this meeting with Bill? I'm sure they're going to want him in a Co-op class."

"That's for sure," agreed Kate. "Amy and Sam have said that they'll go to a fair hearing before they'll send Ben to a Co-op class for kindergarten. Nobody wants that! Although they don't have many illusions about Ben, they've told me that they're not going to budge from their request for a regular kindergarten placement. They figure that if they don't start with kindergarten, they'll never have a chance of having him in classes with regular kids. Things are changing— but they're probably right."

"We need to do two things now," said Jackie. "We need to support Amy and Sam for starters, and then see if we can't come up with some arrangement that everyone could live with and that would be good for Ben."

The next week the group met to discuss ways to provide an appropriate kindergarten experience for Ben. Included in the meeting were Amy and Sam, Bill Frank and Emily Pike from Crestland, and Kate and Jackie from Ben's preschool. The first part of the meeting focused on the results of Ben's recent evaluations and a discussion of long-term goals and program needs. There was little disagreement about Ben's developmental skills. In fact, everyone agreed about the majority of goals for Ben, most of which focused on promoting independence, mobility, and his ability to communicate with others.

It was when the focus of the meeting changed to a discussion of Ben's placement that the participants began to feel uncomfortable. Ben's parents felt strongly that kindergarten should be Ben's primary placement while Bill and Emily still thought a Co-op class would be best. It was the impasse that Jackie and Kate had predicted and discussed earlier. Bill started stacking his papers and placing them in front of him as mute testimony to his professional skills and his knowledge of Ben. Amy sat up straighter and reached for Sam's hand.

"Mr. Frank, we know that you think it won't work to have Ben in kindergarten at Crestland, but we think it can," said Amy. "We know he's not going to read or write like the other kids, but he learns a lot from them about social skills and getting along, and that's what he's going to need to know to be successful when he's older. Besides, we want him to go to his neighborhood school with his brother and his friends."

"That's right," added Sam, "and those are our goals for our son."

"I know they are," said Bill. "I wish I could say that we can meet his needs at Crestland, but I just don't see how."

"Bill's right, you know," said Emily, the special services coordinator. "We've been searching for an OT for the last 18 months and haven't been able to find anyone! Even if we could find a kindergarten teacher who'd be willing to have Ben in his or her class, there's no way we'd be able to provide the kinds of therapy services he's getting this year."

"Amy, you've had a private OT for Ben, haven't you?" asked Kate.

"That's right," answered Amy. "It was a real problem for us when there were school vacations. Ben wasn't getting therapy, and we could see his progress stop. He's been seeing a private OT once a week for the past year, and we were planning to continue using our OT, Jenny, next year. Of course we'd like him to get as much OT at school as he's gotten this year, but, if that's impossible, attending kindergarten is more important to us. I am sure we can increase his private therapy if we need to. And I'm sure Jenny would be happy to consult with his classroom teacher—she's done that before."

"That might solve one problem, but I still don't see how this could work for Ben or for us," said Bill. "Even if therapy's not an issue, Ben needs the one-to-one, small groups, and pre-academic skills that he would get in a special education Co-op class. He can work on social skills at the playground after school. The only way to give him the academic skills he needs is in a small class with other kids who need the same kind of help."

"We know he could learn in a special education class. We also know he could learn by being in a kindergarten class with his peers," said Sam.

"We've spent hundreds of hours thinking about what we want for Ben—what we need to provide him so he can meet his potential," added Amy. "That includes regular kindergarten, and that's where we want to start. We're not afraid to pursue this to a fair hearing. This is our son's life we're talking about!"

"There might be another way to meet all of Ben's needs at Crestland," suggested Jackie. "You have a full-day kindergarten at Crestland. Maybe there's a way to have Ben in the kindergarten class all morning and then have therapy in the afternoon."

"I'm not sure that would work with the therapists," said Emily, "and I don't know how things would work in the lunchroom. But maybe it's a place to start."

"It's really important to us that Ben be with the kids in the kindergarten class," said Sam. "We know that the regular kindergarten curriculum probably wouldn't be appropriate for him most of the time. But some of his IEP goals might fit in well with the kindergarten activities."

"Let me go back and talk with the kindergarten teachers," said Emily. "We need to be sure that something like this would work for them. I think I know one teacher who might enjoy having Ben in her class, but she would have to agree to it. You know, it's in the teachers' contracts that they don't have to take children with special needs if they don't want to."

"It sounds as though we'll still need to talk about how he'll be getting therapy," said Jackie.

"And about an aide and resource teacher for him if he does go into the kindergarten," added Emily. "But I think we have a beginning here. Let's get together again in 2 weeks and see where we are."

As it turned out, three of the four kindergarten teachers refused to have Ben in their classes. One teacher agreed reluctantly and with reservations to "give it a try," partly because she'd known Ben's parents through their church since before Ben was born. During the summer, Kate consulted with her, providing information about his skills and goals, as well as techniques that had been found to be successful in encouraging social interaction in the preschool class. Ben's kindergarten teacher visited the preschool class on several occasions to observe Ben and learn about the adaptations that had been particularly successful for him. Emily Pike arranged for a classroom aide to be in the kindergarten class for 2 hours each day.

She also arranged for a special education teacher to be available 7 hours each week. Sometimes the special education teacher would work directly with Ben, and sometimes she would act as a consultant to the teacher and aide. Ben's schedule would also include participation in physical therapy, occupational therapy, and speech-language therapy every afternoon.

RESERVING JUDGMENT

Bill Frank remained unconvinced that kindergarten was an appropriate placement for Ben, and he told Jackie this in a telephone conversation several weeks after school started.

"Bill," said Jackie, "Ben's parents are so pleased that he's in a kindergarten class at Crestland. They say that Ben loves to go to school, and he really enjoys being with the other children. They feel that he's really improving his social skills. Amy even invited two of the boys in his class to come over on the weekend. She says that worked out really well."

"I know," said Bill. "They've told me that too, but I think they're dreaming. Learning social skills is not what going to school is for. Ben should have more time to work individually on language skills and basic concepts. What we're doing is just plain wrong for him, but it was the only way to avoid a lot of trouble with his parents. Maybe they'll see things differently when he gets a little older and the other kids make fun of him. This just doesn't feel right."

"I'm sorry you feel that way," replied Jackie. "But when you get to the bottom line, I think that our job is to give parents a lot of information about the alternatives and then let them make the decision. There's a lot of evidence that this kind of approach can work."

"I know. Ben's kindergarten teacher says she's even starting to enjoy having Ben in the classroom," acknowledged Bill. "I guess he and his wheelchair have become the center of attention for a lot of the other kids. Well . . . we're giving it our best shot."

"We'll just have to see how it works," said Jackie. "You and Ben's folks are on the same side now. That means a lot. You know they'll do all that they can to help."

SUMMARY OF BEN'S DEVELOPMENTAL STATUS

The following is a summary of Ben's developmental status at the time he left his preschool program and entered kindergarten. This information was excerpted from his files and from the Learning Accomplishment Profile, which was completed before his discharge from preschool.

Health History

Ben has a history of brain trauma, which was followed by a ventriculo-peritoneal (V-P) shunt placement when he was an infant. He has developed seizures over the last 6 months and is currently treated with medication. He is hypotonic and does not walk independently, although he does cruise along furniture and walk with a wheeled walker. For the most part, Ben uses a wheelchair.

Cognitive Skills

Ben's cognitive skills fall at approximately the 36-month level. He can match "like" objects, count by rote to 15, build a block tower in imitation, and sort by color. He does not, however, name colors. He has also not developed size and shape concepts. Ben has a short attention span and needs adult assistance in maintaining concentration on tasks.

Fine Motor Skills

Ben's fine motor skills are close to the 36-month level. He attempts all activities and uses art materials with assistance. He plays with small toys appropriately, although his handling is somewhat awkward. Ben particularly enjoys Play-Doh and kitchen play. He often requires adult assistance to complete tasks and avoid frustration.

Adaptive Skills

Ben needs assistance in all adaptive areas. He is cooperative with toilet training skills, but there has been little success. Adults monitor chewing during snacktime and lunch because Ben needs reminders to chew slowly. Ben is showing an interest in dressing himself, but still needs a lot of help. At school, he makes an effort to remove his coat, requiring some assistance from an adult. Overall, Ben's adaptive skills are within the range of 20–30 months.

Social Skills

Ben approaches both peers and adults and is eager to talk and play with them. Although his skills in interacting with peers are adequate, having an adult present to facilitate more meaningful exchanges is often beneficial.

(continued)

Summary of Ben's Developmental Status (*continued*)

Speech-Language Skills

Ben's articulation of single words is age-appropriate. He speaks in simple sentences and makes his wants known through phrases and gestures. Expressive language is often characterized by "cocktail party" speech. At times, it is difficult for Ben to name familiar objects or to state their functions; however, this appears to vary with his neurological status (i.e., seizure activity). Ben can follow simple, one-step directions, responds to yes-no questions appropriately, and can answer some "what," "who," and "where" questions. His speech-language skills are scattered between 24 and 40 months.

DISCUSSION QUESTIONS

1. Do you think it was appropriate for Kate and Jackie to take such active roles in advocating for Ben's enrollment in a regular kindergarten?

2. Should Jackie and Kate have done more to present the school system's perspective on Ben's educational needs and placement to the parents?

3. Bill Frank presented a number of reasons for not including Ben. These reasons ranged from what was best for Ben to the reactions of other parents at Crestland Elementary School. What were his arguments against inclusion and were they valid?

4. Did Jackie and Kate do all they could to avoid conflict between the parents and the staff of the school system? Could Jackie and Kate have done more?

5. Jackie played an important role in this case. Do you think the outcome would have changed if she had not assumed the role of advocate for the family? That is, would the family have been equally successful if they only had the support of the preschool teacher, Kate?

6. According to Kate, the parents felt that if Ben weren't included in kindergarten they would "never have a chance of having him in classes with regular kids." Do you think this is a valid assumption?

7. In this situation, the kindergarten teacher could come to the preschool to observe Ben. What if she couldn't? How would you facilitate a smooth transition from preschool to kindergarten?

8. In your own state or local school district, would this family have been able to secure full inclusion for their son in a regular kindergarten setting?

9. In the school district described in this case, the teachers' contracts allow them to refuse to have a child with special needs in their classes. What is the policy in your state or local school

district? Do the teachers have any say in the placement of a child in their classes?

10. What is "education" for children with significant developmental disabilities? Is learning social skills an appropriate focus for an elementary curriculum for children with and without disabilities?

11. What is the role of early childhood programs in the transition of children with disabilities from preschool to public school programs? How can preschool and public school programs deal with diverse educational philosophies and still maintain working relationships?

12. Design a 4-hour workshop about inclusion for parents of preschool-age children with developmental disabilities. Be sure to include strategies for advocacy.

13. Visit and observe a regular kindergarten classroom for at least 1 hour. Suppose then that this was the classroom that Ben would attend. Make at least six specific suggestions that you would offer the teacher on how to meet Ben's needs within the routine operation of the class. (Note: The Summary of Ben's Developmental Status as well as the parents' statements about what they want for Ben may be used to identify Ben's needs.)

In Whose Best Interest?

Brandon F. Greene,
Roger C. Lubeck,
and K. Renee Norman

Carol and Steve would probably prefer not to have the weekly home visits they receive. Although they could refuse these services, they would stand a good chance of losing custody of their two young children, Crystal and Aaron. Both Carol and Steve have limited intellectual abilities. Their lack of basic child care skills, as well as the unsanitary and often unsafe home environment, concerns many professionals who have come into contact with the family. To add to these difficulties, Steve has recurrent outbursts of anger and has threatened several professionals in the community. This case describes one of many home visits to this family of four as well as the overall strategy that has been taken in helping the parents to learn basic parenting and homemaking skills. Despite the progress that Carol and Steve have made, questions still remain regarding their ability to provide a safe and nurturing environment for their young children.

T he cool of the fall morning was just beginning to change into the warmth of an Indian summer afternoon when Becky and Aldo found themselves once again at the front door of the Lowell's mobile home. Their knocks at the door were followed by quick, resonant footsteps along the length of the trailer. Then quiet. A few more knocks and, as always, it was Carol who opened the door. Although it was 11

A.M., it appeared that Steve and Carol had just awakened. Carol was still in her robe. Across the narrow, darkly paneled room they could see Steve, sitting in his customary slumped position on the tattered couch. Steve made no eye contact when Becky and Aldo greeted him and Carol. Carol returned their greeting with her usual timid hello, all the time watching Steve.

Stepping in from the crisp country air, Becky and Aldo showed no reaction to the stale, clammy smell of propane heat that carried a faint scent of garbage throughout the kitchen and living area. The subflooring beneath the chipped kitchen linoleum creaked as the two early interventionists stepped carefully, working their way between a nearly empty pizza box and small piles of clean diapers mixed with dirty laundry on the floor. Peering across the width of the dark trailer, Becky could see that Aaron was awake in his pumpkin seat beneath the rickety formica table that Becky and Aldo had helped the Lowells transport from the thrift shop.

PROGRESS AND PROBLEMS

"How's Aaron?" Becky asked, as she lifted the pumpkin seat from under the table and placed it on the couch beside Steve. "I think he's grown."

"He has been growin'," said Carol with a look of satisfaction and relief. "Doctor said he weighs 8 pounds and 2½ ounces now."

"Eight pounds, 2½ ounces! That's great. He's really getting up there," Aldo chimed in to support Carol's feeling of accomplishment.

From the couch, Steve, who still had not looked directly at Becky or Aldo grunted, "Uhmm."

Sensing that no further social amenities were called for, Becky got to work. "Well, we've got a lot to cover today. We're going to work on teaching you how to sterilize bottles and watch you feed Aaron. While I'm doing that, Aldo will check the baby's room to see if the electrical outlets have been covered and to see if the toilet, counter, and tub are clean. Just like we talked about doing last week, okay?" Carol gave an accepting nod. Steve was sullen.

"If those areas are taken care of," continued Becky, "and if you have a meal planned, then you will move up to an extra 15 minutes of unsupervised time with Crystal when she comes from the foster home for her visit today." Carol nodded again.

"If your visits increase by 15 minutes today, that will bring the total time to 3 hours that you spend alone with Crystal," Becky said to remind the couple that they were making progress at gradually regaining custody of Crystal. "Soon we will ask the child welfare department to let her stay overnight with you. Won't that be great?"

"Let me ask you somethin'," Steve said. "Can child welfare make us take Aaron to that Early Start place?" Early Start was a birth-to-3 program for children with developmental delays or children who are at risk for such delays. Crystal had been served by the program last year.

"Well, I . . . ," Becky stammered.

" 'Cause we got a letter from them, and I don't think that's right! How did those Early Start people get Aaron's name? We never said nothin' about him. The child welfare worker's name is on here. . . . Nancy. She probably said somethin' to them about Aaron and that ain't right! That goes against my constitutional law!"

"I don't know, but maybe . . ."

"I'll tell you somethin' else," Steve exploded. "I don't like them comin' over here without askin'! They're tryin' to take Aaron away, and I ain't gonna' stand for it! Cause I gotta' knife what's sharp and I'll gut 'em!"

This wasn't the first time Steve had shown his temper. More than once his gruff manner had intimidated personnel from several human services agencies. Some had refused to return to the family's home after such outbursts. Some also had pointed to Steve's temper as the primary reason for continuing Crystal's foster placement and for continuing to provide services in the home when such services were not always embraced by the parents themselves. Becky reflected on yesterday afternoon's case staffing when these issues had been foremost on the agenda.

A QUESTION OF CUSTODY

The child welfare department had called the staffing to review the Lowell case with each service provider. After this review, the department would begin to formulate a recommendation to the juvenile court about whether to continue Crystal's foster placement and whether the parents should be ordered to cooperate with services for Aaron.

Attending the staffing were persons from the public assistance office and the public health department, the foster parents, and the family's homemakers (i.e., paraprofessionals involved in providing assistance with transportation and other basic family needs). Becky and Aldo represented Project 12-Ways, an in-home intervention program serving a variety of families including families with histories of child abuse and neglect. In the course of serving these families, the staff often identified family members, both parents and children, as having disabilities.

The caseworker, Nancy, had started by reviewing the original reasons for becoming involved in the family's life. Crystal, at 3 years of age, had been taken into foster care following substantiated reports of physical abuse by her father, who was Carol's first husband, Bob. Carol herself had not abused Crystal and, in fact, she too had been beaten badly by Bob. Even so, the court ruled that Carol had failed to provide adequate protection for Crystal and that the conditions in the home were hazardous and unsanitary. As part of Crystal's plan to return home, Carol received weekly supervised visits with Crystal in her home. Staff members from Project 12-Ways supervised these visits. These visits never involved Bob, whom Carol divorced and who was sentenced to prison shortly thereafter on charges of check fraud.

From all reports, Carol had been cooperative and successful in learning appropriate parenting skills during visits with Crystal. Then Steve entered the picture and began to live with Carol. At the time they met, Steve was 25 and Carol was 31. Both were receiving public assistance as a result of their developmental disabilities. Steve had a reputation for making verbal outbursts and intimidating people with his size (i.e., 235 pounds) and angry demeanor. Although never physically violent against another adult, local law enforcement officials had been called by neighbors to quiet Steve during late night shouting matches at his sister's house. His temper surfaced occasionally in public and had made him less than welcome at the offices of several human services agencies.

For the team, Nancy reviewed how she had enlisted the public health department's outreach program when Carol became pregnant with Aaron. When he was born, Aaron weighed 5 pounds, 6 ounces. After Carol and Aaron were discharged from the hospital, a nurse from the health department began to make regular home visits to provide the family with infant formula and to weigh Aaron. At 3 weeks, Aaron weighed only 5 pounds, 9 ounces. He was protruding his tongue from his mouth, spitting up large amounts of formula after every feeding, and often startled whenever Steve spoke.

On one home visit, it appeared to the health nurse that Aaron was dehydrated. She urged Steve and Carol to have Aaron hospitalized, but they both feared that this would lead to their loss of custody. The nurse felt legally obliged to report the matter to the child welfare abuse hotline. Within hours the welfare department conducted an investigation and arranged for Aaron's hospitalization. After 2 days at the hospital, Aaron had gained 7 ounces and was discharged. Carol and Steve were ordered by the court to cooperate with the public health nurse in maintaining Aaron's feeding regimen. They had done so, and Aaron had grown steadily.

Nancy concluded her review of the case by saying, "The real question for me is whether Crystal can ever be returned to the home, particularly as long as Steve is there. He is so volatile. Last week he was removed from the WIC office for causing an uproar. It seems he accused the nurse of holding back on some of Carol's food stamps. Also, you all know that when he was going to the sheltered workshop, folks there said he'd killed his sister's dog with a rubber mallet. I just wonder how much longer it will be before we have a report that something serious has happened to Aaron—something more serious than this last episode."

The homemaker, Bess, quickly responded to Nancy's concluding remarks, "Well, all I know is I won't go back to that home alone. The last time I was there, Steve stood up, stuck his face in mine, and yelled, 'You got no right to be in my home tellin' me what to do with my kid. I don't want you back here no more!' I guess he forgot that the only way he can get to the store or to a doctor's appointment or wherever he needs to go is if we take him."

"I just don't take Steve too seriously," said the nurse. "He huffs and puffs but he's never really scared me. The main problem we have is that they take things very literally. We told them to give Aaron 5 ounces of formula every 4 hours. They do this without fail, even to the point of waking the baby up to feed him. But as far as we are concerned, it's better to be a little too fat than underfed. We don't see the need to continue going to the family's home every week. We'll just furnish them with a large supply of the formula so they'll have what they need for the next few months."

"What about Crystal?" asked Nancy. "How is she getting along in the foster home?"

Dianah, the foster mother, replied, "Well, sometimes she'll act like she's sick so she don't have to go visit at Carol's and Steve's. I just tell her, 'Look, you got to go. Your mother wants to see you. So don't be makin' like you're sick.' Usually she'll quit her actin' then. When she comes home, though, she sometimes will tell me that Steve yelled a lot. She really likes seein' her mama but don't like him too much. I tell her, 'They're married now and you have to try to get along,' but she can be a little manipulator. If she could figure out how to be with Mom without him being there, she would do it."

"Okay," accepted Nancy. "What is Project 12-Ways seeing?"

Becky began, "When we initially began serving the family, Carol was in the process of divorcing Bob. Steve was just moving in, and Crystal came to the home for supervised visits for an hour 1 day each week. The home was filthy at that time. Garbage was piled up in and outside of the house. The plumbing was clogged, the toilet backed up, and piles of dirty clothes and boxes were everywhere. Plus, the baby was due in a few months. We were not optimistic."

"We began by making a contract with the parents—literally a contract to gain longer visiting periods with Crystal and, ultimately, to regain custody of her. As you know, cases like this are tough. One or more family members have a disability and would truly benefit from services but, because of their involvement with the legal system due to child abuse or neglect, they're not necessarily all that enthusiastic about us, especially when we first start. Anyway, our approach has always been to put the cards on the table—to let the parents know that we are happy to provide services but that they can refuse these services. We want them to know, however, that unless some specific changes are made in the household, it is unlikely that the court will allow a child to go home. So, with Carol and Steve all this information was put in a contract."

"Each week we renew the contract. We negotiate some aspect of change that they can achieve within a week's time. For example, a week's objective might be to have the dishes in the sink clean, or the toilet unclogged, and so forth. If they can do that in time for Crystal's visit the following week, then we agree to add 10 or 15 minutes to the length of that visit. If they do not make the changes we agree upon, the visit remains the same length as the week before. More visiting time is added, some of it unsupervised time, as more changes are made and maintained. Right now, the family is spending nearly 3 hours with Crystal, and most of that time they are alone with her."

Becky passed around a graph that showed an ascending set of bar graphs representing the amount of time the family spent together during weekly visits for the last few months. Superimposed upon that were ascending plots with such labels as "Percent of Diapering Steps Performed," "Percent of Kitchen Areas Clean," and "Percent of Praise Statements to Children."

The group took a moment to study it all. Becky interpreted the technical details for them. Then Nancy asked, "So what's your plan for the future?"

"Well," responded Becky, "we'll try to continue to stretch out the amount of time the family spends together and to increase the changes the parents make to receive visiting time with Crystal. We would like to fade Crystal back into the home in this gradual manner."

Nancy furrowed her brow, "I guess the only problem I have is with the unexpected. You've taught the parents to handle specific situations the way that I train a dog to follow specific commands. I don't mean to sound like I'm putting you or them down. It's just that my concern is with what happens when a situation comes up that you simply haven't taught the family to handle. How can you be sure that Steve won't haul off and hurt someone when you're not there? Even if you could teach them to handle every possible situation now, won't you have to retrain the parents over and over for the new situations that come up when the children grow older? Is Project 12-Ways or any other agency prepared to serve this family for a lifetime? And, even if you were, would that be in the family's best interest if it always meant having some involvement with us or the court?"

CONTINUED UNCERTAINTY

Nancy's questions from the staffing echoed in Becky's head as she struggled for the right way to handle Steve's outburst. "I see you are upset," she began calmly. "If you want, we can talk about that more at the end of the session. Right now, we've got the bottles to take care of." Becky rose and walked toward the kitchen.

"Well, I just don't like the way they treat us!" continued Steve.

"Okay, Carol, do you want to do the bottles first or should Steve go first?" asked Becky.

From the corner of her eye Becky could see that Steve was looking away.

"I guess I'll start," said Carol.

In the back of the trailer, Aldo had begun to check the children's room for hazards that Steve and Carol had agreed to eliminate. Things had improved so much, he thought, from the first time he had come to the home. It was filthy then, infested with cockroaches, and without heat except for what was put out by the burners on the stove. Maybe Steve and Carol could manage to regain custody. Maybe it would be all right.

Meanwhile, in the kitchen, Carol was busy at the stove. "How'd I do?" she asked hopefully.

Becky began on a positive note, "You did real well in bringing the water to a boil. You also kept the bottles in the water for a long enough time to be sterilized. Remember, though, you have to use a very clean cloth to drain the nipples after you wash them. If you set them on the side of the sink or in the dishrack, they will pick up germs again."

"Oh yeah, that's right," said Carol, with obvious pleasure at having only missed a simple step. "Your turn, Steve."

Steve appeared disinterested. "I'll get Aldo to go over sterilizing the bottles with you, Steve," said Becky.

Aldo entered the kitchen and, shaking his head, said, "Uh-oh. I'm not sure I can remember all the steps."

"Oh, you remember them," Steve livened up. "You're just saying that to see if you can trip me up!" Then with a broad grin Steve chimed, "I really love you folks—'preciate all you are doin' to help us."

Becky and Aldo shared an uneasy moment of eye contact at this sudden change of mood. They then worked through the task with Steve.

Before leaving that day, Becky reviewed the family's contract. They had kept their part of the bargain. The house was acceptably clean. They had a meal planned for Crystal. They both had been able to sterilize the bottles and feed Aaron. Becky reassured herself that these were tangible indications that the parents could take care of the children. At least the family would be able to manage for the 3 hours they would be alone with one another.

There was a knock at the door. Carol opened it and there stood Crystal, grinning.

"Hi, baby!" said Carol.

Crystal just grinned and walked in. She went to the table and picked up an orange. "Baalll," she said, holding it for Aldo to see.

"It's like a ball. It's an orange. O-r-r-a-a-n-n-ge," enunciated Aldo while bending low for Crystal to see his mouth.

Crystal smiled and put it back on the table.

"Well, you have 3 hours alone together with your family," said Becky. When she walked over to Aaron to say good-bye, she caught a whiff of urine. "Looks like the baby's diapers are wet."

"Yeah, but those are large Pampers, not like the littler ones you taught us with," Steve said confidently. "They hold a lot more."

"Yes, but wet diapers cause a rash," Becky sighed. "Let's go over diaper changing before we go."

Becky and Aldo said good-bye, squinted in the sunlight, and stepped onto the makeshift steps at the trailer door. They looked at each other hesitantly. What were the options? The child welfare agency could consider terminating parental rights to Crystal, but the agency's case would not be a strong one. After all, neither Carol nor Steve had perpetrated any abuse. Termination and adoption proceedings also take time. Meanwhile, Crystal's delays were already apparent, and Becky suspected that Aaron's development would follow a similar course. Would either or both children be in great demand and would someone want to adopt both to keep them together? If not, Becky knew that the children would probably drift from one foster home to the next.

But why agonize over such questions? For all Steve's roaring, he had shown no bite. Becky and Aldo walked to the car reassured that they were doing the right thing.

They paused as they heard the sound of Steve's raised voice, the slamming of a door, and the baby's cry muffled by the tin siding of the mobile home.

DISCUSSION QUESTIONS

1. Does the contracting approach Becky and Aldo have chosen to take with the Lowell family exemplify family-centered practices? Are their interactions with the family respectful and empowering?

2. Is Steve's complaint about the referral to Early Start a valid one?

3. Becky chose to ignore—or at least postpone dealing with—Steve's outburst about Nancy's referral of Aaron to the Early Start program. Was this the best way to handle his outburst?

4. In this case, Becky and Aldo make home visits to the Lowell family together. What are the advantages of co-visits in this case? Under what circumstances should co-visits be considered given the increased cost of assigning two staff members to a family?

5. Carol's and Steve's cooperation with the various agencies and professionals described in the case seems largely a function of court orders and threats. Can a family-centered approach be implemented under such circumstances?

6. If you could turn back the clock to the time when Crystal's abuse was first discovered, how would you have proceeded with this family? To what degree do you think you could have avoided the use of court orders and threats?

7. Becky and Aldo seem somewhat more positive about the Lowells than other professionals who work with the family. Is there anything that Becky and Aldo can do to influence others' perceptions of the family or to persuade them to take a more family-centered approach?

8. Will the apparent developmental delays of the children be exacerbated by the fact that Carol and Steve have disabilities? If so, should this affect decisions about the placement of the children?

9. If, as the caseworker suggests, the Lowell family will need supportive services throughout their lifetime to avoid further

incidences of abuse or neglect, would you favor providing such services over terminating the parents' rights? Should the economic costs of services versus termination be considered in resolving this question?

10. Have the best interests of Aaron and Crystal been taken into consideration in the decisions made by the court and the human services agencies? What are these children's rights and can they be honored while adhering to a family-centered approach?

11. In this case, have the necessary precautions been taken to guard against child abuse or neglect? What possible indications of abuse or neglect should Becky and Aldo watch for in order to guard against its occurrence.

The Go-Between

Irene Nathan Zipper

No one knew the extent of Luisa Ramirez's drug use. A urine test had revealed that her son, Ramon, was exposed to cocaine shortly before his birth. Ramon was at risk for developmental delays and, therefore, eligible for early intervention services. Elaine York was assigned as the service coordinator for Ramon and his family. This assignment was fortunate because Elaine speaks fluent Spanish, Luisa's only language. This case study describes a situation in which the mother, Luisa, is motivated to work for change that will benefit both herself and her children. It is soon discovered, however, that the services she desires to make changes in her life are unavailable for a variety of reasons. Agency policies and procedures prevent access, "turf" issues among agencies impede effective collaboration, and complex questions about the financing of services cannot be easily resolved. Elaine York tries to be supportive of Luisa and respect her role as decisionmaker in matters that affect her family, especially development of the individualized family service plan, but other service providers in the community do not necessarily share this respect.

Elaine York had been working at the Department of Public Health for 3 years when she met Luisa Ramirez shortly after Luisa's second child, Ramon, was born. Routine tests showed that the baby had been exposed to cocaine prior to birth. The hospital made a referral to the Department of Social Services to determine whether Ramon's mother would be allowed to take him home from the hospital. After an investigation that included interviews with Luisa and with the teacher at the child care center attended by Ramon's sister, Tina, it was decided that Ramon would be released to his mother. Ramon was classified as at risk for developmental delay, making him eligible for early intervention services. Elaine York was assigned the role of service coordinator.

MAKING ARRANGEMENTS

Elaine's first meeting with Luisa was a home visit shortly after Luisa returned home from the hospital. Luisa, Ramon, and Tina were there when Elaine had arrived at the home. Luisa seemed very proud of both Ramon and his sister. There were photographs of Tina, Luisa, and a man about Luisa's age on the living room wall. In response to Elaine's questions about the photographs, Luisa said that the children's father had left the area shortly before Ramon was born and that she had not had contact with him since his departure. Elaine explained that, as their service coordinator, she would do her best to see that Luisa and her family received the services they wanted and were entitled to, and that they were provided in the way that Luisa wanted.

Elaine explained that Ramon would be eligible for well-baby care through the Special Infant Care Clinic at the Department of Public Health where her office was. The clinic provided comprehensive health services for babies who were at risk for developmental delay. Luisa was glad she would not have to take Ramon to the clinic at the hospital, where she had had to wait 2 hours or more to see the doctor. Luisa volunteered that she was not currently taking cocaine, although she said that she had done so in the past. She said she wanted to take advantage of the services being offered and was pleased that they were available to her. The fact that Elaine spoke fluent Spanish made everything much easier than it would have been if an interpreter had been needed.

An IFSP meeting was held the next day at the Department of Public Health, which was near Luisa's apartment. The meeting was attended by Luisa, Elaine, the nurse from the Special Infant Care Clinic, and Suzanne Smith, the protective services worker from the Department of Social Services, who had conducted the investigation while Ramon was at the hospital. When Suzanne suggested substance abuse counseling, Luisa said she did not see the need for counseling because she was no longer using drugs. The subject was dropped. It was agreed that Luisa would bring Ramon to the Special Infant Care Clinic monthly, that Tina would continue at her preschool, and that Elaine, as the service coordinator, would maintain regular contact with Luisa. Suzanne would keep informed of the situation through Elaine. Finally, the Department of Social Services would provide financial support through Aid to Families with Dependent Children payments, and the family would also qualify for food stamps.

Over time, Elaine and Luisa saw each other frequently, as Elaine visited Luisa at home regularly. When Ramon was 3 months old, he began attending the same child care center that Tina attended 2 days a week, and Luisa began to look for work. Luisa kept her appointments for Ramon at the Special Infant Care Clinic and, although he remained slightly hypertonic, Ramon seemed generally healthy. Elaine kept in touch with the lead teacher at the child care center, who had grown quite attached to Ramon. His interactive skills seemed age-appropriate, and his motor development was within normal limits. Overall, things were going quite well for Luisa and her children.

The only issue that had not been resolved was finding a job for which Luisa was qualified. Luisa brought up this concern during several home visits, saying she was growing tired of being home all of the time and really wanted to work. Elaine gave her the name and telephone number of a counselor at the Employment Security Commission. Luisa had an interview with the counselor and passed a test qualifying her for classes at the Employment Security Commission. Luisa, however, took no further action toward attending the classes.

A CRY FOR HELP

Elaine continued to visit Luisa. Ramon, who would be 1 year old in a few weeks, remained healthy, and his delays were minimal. During one visit, Luisa asked Elaine if she could drive her to a doctor's appointment the next day because her car was not working. She said that she did not like relying on others for rides, and she hoped her car would be fixed in the next few days. Elaine was not available to drive Luisa, so she gave her the number of the County Ride Service. Elaine sensed that something else was bothering Luisa and asked if there was anything else she wanted to discuss. Luisa assured her that everything was fine, but Elaine was not convinced.

Luisa called a week later to ask if Elaine could come to her apartment. A meeting time was arranged for the next day, and Luisa was waiting for Elaine when she arrived. Luisa began to cry as soon as Elaine entered the apartment. She said she had learned last week that she was pregnant. After Luisa regained her composure, she said she had to tell Elaine something else. She began by saying she had used cocaine on occasion since before Ramon was born. Although she hadn't used it regularly and knew it hadn't affected the way she cared for her children, she had realized after Ramon's birth that it could be harmful to use cocaine during pregnancy. She didn't want to hurt the baby she was carrying, and she really wanted to stop using drugs altogether.

Ramon's and Tina's father had come to visit the month before and was the father of the baby she was now carrying. He was a drug user and had introduced her to cocaine. He had left the area again, and she hoped he would not return. As she put it, "I want to turn my life around." Luisa and Elaine talked for a long time. During their conversation, Luisa played down the seriousness of her drug use, insisting that she used cocaine only occasionally. At the same time, she talked about a close friend who had become addicted to drugs and lost her job and custody of her children. It was clear that Luisa was afraid the same thing could happen to her.

Luisa was definite about wanting to begin substance abuse treatment as quickly as possible and said that she hoped to be able to receive treatment on an inpatient basis. She didn't see how she could do that while taking care of her children and asked Elaine to help her sort out her options. Luisa thought Medicaid would cover inpatient substance abuse treatment, but had several questions: Could the Department of Social Services arrange for child care while she was in the treatment program? Would her AFDC payment continue during the treatment? Could she go to a treatment program on an outpatient basis and live at home while getting treatment? Would Medicaid cover outpatient treatment? Should she tell her obstetrician about her drug use?

As they talked, it became apparent that Luisa needed considerable support. In order to plan for herself and her children, she needed information about substance abuse, funding for treatment, the treatment program, and the assistance available through the Department of Social Services.

Elaine suggested that they meet with the DSS caseworker and a representative from the drug treatment center to consider how to proceed. Although Luisa did not want to discuss the issue openly, she realized that she needed information and assistance from DSS and from the treatment center and agreed to a meeting. Luisa said she would like Anna MacKenzie, the lead teacher at Tina's and Ramon's child care center, to attend the meeting because she respected her opinion and considered her a friend. She also felt that Anna needed to know what was happening. Elaine agreed to arrange the meeting as soon as possible. Elaine also offered to talk with Suzanne Smith, the DSS caseworker, prior to the meeting to tell her about Luisa's desire for substance abuse treatment, and to gather some background information. Luisa agreed that this might be helpful.

THE SYSTEM'S RESPONSE

Elaine called Suzanne Smith the day after she and Luisa had their long talk. Elaine told Suzanne about Luisa's desire to enter a substance abuse treatment program and suggested the joint planning meeting. Elaine was unprepared for Suzanne's reaction. Suzanne said that, in light of this new information, she needed to reassess Luisa's ability to care for the children immediately. She would visit Luisa that afternoon to decide whether Ramon and Tina would be placed in foster care. There was a long pause while Elaine thought about what Suzanne was saying. She understood that Suzanne was responsible for ensuring the safety and well-being of the children, but she was also convinced that Luisa was providing adequate care for Tina and Ramon. Elaine was afraid that Luisa would, in effect, be punished for becoming motivated to deal with her problems. Elaine tried to discuss this with Suzanne, but Suzanne didn't seem to listen. Elaine offered to go to Luisa's home with Suzanne and serve as an interpreter. Suzanne refused her offer, saying she thought it would be best if she arranged for a certified interpreter to attend. Suzanne said she would call Elaine after she saw Luisa and hung up the telephone. Elaine wondered whether she had somehow betrayed Luisa by talking to Suzanne. She had other home visits scheduled for the afternoon, so there was little she could do but wait until the morning.

The next morning, Suzanne Smith called. She had gone to the home the previous afternoon and talked at length with Luisa. Suzanne was satisfied that the children were safe with Luisa and would not proceed with alternative living arrangements. Elaine was relieved and again suggested a meeting to discuss how Luisa could be supported in caring for the children and considering the choices she faced. Suzanne gave Elaine some times when she would be free to meet. Elaine said she would check with Luisa to see which times were convenient for her, but Suzanne responded by saying that was unnecessary since Luisa did not need to attend the meeting. She said that the professionals working with Ramon, Tina, and Luisa had to decide on an appropriate plan for the family so that they could make a single recommendation to her. Luisa and the professionals could make specific service plans at an IFSP meeting, which was to be held soon anyway.

Elaine strongly disagreed with Suzanne and now was faced with a dilemma. Elaine believed that Luisa should be present at the meeting. In fact, she saw little point in meeting without her. After all, she thought, the meeting was in response to Luisa's request for information about her treatment options. Its purpose was to support Luisa in making an informed decision about how to proceed. Elaine knew that no plan would be successful unless Luisa was fully committed to it, and Luisa was not likely to be committed to a plan that she had no part in formulating. Elaine also knew that the service providers in this situation could not possibly understand Luisa's priorities without her direct involvement. When Elaine voiced her objections, Suzanne reiterated that she felt it was up to the professionals to determine what was best for Luisa under the circumstances. She thought it was their responsibility to decide on an appropriate plan and to present Luisa with a single recommendation, rather than with a number of options that might be confusing.

Elaine reluctantly agreed to a meeting without Luisa. She was afraid that if she insisted on Luisa's presence, the meeting might not take place at all. Perhaps a group discussion in which all of the options were considered would provide helpful information, even in Luisa's absence. After she hung up the telephone, she thought more about what she could do to ensure that Luisa's decisionmaking authority was not undermined. She decided that after the meeting she would discuss the various options that had been presented and any other issues that were raised with Luisa. She would tell her about the group's recommendations, but be sure Luisa knew that it was up to her to decide how to proceed. Elaine discussed her plan with Luisa, who, instead of being upset, seemed almost relieved about not attending the meeting. Luisa asked Elaine to tell the group about her pregnancy only if it became necessary and relevant to the discussion.

SURVEYING THE POSSIBILITIES

It was 2 P.M., and the meeting would begin in half an hour. Elaine was making coffee and setting out cookies when Suzanne arrived at the front desk. Anna MacKenzie, Ramon's child care teacher, arrived a few minutes later, followed by Richard Downs from the Substance Abuse Treatment Center. After everyone had helped themselves to refreshments, Elaine welcomed them to the Department of Public Health and asked them to introduce themselves to each other. Although she had explained the purpose of the meeting to each of them when it was scheduled, she began by explaining the purpose of the meeting again in order to set the tone and ensure that expectations were clear. They were here to discuss Luisa's request for substance abuse treatment and consider how they could support her desire to "turn her life around."

Richard Downs began the discussion, saying that he could add Luisa to the waiting list for admission to the inpatient program at the Substance Abuse Treatment Center, but that their current waiting list was 8–10 weeks long. Suzanne was surprised to hear there was a waiting list, as clients she had referred in the past had entered the program immediately. Richard agreed that that had been true in the past, but over the past several months requests for admission had increased dramatically and the staff had had to resort to a waiting list. The group was momentarily stymied. Suzanne finally broke the silence by pointing out that the wait would allow her time to plan for Ramon's and Tina's care while Luisa was in the program. She said Luisa could choose from among several options, including temporary foster care, having a home visitor come to the apartment, or full-time child care if she chose outpatient treatment.

Elaine realized that a 10-week delay meant Luisa would be almost half-way through her pregnancy before she began treatment. She decided that the group needed to be made aware of the pregnancy. She calmly announced that Luisa was pregnant, and that the pregnancy meant that treatment could not be delayed. Richard responded with surprise. He had assumed that everyone knew of his center's strict policy against serving pregnant women. He said there was a drug treatment center in a neighboring county with a short waiting list that might be able to accommodate Luisa. He could get the name of a contact person at that center for Elaine. It had not occurred to Elaine that Luisa's pregnancy might limit her access to treatment. She knew that Luisa would be very disappointed to learn that the local treatment center would not serve her. Now the group needed to determine what other options Luisa had.

Elaine asked Richard about the other center, and he described the program in some detail. Suzanne, who had been listening closely, responded, "There's no point in contacting the center in that county. They don't accept Medicaid payment for inpatient services. Since Luisa doesn't have any other medical insurance she has no way of paying for that program."

To Elaine, Suzanne sounded as though she were speaking to a group of children who should have known better. Elaine had the distinct feeling that Suzanne thought Luisa "belonged" to her department because Luisa needed financial support in order to get services. She decided not to address this issue directly, but felt herself becoming frustrated with Suzanne and with the progress of the meeting.

Elaine asked whether there were other inpatient programs in their county that might be able to serve Luisa. Richard knew of a small program at the southern end of the county, but said that it had a very long waiting list. Elaine asked whether outpatient treatment was a possibility. Suzanne said that the local mental health center accepted Medicaid payments for outpatient services, but that she knew of several clients who had been disappointed in their outpatient treatment at the substance abuse unit. She thought they should consider it only as a last resort.

Anna MacKenzie had said nothing up to this point. Now she asked the group whether the substance abuse program would also help with job training. She told the group that Luisa had been working hard to find a job, but that she had not been successful and the situation did not look promising. Perhaps more job opportunities would be available to her if she had additional training. Richard said that the treatment program Luisa had expected to attend worked with the Employment Security Commission to help residents gain job-related skills. Elaine proposed that she talk with Luisa about the job training programs available at the Employment Security Commission again and about including job training as one aspect of her involvement with any treatment program.

Suzanne then warned the group about some additional hazards of postponing treatment. If Luisa did not begin treatment quickly, her continued drug use could disqualify her and the children from receiving the assistance to which they were currently entitled. Almost as an afterthought, Suzanne added that Ramon's eligibility for early intervention services should be re-evaluated at the next IFSP meeting. Elaine became alarmed. Her involvement with the family could continue only as long as Ramon was receiving early intervention services. Luisa needed an advocate now more than ever, and, although Ramon was progressing well, he was still at risk for developmental delays. Elaine agreed to plan for a discussion of Ramon's progress and eligibility at the IFSP meeting, but her thoughts raced ahead in planning ways to ward off Luisa's loss of her services. She planned to suggest to Luisa that a comprehensive evaluation be carried out before any final decisions were made.

There was more discussion and, in the end, everyone agreed that further information was needed about treatment options and service availability. Elaine said she would research other inpatient and outpatient facilities. They agreed it was unfortunate that the local program did not serve pregnant women and that this issue should be addressed in future discussions. The meeting ended after an hour and a half, leaving many unanswered questions.

BREAKING THE NEWS

As planned, Elaine went to Luisa's apartment immediately after the meeting. She reviewed the entire meeting, listing who had attended and what they had said. When Elaine told Luisa about the local treatment center's policy against accepting pregnant women, Luisa was stunned. She didn't understand why her pregnancy should disqualify her from inpatient treatment. She began firing questions at Elaine. Had she misunderstood that drug use during pregnancy could hurt the baby? If it could, why would they refuse to accept her in treatment now? Luisa began to cry. Elaine felt helpless. She realized that she could not answer Luisa's questions because she did not fully understand the reasons for the policy. She suspected that it had been established to protect the center from liability for medical problems related to pregnancy and substance abuse. The policy certainly didn't reflect sensitivity to the issues faced by women in Luisa's situation. Elaine told Luisa that she did not fully understand the reasons for excluding pregnant women from treatment, but that she planned to find out more about it. She said she would tell Luisa what she learned, but cautioned that it might take some time.

Luisa agreed that she needed to consider her other options. Elaine brought up the outpatient treatment program at the local mental health center. They talked at length about its positive and negative aspects. Luisa said outpatient treatment had helped her neighbor, but she had heard that others did not like the program. She was also afraid that Carlos, the children's father, might come back while she was in treatment and "mess things up." Luisa began to cry again. Through her tears, she told Elaine about Carlos. He and his brother had been using drugs for years, and she was really afraid for him. She had seen enough of what had happened to others like him to know the dangers he faced. Although she did not know where he had gone, she thought he would eventually come back because, in his own way, he cared about Ramon and Tina. Luisa had said little about Carlos before that day, and Elaine had not realized how much she cared for him.

Luisa told Elaine about how she and Carlos had met, about his drug use, and how she had begun taking drugs with him. She said that after he left the second time, she had realized that her own drug use had become a problem and that she needed to get treatment for herself. Luisa was worried that she might have harmed Ramon and didn't want to do the same thing to the child she was carrying. She said she had to begin the program now, while Carlos was gone. One advantage of the outpatient program was that she could begin there immediately. She also liked the fact that Tina and Ramon would not need to go into foster care while she was in treatment. Elaine brought up the issue of job training, asking if Luisa would be interested in some combination of job training and outpatient treatment. Luisa became more animated as she talked about job training and the jobs she might qualify for if she took some classes. They talked for a while longer, until Luisa had to leave to pick up Tina and Ramon from child care. She said she wanted a few days to think about everything. They arranged to meet again 2 days later to plan how to proceed.

As she left Luisa's apartment, Elaine reviewed the day—the meeting with the service providers and her conversation with Luisa. Elaine was glad that Luisa had told her about Carlos. Although Elaine knew relationship building took time, she was struck again by the fact that it had taken almost a full year for them to establish enough trust for Luisa to share these personal concerns. Elaine now understood that Luisa's sense of urgency about treatment was the result of more than just her pregnancy.

Elaine thought about all of the issues as she drove back to the office. Anyone who wanted treatment for substance abuse had to wait at least 10 weeks for admission to the local inpatient program, and pregnant women were excluded from the program altogether. Ironically, the very fact that Luisa had cared about her children enough to request substance abuse treatment meant she risked having them taken away from her. Elaine wanted more information about the Substance Abuse Treatment Center. What exactly was the policy? Why had it been established in the first place? Could anything be done about the waiting list? It seemed that Luisa had decided on outpatient treatment as an acceptable alternative. However, she still needed vocational training to increase her chances of finding work. Would it be possible to coordinate Luisa's outpatient treatment with a job training program? Elaine decided to discuss the situation with her supervisor, Anita. Anita was a social worker who had been with the agency for approximately 12 years. Elaine respected her and often sought her advice. This time, she wondered if even Anita could help.

WORDS OF ENCOURAGEMENT

The next morning Elaine saw Anita in the hall and asked if they could talk for a few minutes. They went into Anita's office, where Elaine presented her with a complete picture of Luisa Ramirez's situation. Anita was surprised that Elaine had not known that the Substance Abuse Treatment Center did not accept pregnant women and had a long waiting list. Anita made a mental note to schedule a meeting for the agency's service coordinators. She knew that service coordinators needed complete and up-to-date information about local agencies and services in order to be effective. Elaine's description made it obvious that they did not have all the information they needed. The purpose of the meeting would be to consider possible strategies for ensuring that their information about resources was current. But now Anita needed to address Elaine's specific concerns.

Anita asked about the severity of Luisa's drug problem, about Luisa's informal and formal supports, about Ramon's development and prognosis, and about the financial support available to the family. They discussed Luisa's options and possible strategies for dealing with the agencies offering the resources Luisa might need. In talking about Luisa, Elaine expressed her concern about the local treatment center's policy regarding pregnant women and wanted to know if Anita thought anything could be done about it.

Anita knew the history of the treatment center's policy. She said it had been established several years ago under a director who had been concerned about issues of liability and had decided that the center could not risk serving pregnant women. That director had since left. Anita agreed that the need for substance abuse treatment for a woman in Luisa's situation was urgent. They talked about the issues and brainstormed about possible solutions. Maybe someone from the state medical school could consult with the treatment center. Maybe an interagency agreement could be developed, whereby several agencies would share the cost of hiring a local obstetrician to consult so they could more safely serve pregnant women. Anita decided to meet with the new director to raise the issue again. If he agreed to rethink the policy, she would support his efforts in any way she could.

Aside from the issue of pregnant women, a 10-week waiting period for inpatient treatment was unacceptable for those who had resolved to seek services. Anita did not know how many people were currently using substance abuse services in the county or how many women could benefit from a change in the center's policy regarding pregnancy, but she realized that the adequacy of substance abuse treatment programs within their community should be examined. To do so, local agencies would have to collaborate to determine the need for expanded services and improvement of available services. Anita decided to arrange an interagency meeting to consider these issues. She told Elaine she would begin making telephone calls that afternoon. What she didn't tell Elaine was that she doubted she would get the cooperation necessary to make a difference. Nevertheless, she would try.

They talked about Luisa's tentative plan to enter the outpatient program and Elaine said that Luisa also needed job training. Elaine mentioned the collaboration Richard Downs had described between his center and the Employment Security Commission. Anita said she would mention the need for close coordination between employment training and substance abuse treatment at the interagency meeting when it was held. In the meantime, she suggested that Elaine work with both the outpatient program and the staff at the Employment Security Commission to ensure that they collaborated on Luisa's behalf.

Anita asked for Elaine's ideas about collaborating with Suzanne Smith. Elaine had given this more thought since yesterday's meeting and had decided that the process of developing the IFSP could, in fact, be very beneficial. It would provide important information about Ramon's progress and status as well as information about Luisa's concerns. Maybe Suzanne would be more supportive when she was more aware of Luisa's priorities and concerns. Development of the IFSP might also provide a structure for facilitating collaboration among the service providers and she would coordinate that effort. Finally, Elaine thought that she might try to involve Suzanne more directly in the assessment process so she would have firsthand knowledge of Luisa's priorities for her family. Anita thought her ideas were good and suggested she begin planning with Luisa as soon as possible.

Elaine left Anita's office feeling more hopeful. As a service coordinator, she was responsible for helping Luisa to obtain services. Although she couldn't create services herself, she could advocate for needed services and resources. She was glad that she had taken the issues to Anita. By involving Anita, she had taken a first step toward improving services. She hoped the multi-agency problem-solving that Anita was about to initiate would be successful in improving substance abuse services. Even if Luisa would not benefit from a change in the policy for pregnant women, others might benefit in the future.

DISCUSSION QUESTIONS

1. The service coordinator's liaison function between the family and other service providers can sometimes be quite difficult. How is that illustrated in this case?

2. If you had been assigned the position of service coordinator for the Ramirez family, would you have handled any aspect(s) of the situation differently? Why?

3. The service coordinator's role often includes facilitating group meetings. How did Elaine set the tone for this meeting? How did she facilitate the meeting? What else might she have done?

4. Part of the service coordinator's role is to keep up-to-date information about local agencies, services, and resources. It would have been helpful if Elaine had had more information prior to meeting with the service providers. What information might have been helpful? What strategies can be used to ensure that information is kept current?

5. Was it appropriate for Elaine to divulge the fact that Luisa was pregnant when she did? Did Elaine say or do anything that betrayed Luisa's trust in her?

6. When working from a family-centered perspective, parents should have the opportunity to attend any meeting at which their situation is discussed. In this case, Suzanne Smith does not want Luisa to attend the meeting. How might the presence of the parent make the meeting proceed differently? What are the advantages for the parent of being present? What are the advantages for professionals when the parent attends the meeting? Do you think there are times when parents should not be included in meetings? Why?

7. Collaboration among service providers can be a difficult process. What factors made collaboration difficult in this situation? What strategies might be used to promote collaboration?

8. Some issues must be addressed at the agency level (i.e., among supervisors and administrators) in order to support collaboration among direct service providers. From your own experi-

ence, give some examples of decisions that were made by agency supervisors and administrators that facilitated collaboration among service providers.

9. Think about the community in which you work or live. If you wanted to plan an interagency meeting similar to the one that Anita is contemplating, which agencies would you invite? What information would you want to have before the meeting? Where would you get this information? Draft a letter to the agencies you would ask to participate in the interagency meeting.

Situations for Problemsolving

The Team Meeting

P.J. McWilliam

This case describes a conflict among members of an interdisciplinary early intervention team. The conflict arises over the case of Adam Goodman and his family. Adam is a 2-year-old who has significant developmental delays in all areas. His behavior is a problem for his parents, Stan and Tracy. The family is also concerned about Adam's speech, motor development, and poor eating habits and has asked for additional assistance from the team. Marilyn is the member of the team who provides regular visits to the Goodmans' home. She relates the family's requests to the other team members at a meeting, but the other team members disagree about Adam's need for additional services. Marilyn is infuriated with them and their airs of superiority.

"**I** suppose they're all too good to make the coffee too," Marilyn mumbled as she put the empty pot back on the warming pad. She turned toward the Coca-Cola machine and fiddled through her pockets for change.

"They really got to you, didn't they?"

Marilyn startled at the sound of the voice behind her. It was Juanita. Marilyn hoped she hadn't been there long enough to hear her grumbling at the coffeepot. "Yeah, I suppose they did a bit," Marilyn replied. "I don't know why I even bother sometimes. They just seem to do as they please. It makes you wonder if they ever really listen to what the rest of us say." She popped the top on her can as Juanita's coins jangled through the machine.

"It's stuffy in here. Do you want to step outside?" asked Juanita.

"Sure," said Marilyn. "Maybe that will help me get through the rest of the meeting."

The two women stood just outside the side entrance to the building. Marilyn sighed and leaned against the brick wall. Juanita chose a spot of sunlight on the sidewalk nearby. "I don't understand how they can get away with choosing who they will or won't work with," Marilyn began. "So what if Adam has mental retardation? Doesn't he have the same rights to physical therapy and speech-language therapy as any other child in this program? The only kids they want to work with are the smart, little kids with cerebral palsy who have braces on their legs and Coke bottle-bottom glasses. That way they can perform their miracles and get their egos stroked. Well, there isn't much applause for working with the Adams in this world, but that doesn't mean he doesn't have the right to everything the other kids get." She sighed and took a drink from her can before continuing, "To tell you the truth, I think that kids like Adam may need therapy even more. Those other kids will probably make it no matter what. But what chance has Adam got without being pushed along?"

"I know what you mean," agreed Juanita, "but being smart and cute isn't their only criterion for working with a kid. They also have a strong aversion to roaches and trailers. They get the lower class kids off their caseloads just as fast as they can. They always give a good reason, but isn't it funny how they seem to keep the cute kids with middle-class parents on their caseloads forever?"

"Yeah, real funny," replied Marilyn looking down at her watch. "I suppose we better get back. After all, we wouldn't want to waste any of their precious time," she said sarcastically. "It's so much more valuable than ours."

FAMILY CONCERNS

Stan Goodman, age 27, and his wife, Tracy, who is 25, have been married for 3 years. Stan has worked as a police officer for a local department for the past 5 years and has earned several promotions. Tracy is a clerical worker in a large lumber yard on the outskirts of town. She handles requisitions and does some work on the company's accounts. The Goodmans have a 26-month-old son, Adam, who has developmental delays. The family lives in an apartment complex in the suburbs of a metropolitan area.

Adam's problems were not detected at birth. It was a normal pregnancy and delivery, and Adam seemed to be a typical baby—for a while. Adam was an extremely irritable newborn. He rarely slept for more than an hour at a time and had long crying bouts.

"Colic," the pediatrician said. Tracy noticed early on that Adam was not as alert as most babies nor was he very responsive to his parents' attempts to play with him. For a while, it was easy to blame it on the colic.

When Adam was 7 months old, he was still not sitting up by himself and made few attempts to play with toys or people. The pediatrician then confirmed Tracy's and Stan's suspicions of their son's delays and suggested that they look into the early intervention program in their area. It took the Goodmans a while to adjust to the idea, but they called the program and began receiving home-based services when Adam was 10 months old. Marilyn, the special educator on the team, became the primary service provider for the family and has visited the family once a week for nearly a year and a half.

Adam has made slow but steady progress since his entry into the program, but still has considerable delays in his development. Although he is 26 months old, his skills are more similar to those of a 9- or 10-month-old child. Adam is also quite small for his age and is underweight. Recently, Stan and Tracy were told that Adam has microcephaly (i.e., small head circumference); however, the size of his head is proportional to his small stature and frame. Overall, Tracy and Stan seem to be adjusting to their son's diagnoses remarkably well. They are, however, having difficulty handling the situation that has developed since Adam began trying to walk on his own about a month ago.

Adam's walking is a marvel to behold. He never learned to crawl. Instead, he scoots on his bottom to any vertical surface and pulls himself to a stand. Then he starts to walk, moving his little feet as fast as he can with his upper body lunging forward. Gravity eventually wins out and Adam goes crashing to the floor. His stiff-legged, wide gait looks awkward, and he doesn't appear to have any protective reactions as he is falling. Consequently, he is covered with bumps and bruises. Both Stan and Tracy are concerned that he might be seriously hurt one day.

Stan refers to Adam as the "kamikaze pilot" in light of his unique style of walking, and Tracy calls him her "little tornado" because of the chaos in their home since he has begun to pull to a stand and walk. Adam can clear the coffee table, or any other horizontal surface, in 2 seconds. He will pull, push, or otherwise tumble any object that he comes across. Although his actions are quite destructive, Adam hardly seems aware of what he is doing. He just moves along calmly to the next thing in the room. Tracy, however, is totally exasperated. She has "Adam-proofed" the apartment as much as possible, but he still requires constant supervision. It's next to impossible to clean, cook, or even go to the bathroom when she has him on her own. Unfortunately, Stan works long hours and often works evenings and weekends.

On the advice of the team psychologist, the Goodmans have tried a "time-out" procedure to control Adam's destructive behavior. This involved saying "No" very firmly whenever he toppled or threw an object and placing him immediately in the playpen for 3 minutes. They tried it for about a week and a half but, according to Tracy, he never seemed to catch on to why they were putting him in the playpen. "I guess the wiring just isn't there," said Tracy on one visit as she gently patted Adam's head. In additon to the chaos Adam has been creating at home, the director of the child care center that Adam attends has spoken to Tracy several times about his behavior. The center is the only classroom program in their community for children with special needs, and Tracy is afraid that they might kick him out of the program.

The Goodmans are also concerned that Adam does not talk and has poor eating habits. Adam rarely makes any attempt to communicate verbally. Sometimes he makes a grunting noise when he wants something that is out of reach, such as a favorite food on a countertop. He may or may not accompany this grunting with a hand raised in the direction of the desired object. Adam also has a high-pitched squeal he makes when he is stopped from doing something or when something is taken away from him, but he makes this sound at other times as well. For the most part, Adam is silent. Tracy has recently asked Marilyn about the possibility of obtaining speech-language therapy through the early intervention program.

Adam is an extremely picky eater. There are only a few foods that he will eat. Among these are vanilla yogurt, bananas, cheese, crackers, and peanut butter sandwiches—smooth not crunchy. He also loves milk and apple juice. Although Adam is constantly offered new foods, he quickly rejects them. The parents have thought about withholding these favorite foods until he tries something new, but they have rejected this idea because Adam is underweight. It's hard to get enough food into Adam to maintain his weight, let alone increase it.

A DIFFERENCE OF OPINION

The early intervention team consists of six core members: a special educator (Marilyn), a social worker (Juanita), a psychologist (Brenda), a physical therapist (Carol), a speech-language pathologist (Scott), and a pediatrician (Jim). Other services and consultations are available through several community agencies that collaborate with the program. All team members provide both assessment and intervention services to children and their families.

Once a week, the team meets to handle routine administrative matters, plan and discuss upcoming assessments, and review one or two ongoing cases. During these case reviews, the primary service provider updates the rest of the team with the progress that the child or family is making toward established goals and objectives, notes any new or proposed changes in the intervention program, and enlists the assistance of other team members in problemsolving or service delivery. Today, it was Marilyn's turn to review Adam Goodman.

Marilyn went through the standard review of the Goodmans' goals and objectives and quickly updated her colleagues on their progress. She wanted to get to the heart of the matter.

"Tracy and Stan are really under a lot of stress right now," she told the team. "They're tickled pink about Adam learning to walk but they are scared to death that he'll really injure himself in the process. Maybe Carol could get more involved in the case and visit the family."

"I really don't see what good that would do," Carol said. "Adam isn't a good candidate for physical therapy right now. He's too out of control. I'd just be putting him through the motions, and he'd be screaming. Besides, his motor skills are about on par for his overall developmental level. It's just that he doesn't have the protective reflexes. Protection may be about the best that can be done for him right now. I could order a lightweight helmet if you think the parents would go for it."

"Well, I don't know," replied Marilyn. "I'll think about it. There are a few other issues I wanted to mention. Adam's speech-language development is one of them." Marilyn went on to explain the parents' concerns and described the types of sounds Adam was making as well as his nonverbal communication. "The parents have asked about getting speech-language therapy for Adam," she said in closing.

"My caseload is full," said Scott quickly. "Besides, I think that it would be better to help the Goodmans understand that Adam's delayed speech is probably a direct function of his cognitive delays. You know what I mean. Adam can't talk about something he doesn't understand. Of course Adam could use some communication training, but he doesn't need my services. Marilyn, you can work with Adam on basic communication skills."

"Maybe it would help if you explained that to the family," replied Marilyn bitterly.

"Maybe," said Scott, "but you've had a long relationship with them, and I can't help thinking that they'd rather have it come from you."

Perhaps sensing the tension building, Jim interrupted the discussion, "Why don't we stop here and take a 10-minute break. Marilyn, we'll continue with the Goodman family when we get back, okay?" Marilyn left her papers spread out on the table and headed down the hall toward the coffeemaker—only to find the pot empty.

DISCUSSION QUESTIONS

1. What factors may have contributed to the anger or bitterness that Marilyn feels toward the other team members?

2. Is there anything that Marilyn might have done or failed to have done that may have contributed to the current situation?

3. What options does Marilyn have when she returns to the meeting after the break? What are the possible outcomes of each option?

4. What is the wisest course of action for Marilyn to take and why? Specifically, what should Marilyn do or say upon reconvening?

5. Jim, the team's pediatrician, appears to function in a leadership role. What, if anything, could he do or say to rectify the situation?

6. The difficulties of this team appear to go beyond the issues surrounding Adam Goodman and his family. If you were the director of this program and were responsible for supervising all of the team members, what approach would you take to strengthen team cohesion? How would you begin the process?

7. What are the options for addressing the Goodmans' concerns about Adam's walking, talking, and destructive behavior? List the options available: 1) if the speech-language therapist and physical therapist are able to work directly with the family, and 2) if they are only available as Marilyn's consultants. How would you determine which course of action to follow?

8. Can this team adequately address the issues presented by the Goodman family or are additional resources needed? If so, who or what would they be?

9. In general, how should it be decided which children receive related services such as speech-language therapy, physical therapy, or occupational therapy when the availability of such services is limited within a program?

Close to Home

P.J. McWilliam

The last few months have often seemed like a nightmare for Bill and Carla Johnson. Ryan Johnson, age 2½, has also felt the effects of the recent changes in family life. Bill's and Carla's 5-month-old daughter, Elizabeth, was born with a chromosomal abnormality that usually results in death before a child is 2 years old. Elizabeth has severe developmental delays and has spent the better part of her short life going in and out of the hospital. Linda Cummings has worked with the family since Elizabeth was 4 days old. The case describes a visit Linda makes to the hospital the day before Elizabeth is scheduled for another surgery. On this visit, Linda is made aware that Carla's feelings about the child are not necessarily shared by her husband, Bill. This case also touches upon the sometimes inevitable effects of the professionals' personal lives on their work with children and families and vice versa.

Since the hospital was on her way home, Linda decided to stop and see Bill and Carla after she had finished her other visits. Parking was a bit of a problem this late in the day, but Linda didn't mind walking. It was one of those unusually warm days in February that made you glad you lived in the South. The moist, earthy smell of spring floated on the light breeze—a real tease at this time of the year. Linda took off her sweater and strolled across the lawn in front of the hospital.

As her heels clicked on the polished granite steps, she had a sudden sinking feeling in her stomach. Linda always experienced this sense of dread before she saw Bill and Carla. She grabbed the brass handle of the oversized glass door and took a deep breath. "Get a grip on it, Linda," she told herself. "You've been working in this job for 6 years now. So, just do it." She pulled the door open and stepped into the lobby. Inside the air was warm and stuffy with an antiseptic smell that took her back to the first time she met the family. It was only 5 months ago, but somehow it seemed much longer.

BABY GIRL JOHNSON

The neonatal intensive care unit called the early intervention team to say that a baby with a chromosomal abnormality had been born 4 days ago. The baby's condition was still quite tenuous; however, she appeared to be stabilizing. If her current progress continued, it was possible that she might go home in 2 or 3 weeks—that is, if the parents decided to take her home. The infant's mother was scheduled for discharge in the next day or two, and the NICU staff thought the team should get involved and meet the mother before she went home. Linda volunteered to stop by the next morning since the hospital was on her way to work. Linda's memory of that first meeting was vivid.

"Mrs. Johnson?" Linda asked as she poked her head into Carla's room on the maternity floor. Carla startled at the sound of her name. She was dressed in a white velour robe and was just tying a band of pink ribbon in her hair as Linda entered. "Mrs. Johnson," Linda continued, "I'm Linda Cummings from the early intervention team. Did Dr. Parker tell you I was coming?"

"Oh, yes. . . . Yes, he did. Please come in," Carla answered softly.

Sensing Carla's discomfort, Linda took up the conversation, "Well, congratulations! I hear you have a new little girl. Is this your first child?"

"Thank you," Carla said. Her eyes filled with tears. "No. This is my second. I have a boy, Ryan, who's 2 years old."

"I'll bet he misses his mommy. What's your little girl's name? Or haven't you decided yet?"

"Elizabeth," said Carla, "Elizabeth Paige Johnson." A faint smile came over her face.

"Elizabeth Paige. . . . how pretty. I'd love to see her. Do you think we could take a peek?" Linda waited for her response.

"I'm not sure," said Carla. "Let me check first. She had a rough night. She started having. . . ." A tear trickled down her cheek and she grabbed a tissue from the bedside table. "She had some seizures last night." Carla reached to the other side of the bed and picked up the telephone.

While Carla was checking on the status of the baby, Linda glanced around the room. She couldn't help noticing the absence of flowers and cards. Only a single vase of pink roses sat on the shelf beside two cards. She supposed the roses were from Carla's husband, Bill. On the chair beside the bed were two skeins of pink yarn and a pair of knitting needles with just the beginnings of "something pink" attached. Through the half-opened bathroom door, Linda could see bottles and a breast pump sitting on the counter.

"They said she is doing better now," said Carla. "We can go see her for a few minutes."

The two women scrubbed their hands and put on masks and gowns. They entered the NICU and Carla led Linda to one of the small isolettes. The card above the tiny bed said "Baby Girl Johnson" but someone had written in "Elizabeth" as well. The baby was enmeshed in a tangle of wires and tubes. A barrage of machines with blinking lights, buzzers, and bleeps formed a semicircle around the clear plastic bed. Linda admired the baby and asked questions of Carla. Linda was very impressed by Carla's knowledge about Elizabeth's condition and status. While they talked over the isolette, Carla gently stroked a small patch of skin on the baby's thigh, about the only spot without wires, tubes, or bandages.

The prognosis for Elizabeth at that time was quite grim. It still is. Most children with the syndrome she has die before they are 2 years old. Severe mental retardation and heart abnormalities head up a long list of difficulties associated with this chromosomal abnormality. The Johnson's pediatrician and the NICU neonatologist provided Bill and Carla with this information within a few days of Elizabeth's birth.

Carla went home the day after Linda's visit, but she came back every evening to spend about 2 hours with Elizabeth in the NICU. When she could, she visited with the baby twice a day. Linda continued to see the Johnson family at the hospital during the next few weeks. Then Elizabeth was discharged and Linda visited in their home on a regular basis. Talking to Carla was easy. She was open about her fears, worries, and hopes about Elizabeth. Carla wanted to know everything she could to help her daughter both medically and developmentally. Bill was another story. Although he worked long hours, he was home for Linda's visits whenever he could be. Even so, he said very little, leaving most of the talking to Carla.

LIFE BEFORE ELIZABETH

During the past 5 months, Linda learned a great deal about the Johnsons from Carla. Carla was born and grew up in a small town in the southeast, just 200 miles away from where they live now. Her father still practices law there, and her mother has her own greenhouse where she raises and distributes hybrid orchids. Carla speaks highly of her family, including her two older sisters. She appears to rely on her family for a great deal of emotional support.

Bill is from a large city in the northeast. According to Carla, Bill doesn't talk about his past very much, not even to her. His father was an alcoholic, which led to his parents' divorce when Bill was 10 or 11 years old. Carla has never met Bill's father. Sometimes she wonders whether he is dead or alive, but Carla says she knows better than to bring up the issue with Bill. Bill's mother still lives in the city and works in a large department store. They visit her about once a year, but she has only come to visit them twice since they were married.

Bill and Carla met in graduate school. Bill had moved to the southeast to pursue an advanced degree in chemistry, and Carla entered the same program a year later. The following year they were married and Carla dropped out of the program, content with her master's degree. She took a job as a research assistant at the university, and Bill continued in the program in pursuit of a doctoral degree. Bill's scholarship money dried up a year later, so they had to live on Carla's salary alone. They experienced some financial difficulties when Carla unexpectedly became pregnant and gave birth to their son, Ryan. Nevertheless, they weathered the tight times and Bill earned his doctorate.

Shortly after graduation, Bill was offered a position as a senior-level researcher at a large pharmaceutical firm in a neighboring state. He accepted the offer and the family moved. Carla regretted leaving her friends and colleagues at the university, but she enjoyed becoming a stay-at-home mom. When Carla became pregnant again, the family bought their first house.

BILL'S STORY

Linda walked across the lobby to the bank of elevators on the far wall. It was only a matter of seconds until she heard the "ding" and looked up to locate the right set of doors. The far elevator opened, and Linda waited on the side while the passengers got off. Among them was a woman in a wheelchair who was escorted by her husband and a nurse. In the crook of her arm, the woman held a newborn baby swaddled in a pink blanket with satin edging. The new mother's gaze was intent upon the baby's face as she outlined the child's cheeks and brow with her index finger. Linda had to laugh at herself. "I suppose I forget that there actually are some babies who escape birth defects," she thought.

Once on the pediatrics floor, Linda quickly found Elizabeth's room. Bill and Carla were both standing beside the shiny metal crib where Elizabeth was lying motionless. "How's my gal doing today?" Linda asked cheerfully as she entered the room.

"Hi, Linda!" Carla answered. "You just missed the doctor. They've scheduled the surgery for 7:30 tomorrow morning. He says everything looks good."

Although Carla sounded cheerful enough, Linda knew better. She could read the worry on her face. It was the same look Carla wore every time Elizabeth was admitted to the hospital. This time, however, Linda chose not to deal with it. Instead, she looked down at Elizabeth and pretended to hold a conversation with the unresponsive infant in an attempt to lighten things up. Elizabeth's hospital gown had lavender embroidery around the neckline and cuffs and a pink appliquéd bunny over her heart. A set of matching slippers lay on the corner of the mattress. Carla had really outdone herself this time, thought Linda. Carla made beautiful clothes for Elizabeth and always had her dressed to the nines. But even the beautiful clothes couldn't conceal the fact that Elizabeth looked different from other infants. Her odd face, floppy muscles, and vacant stare were easily detected.

Linda and Carla talked for about an hour. They discussed the revision of the colostomy that was to take place the next day, and they talked a little about Ryan. Ryan had evidently put on quite a display of anger when Bill and Carla left for the hospital and left him with Carla's mother. Bill had little to contribute to the entire conversation. For the most part, he just stared out the window at the parking lot below. At the end of the hour, Linda offered to stay with Elizabeth for 20 minutes so Bill and Carla could go for a walk or get a cup of coffee. When they returned, Linda picked up her things, said her good-byes, and started toward the door.

"Wait a minute," said Bill. "I'll walk down to the lobby with you. I forgot to pick up a newspaper earlier." He turned to Carla and said, "I'll be right back, honey. Do you want anything?" Carla shook her head.

"I'll give you a call tomorrow," Linda said to Carla on her way out the door. "Give my gal a kiss for me in the morning." Linda walked toward the elevator with Bill at her side. It felt strange, and she realized that she had never been alone with Bill.

Linda managed some small talk on the elevator, but Bill didn't cooperate. He seemed to have something else on his mind. After what seemed like an eternity, the elevator doors opened onto the lobby floor. Linda gave a little sigh of relief as she stepped off but, instead of heading toward the giftshop, Bill followed her toward the front door.

"Linda, do you have a few more minutes?" Bill sounded as though he was almost pleading.

"Sure," Linda replied.

"Mind if we step outside?" asked Bill.

"Not at all."

Bill held the big glass door open for Linda, and they both stepped out onto the granite steps. Bill turned his back to Linda and stared out at the setting sun. Linda stood silent.

"Sometimes I just wish she would die," he began. "I wish she would die and put us all out of this damn misery. I know I shouldn't feel this way. . .but I do. I can't help it." Bill's voice grew louder with each word. He turned to face Linda. "Every day I see Carla getting closer and closer to her and I know that the more attached she gets, the more it's going to hurt her when Elizabeth dies. She's going to die, Linda. We both know it. I just wonder if Carla knows it. My God, how can a father feel this way about his own child?"

Linda was in shock, but she sensed Bill's need for comfort. Even so, she didn't know what to do or say. The two just stood and stared at each other for a few seconds. It was Bill who finally broke the silence.

"Listen, I'm sorry," Bill said in a soft voice. "I shouldn't be laying this on you. I should be thanking you for all you've done for Carla and Elizabeth. You mean the world to her, you know."

"No, don't be sorry," Linda said, as she began to regain her composure. "I'm glad you told me."

"Well, I've taken up enough of your time. You have your own family to get home to." He squeezed her shoulder gently as he walked by her, pulled the brass handle, and disappeared behind the glass doors.

Linda stood motionless on the steps. No, she wasn't glad that he told her. Now she was the one who was upset. For the past 5 months she had done nothing but talk about how well Elizabeth was doing—even when she wasn't. She was doing all she could to help Carla keep Elizabeth alive. How could she have been so blind to Bill's feelings?

There was a chill in the air now. Linda put on her sweater and held it tightly around herself. The lights in front of the hospital gave off an eerie orange glow as they flickered on and Linda hurried across the lawn to the parking lot. She jumped into her car, still warm from the afternoon sun, and took a deep breath. She thought about the woman on the elevator with the newborn baby. She thought about Elizabeth lying motionless in the crib with the pink appliquéd bunny over her heart. She thought about the baby in her own womb. . . . only the size of a peanut.

DISCUSSION QUESTIONS

1. What might have caused Bill to feel the way he did? Why would Bill want to express his feelings about Elizabeth to Linda?

2. What could account for the different reactions of Bill and Carla to the crisis with Elizabeth?

3. Was there anything that Linda did or did not do that may have contributed to Bill's current emotional struggle?

4. Should Linda have responded differently to Bill when he expressed his feelings about Elizabeth and Carla?

5. Given the events that have taken place, should Linda be concerned about Bill? In other words, just how serious do you think Bill's emotional upheaval is?

6. Should Linda tell Carla about what Bill said to her?

7. If you were Linda, would you feel compelled to do anything to resolve this issue during the same evening that Bill talked to you? The following day? At a later time? If so, specifically, what would you do?

8. In general, what are the purposes or goals of early intervention in the case of a child like Elizabeth? Is, in fact, early intervention an appropriate service in such situations?

A Matter of Policy

P.J. McWilliam

Susan Berkowitz is a single parent who works full time and tries to do her best to meet the needs of her 10-month-old daughter, Jennifer. Jennifer was born with multiple congenital anomalies, which included a tracheoesophageal fistula, a heart defect, hearing impairment, and facial paralysis. She has frequent ear infections and has been hospitalized for pneumonia several times. Jennifer attends a half-day classroom program for infants with developmental disabilities. This case describes an instance of parent–professional conflict between Susan and the classroom teacher, Kathy. The conflict arises over the program's policy of not allowing children to return to class until they are fever-free for 24 hours. The teacher doesn't understand this mother's strong emotional response when she tries to enforce the policy and sends Jennifer home because she had been running a fever the previous day.

The little blue Mazda stopped at the corner of Rosewood and Vine. As Susan stared at the traffic light ahead, she felt the engine shuddering. She just had it worked on last week and it was acting up again already. "Damn!" she said out loud, giving the steering wheel a whack with the heel of her hand. A woman pushing a baby stroller passed in front of the waiting car. Susan pretended to adjust the sun visor to avoid eye contact with her. Once the woman and baby had passed, Susan resumed her watch on the interminable stop light.

Susan felt her chest tighten and her throat swell. The inside of her nose began to burn. It was difficult to see the light as her eyes started to flood with tears. Even so, she maintained her watch, knowing that if she looked down, the precariously perched tears would fall. This was the third incident in less than a month and a

235

half. They must really think she was losing it now, she thought. She could just imagine them writing off this latest outburst as some deep-seated psychological disturbance. She was certain that they couldn't see how wrong they had been this time—but she could. Another wave of anger flowed over her. "Damn!" she said, giving the steering wheel another whack. "Damn, damn, damn!"

It was the movement of the blanket that caught her eye then. Susan turned toward the passenger seat where two familiar blue eyes were laughing at her. "So, you think this whole thing is a big joke, do you?" teased Susan. Since she'd succeeded in gaining her mother's attention, 10-month-old Jennifer gave a squeal of delight, pulled the clutched blanket up to her chin, and kicked her feet against the edge of the baby carseat. "Oh, so you're real proud of yourself for causing all this mess are you?" continued Susan. "Well, little Miss Smarty Pants, what are we supposed to do now? I suppose you think we should go to the park and just play all day?" Jennifer shot her mother a crooked little grin, causing Susan to smile back at her. As she did, the tears lost their balance and tumbled down her cheeks. Just then the light turned green. Quickly, Susan wiped away the tears with the back of one hand and headed off toward the downtown area.

Susan turned the car into the parking lot of Anthem Publishers on Broad Street. She looked up at the clock on the bank tower across the street. "Well, Jennifer, Mommy's late for work again. If we end up on welfare, I suppose we will be able to spend all day at the park."

The baby just stared back at her. Susan checked her face in the rear view mirror and ran a brush through her hair. She started to pull out her cosmetic bag but, on second thought, put it back in her purse and opened the car door. She pulled the stroller out of the trunk and loaded it up with her briefcase, a few of the baby's things, and Jennifer. Within minutes they were in Susan's office. Susan placed Jennifer on a blanket with a few toys in the corner of her office and started working on a manuscript that was due the following day.

Debbie, a colleague, poked her head into Susan's office. "Hey! What's this? . . I thought the exterminators came by here yesterday!"

"Huh? . . . What do you mean?" asked Susan.

"Would you just look at that big ol' linoleum lizard over there in the corner!" said Debbie, smiling and pointing to Jennifer.

"You're going to have to stand up to this woman's insults by yourself, Jenn," said Susan to the baby. "I've fought enough of your battles for one day."

"Is she playing hookey from school today?" Debbie kidded.

THE POLICY STATED

Susan described the morning's events to Debbie. Jennifer had gotten sick in the classroom the previous day. She had had a temperature of 102 degrees. They called Susan at work, and she took the baby straight to the doctor. Not surprisingly, it was another ear infection. Susan had specifically asked the doctor whether it was all right for Jennifer to go back to school and her child care the next day. He said that Jennifer was not contagious and returning to their routine would be fine as long as she was feeling up to it. After two doses of antibiotics, Jennifer's fever was completely gone, and she was back to being her old self by bedtime. So, Susan took her into the classroom this morning. Her classroom, a half-day early intervention program sponsored by the county, was held in the annex of the Mental Health Center. There were two other babies in Jennifer's classroom: Jason, who was 16 months old, and Lisa, age 6 months.

When Susan walked in this morning, she met Yolanda, the social worker for the early intervention program, at the front desk. They were talking together and playing with Jennifer when Kathy walked by them. Kathy was Jennifer's teacher, so it seemed odd to Susan that she didn't stop to talk or at least say "hello." Susan assumed that Kathy must have had some work to finish before class started and was in a hurry.

A few minutes later, Susan carried Jennifer down the hall and into the classroom. Kathy was straightening some toys on the shelf. "Good morning!" Susan said. "Where are our buddies, Jason and Lisa?"

"They're both absent today," answered Kathy. She continued to sort through the toys.

Susan sensed that something was wrong. Kathy was usually chipper in the morning and always talked to Jennifer the minute they arrived. Not knowing what to say next, Susan stalled for time by laying Jennifer on the mat and fiddling in the diaper bag.

"You really shouldn't have brought Jennifer today," Kathy finally said. "She was sick yesterday."

Susan turned around to face her, surprised at the cool tone of Kathy's voice. Then she remembered, "Oh, I forgot to tell you. The doctor said it was just another ear infection. She's on antibiotics. She doesn't have a fever now and she's not contagious." She turned back to the baby. "You're back to your old rotten self again. Aren't you, Jenn?"

"Susan, you know our policy," said Kathy. "Children can't come to the Center if they've had a fever in the last 24 hours."

"But, she's not contagious," replied Susan, now using a rather cool tone of voice herself. "The doctor said it was all right for her to come back to school."

"I'm sorry, Susan. I really am. It's just our policy."

At this point, the conversation had become a standoff. There were a few more exchanges between the two women. Susan argued that since Jennifer wasn't contagious, she wasn't violating the intent of the policy by bringing Jennifer to school. Kathy kept saying that she had to follow the program policy and eventually said something about Susan being unfair by putting her in this situation. Although Susan maintained her composure in front of Kathy, inside she was seething with anger. She couldn't believe this was happening. Susan finally picked up Jennifer and left, saying that she really didn't need this and was already late for work.

CONCERNED COLLEAGUES

Debbie listened attentively to Susan's account of the morning's events and agreed that Kathy had been a real jerk about the whole thing. Debbie was a good listener. Susan always felt better after they talked. Even so, she felt guilty about laying her problems on Debbie. She didn't want to become a whining and complaining friend that Debbie would learn to avoid. So, for the most part, she tried to keep her problems to herself.

"I suppose I've bent your ear for long enough," she told Debbie. "Besides, I'm a full day behind on this editing already. The time I lost yesterday really hurt. With any luck, I'll be able to take Jennifer over to Lucy's house early. I know she had to go somewhere this morning, but maybe she'll be back before lunch." Susan turned back to her desk and picked up the telephone. Debbie walked back down the hall toward her office.

Carmen, another colleague, walked past Susan's open door. She saw Jennifer lying in the corner and stuck her head in. "Hi, Susan," she said. "Is the baby still sick?"

"No, she's just playing hookey," Susan answered, barely taking her eyes off the manuscript spread out in front of her.

"Listen," continued Carmen, "I hate to bug you, but I was just in Bill's office. He was asking about your progress on the manuscript. He really wants to get it out by the end of the week. I just thought I'd let you know."

"Thanks. I'll get it to him on time," said Susan.

"Great. I'll see you later then. Let me know if I can help." Carmen left and headed down the hall toward Debbie's office.

Susan picked up the telephone again. Lucy, her child care provider, was home, and she could take Jennifer early. Susan packed up Jennifer's things and picked up the baby. She hurried down the hall and stuck her head in Debbie's office. She was surprised to see Carmen sitting across the desk from Debbie, but ignored her presence. "Debbie, I'm going to run across town to take Jennifer to Lucy's house. I'll be back in about 45 minutes." Susan left without waiting for a reply.

Carmen looked around the corner of the door to see if Susan had left, then she turned back around to face Debbie. "Is she all right?" Carmen asked, referring to Susan.

"I think so," said Debbie. "She just had a rough morning."

"I don't know how she thinks she's going to have that manuscript ready for Bill by tomorrow," said Carmen. "He's really itching for it, you know. I've offered to help her, but she won't accept any help."

"She'll get it done," assured Debbie. "She's pretty amazing. I roomed with her my first year in graduate school and she'd stay up all night long to finish assignments. Her school papers were always top-notch. If I did that, my writing would be reduced to a mere dribble by about 1 A.M."

"Well, she looks as though she's stayed up all night for the last three nights, if you ask me," said Carmen. "She looks awful! She couldn't weigh much more than 100 pounds and she looks absolutely gray. As a matter of fact, I tried to talk to her one day about eating right. She said she didn't have time for breakfast in the morning, but I told her it didn't take much time to eat something with a little protein in it. You know . . . an egg, some yogurt, a little bowl of instant oatmeal, or just a glass of milk. She just seemed to keep making excuses."

"It hasn't been easy for her, Carmen," said Debbie. "What with all the doctor visits, missing work when Jennifer is sick or in the hospital, and the divorce. Even when Jennifer is well, she has to get up every 2 or 3 hours to feed her. You know, she still has to be fed through that tube in her stomach."

"Divorce?" asked Carmen. Obviously, she hadn't heard about Susan's separation.

"He moved out about 3 or 4 months ago," explained Debbie. "I never trusted him anyway. If you ask me, she'll be better off without him in the long run. What a jerk! He hasn't even been paying child support."

"Maybe I should talk to her," suggested Carmen.

"Ummm. . . well, she really doesn't like to talk about it much. Maybe you should hold off until she comes to you about it," said Debbie. She realized now that Susan had probably been quite purposeful in not telling Carmen about the separation. She wondered if Susan had told anyone else in the office.

"Does Susan have anybody at all to help her?" asked Carmen, sounding quite concerned.

"Not that I know of," said Debbie. "After she got married and moved out of the apartment, I didn't see much of her outside of class. Then she had Jennifer and dropped out of graduate school. I hardly saw her at all after that—that is, until she took the position here. To tell you the truth, I couldn't stand being around her husband. And when the baby was born, I didn't know what to do. I saw her at the hospital, but that was about all."

"I didn't realize that you've known Susan that long," said Carmen.

"Yeah, we used to have great fun together in grad school," replied Debbie. "Susan was a real card. She could even make washing the kitchen floor seem like fun. We used to go out to the Beach Club every Friday night to go dancing. I really miss those times now."

"It's hard to imagine Susan ever being like that," said Carmen. "She always seems so serious to me."

"I guess she's changed a lot since then," said Debbie. "I don't think she's been away from Jennifer for one night since she was born. I've thought about offering to babysit for her but that kid is just too damn scary. I wouldn't know what to do."

"What about her family? Don't they help?" asked Carmen.

"They live in Virginia, a good 500 miles away. I met them once a long time ago. They were real nice people. . . not a lot of money though. Susan seemed to have a good relationship with them." Just then, the telephone rang. Debbie stopped talking and reached for it. Carmen signaled that she was leaving and walked out the door.

DEALING WITH AN IRATE PARENT

It didn't take Susan long to leave the building after her standoff with Kathy. Kathy didn't try to stop her either. Instead, Kathy went straight to Ron Thompson's office. Ron was the director of infant and preschool services at the Center and Kathy's supervisor.

"Ron, do you have a few minutes?" asked Kathy. Ron motioned for her to sit down, and Kathy continued, "It's Susan Berkowitz again. I'm afraid I've upset her."

"Is she here?" asked Ron.

"No, she just left with Jennifer," answered Kathy.

"Okay then, let's hear what happened." Ron settled back in his chair and folded his arms across his chest in a relaxed pose.

Kathy told Ron about everything that had taken place, from Jennifer's getting sick yesterday right through to Susan walking out the door. Then she added, "I'm not sure what Susan might do about this. She said something about not needing to deal with all of this and that she felt like pulling Jennifer out of the program." She paused for a moment to think and then concluded, "She might just do it, Ron. I don't think she realizes just how severe Jennifer's disabilities are aside from her medical problems. Susan talks to that child as though she were perfectly normal."

Kathy and Ron talked for a while about what to do next. In the end, they agreed that Kathy should call Susan Berkowitz at home and see if they could work things out. Kathy wasn't exactly thrilled about the prospect of calling Susan, but she knew it was probably the best thing to do.

Kathy walked back to the staff lounge for a much-needed cup of coffee. Julie, the physical therapist, was sitting at the table with a cup of coffee working on some files. "Mind if I join you?" Kathy asked Julie.

"Be my guest," answered Julie, pulling out a chair for Kathy. "Are you taking the morning off or something?"

"No, but I should have," responded Kathy.

"Something wrong?"

"It's Susan Berkowitz. . . ."

"Say no more!" interrupted Julie. "I've had it up to here with that woman. Tell me, is that kid still scooting on the back of her head?"

"Yeah, I suppose so. . . ." said Kathy, hesitantly.

Kathy didn't want to say too much about that issue. She hadn't entirely agreed with Julie's position in the rather heated disagreement between Julie and Susan concerning Jennifer's physical therapy needs. It had happened just about a month and a half ago. Jennifer hated being on her stomach. The gastrostomy tube she was fed through may have been part of the problem, but she also seemed to have a structural abnormality in her shoulders. Her shoulders

seemed at least partially dislocated and she appeared to have very
little strength in them. Whatever the reason, Jennifer cried whenever she was forced to lie on her stomach. She made no attempt to
get in a crawling position, but had created her own way of getting
around while lying on her back. She arched her back until the top
of her head was touching the floor. Then she pushed with both feet,
which propelled her across the floor. She did this repeatedly and
could travel quite a distance in a fairly short time. She had actually
worn a bald spot on the back of her head from the friction on the
carpet. But the real friction was between Susan and Julie.

Julie had insisted that scooting on her back was bad for Jennifer because she would develop atypical motor patterns. Initially,
Susan had agreed to Julie's recommendations, and Susan had tried
to get Jennifer to spend time on her stomach, but Jennifer just cried.
Then one day Susan came to pick up Jennifer early. Julie had just
caught Jennifer scooting on her back and said, "No" in a firm voice
while turning her over on her stomach. Jennifer started to cry. Unfortunately, Susan had witnessed the event and become upset. There
was a showdown, and it ended up with Susan saying that she felt
it was more important for Jennifer to be able to get around on her
own than it was for her to tolerate being on her stomach. In the
end, Susan decided that she didn't want physical therapy services
for Jennifer anymore.

A TELEPHONE CALL TO SUSAN BERKOWITZ

The encounter with Susan Berkowitz bothered Kathy for the rest of
the morning and into the afternoon. Even so, Kathy couldn't bring
herself to call Susan. Just the thought made her stomach tighten.
Kathy thought if she waited until the evening, Susan would have
a chance to cool off and think about it.

After dinner, Kathy gave her 3-year-old a bath, read him a story,
and tucked him into his bed. Then she returned to the kitchen where
her husband was rinsing dishes. While Kathy loaded the dish-
washer, she told her husband about what happened with Susan
Berkowitz. He suggested that Kathy go ahead and make the call so
she could enjoy the rest of the evening. "After all," he said, "what's
the worst thing that could happen?" He always made things seem
so simple, but Kathy knew he was probably right. She decided to
make the call.

"Hello," said Susan, picking up the telephone on the fourth
ring.

"Hi, Susan. This is Kathy, Jennifer's teacher."

"Oh . . . Hi," said Susan.

"I hope I'm not interrupting anything."

"No. I just finished giving Jennifer a bath. She's playing on the floor."

"How's she feeling?" Kathy knew it was the wrong thing to say the minute it came out of her mouth.

"Just fine," Susan replied icily.

"Listen, Susan, I'm really sorry about what happened this morning."

"That's okay," said Susan. Her voice was still cool.

"I mean it, Susan. I really am sorry. I didn't handle the situation well, and I hope you accept my apology."

"Sure," said Susan, "I just didn't understand. . . ."

"Susan," interrupted Kathy, "it seems to me that there's a lot more going on than just what happened this morning. You don't seem very happy about a lot of the things we're doing with Jennifer. You do know that I really care about her, don't you?"

"I think so," said Susan, softening up a little. "I suppose that's what hurt my feelings this morning. I've always thought that you liked her, but it seemed like you were trying to get rid of her this morning. You didn't even say hello to her—like she wasn't there or wasn't a real person."

"I could never stop liking Jennifer," said Kathy, "but I think we need to talk about the other things that seem to be bothering you so you don't stop liking us. Do you think that you could stay for about an hour when you bring Jennifer in tomorrow morning?"

"No. I really can't," answered Susan. "I have a deadline at work that I need to meet and I'm behind on it." She hesitated for a moment before continuing. "Kathy, I don't think I'll be bringing Jennifer to the classroom anymore. I've thought about it a lot today and it seems like the best thing to do. Lucy said she'd keep her full-time."

"Is it just because of this morning? Because if it is, I. . . ."

Susan interrupted her. "No, Kathy. It's not just because of this morning. I suppose this morning was just the straw that broke the camel's back. I'm tired of trying to hold my life together with string and Elmer's glue. As much as I'd like to think I can, I can't do everything. Something has got to give for a while. Besides, I feel as though I've caused nothing but trouble at the Center lately. I've become the witch of a mother who everyone avoids."

"That's not true, Susan."

"That's how it feels to me. I've got to work full-time. I don't have a choice. I provide the roof over Jennifer's head and the med-

A BRIEF HISTORY

Jennifer Berkowitz was born after a full-term pregnancy, which was complicated by polyhydramnios. There was no history of infection, illness, or drug ingestion during pregnancy. Delivery was to be by Cesarean section because of cephalopelvic disproportion (CPD). At delivery, the baby was noted to have right facial palsy and malformed, low-set ears. Birth weight was 7 pounds 8 ounces. Apgar scores were 3 at 1 minute, 6 at 5 minutes, and 8 at 10 minutes. In attempting to suction via nasogastric (NG) tube, the catheter did not pass to the esophagus. A small amount of barium revealed a type III tracheoesophageal (TE) fistula. This was surgically repaired within the first 24 hours of life with the only complication being a pneumothorax that required insertion of a chest tube. Jennifer required a respirator for 4 days after the initial surgery. The chest tube was removed in 6 days. A renal work-up revealed normal kidney functioning, and a computed tomography (CT) scan was also normal. Chromosomal studies were normal. While Jennifer was still in the neonatal intensive care unit (NICU), follow-up barium swallows showed no obstruction; however, the baby was still unable to handle secretions. In addition, the baby was unable to obtain nourishment from a nipple. At 2 weeks of age, surgery was performed to insert a gastrostomy tube for feeding.

A heart murmur was noted on the 1st day of life. This was a grade 3 of 6 systolic murmur. An electrocardiogram (EKG) obtained on the 15th day of life appeared to be normal, and chest X rays during the first month of life were read as normal. On the 10th day of life, Jennifer began to have seizures that were tonic-clonic, lasting 4 minutes, and generalized in nature. Phenobarbital was given; however, seizures continued despite therapy. Blood levels later revealed lowered calcium levels. Calcium was then administered directly (IV push) and added to the hyperalimentation. Calcium rose steadily, and no further seizures were noted. Phenobarbital was discontinued.

Jennifer was discharged from the NICU to the care of her parents 1 month and 3 days after her birth. Her mother was taught how to suction the child and instructed in feeding the child via the gastrostomy tube. The baby was to be fed a small amount of breast milk every 2 hours.

In the 9 months since her discharge from the NICU, Jennifer has had numerous upper respiratory infections. She has been treated for seven instances of ear infections. About half of these illnesses were in conjunction with throat infections or acute bronchitis. Jennifer has been hospitalized once for pneumonia and once for a high fever (106 degrees) and pneumonia that was discovered to result from a blood infection (i.e., Haemophilus influenza). She was hospitalized a third time for dilation of the

(continued)

A Brief History (*continued*)

gastrostomy. Jennifer is scheduled for outpatient surgery in 2 weeks for insertion of ventilation tubes in her ears (i.e., myringotomy).

Jennifer was seen by a cardiologist at 6 months of age. A chest X ray at that time was read as mild cardiomegaly, with prominent vasculature. This has been diagnosed as patent ductus arteriosus (PDA) and will require surgery at some time—probably between the ages of 2 and 3 years. Jennifer becomes slightly cyanotic around the head and extremities and diaphoretic with crying.

Two months ago, when Jennifer was 8 months old, her mother took her to an audiologist upon the advice of her pediatrician. Testing at that time indicated a bilateral hearing loss, with a stapedius reflux present at 70 decibels in the right ear and absent at 90 decibels in the left ear. Further testing will be done after the myringotomy.

A relative weakness of her upper extremities has become apparent. Although she has been seen by specialists for this problem, no diagnosis has been made. At this point, a partial dislocation of the shoulders is suspected. Jennifer has remarkably well-preserved fine motor movements of the hands (i.e., inferior pincer grasp).

Last month, at 9 months of age, Jennifer was admitted to the large regional hospital for a full diagnostic work-up. The pediatrician suggested this to the mother and made the referral primarily to obtain information about the persistence of Jennifer's difficulties in handling secretions and not swallowing.

ical insurance. Believe me, I'd much rather be providing the love and the therapy. But this is how it is and I might as well accept it. So, to do a good job at work, Jennifer is going to have to do without. I'll do whatever extra it takes with her at home in the evenings and on the weekends."

"Susan, I know it's been hard on you," said Kathy. "I guess I didn't realize just how hard it has been. But, I hate to see Jennifer leave the program. I'll miss her."

"I'm sorry, but it's just the. . . ."

"There's no need for you to say you're sorry," said Kathy. "There must be something else we can do. I don't know what, but there must be something. Would you be willing to look into some other possibilities?"

"Well, I suppose so. . . ."

"Good," said Kathy, snapping up the opportunity. "Maybe we could get together and talk about it in the next day or two."

A DIAGNOSTIC WORK-UP

Growth: Head circumference: Approximately 10th percentile
          Height: Approximately 5th percentile
          Weight: Below 5th percentile

Persistent Dysphagia: The results of the cine-esophagogram and the presence of a good gag reflux suggest that this is primarily a problem of esophageal motility and not a result of central nervous system dysfunction. Barium swallow revealed propulsion of barium into proximal esophagus with minimal, but present, aspiration. There was a delay of barium movement in the distal esophagus. Considerable aerophagia was seen with regurgitant movement of air in the esophagus. The neurologist felt that there might be a right hypoglossal palsy in addition to facial palsy (causing tongue to deviate to the right).

Right Facial Paralysis: Much improved since birth; however, recovery appears to have plateaued. Permanent damage to 5th cranial nerve is suspected.

Patent Ductus Arteriosus: Aortic shadow is now prominent, suggesting increased shunting since last examination at 6 months of age.

Motor Development: Greater than 2 standard deviations below the mean (Bayley Motor Scale). Psychomotor Development Index (PDI) = 54; 6-month age equivalent. Lifts head in prone for about 30 seconds with much encouragement. Rolls from back to front and front to back using mostly her feet to throw herself over. Cannot sit or creep. Complete head lag in pull-to-sit but can hold head steady in supported sitting. She cannot elevate herself by arms in prone. She is able to bear weight on both arms despite the fact that her shoulder stability is very poor. Nevertheless, she fusses a great deal during weight-bearing activities. Reaches for objects and uses an inferior pincer grasp. Combines objects in midline.

Mental Development: Greater than 1 standard deviation below the mean (Bayley Mental Scale). Mental Development Index (MDI) = 74; 7-month age equivalent. She did not demonstrate object permanence (e.g., did not look for fallen spoon, did uncover toy). She reaches persistently, retained two out of three cubes, but did not attempt to secure the third. She did not attend to scribbling, nor finger holes in a pegboard. She did, however, look at pictures in a book and "turn pages." She was able to secure a small pellet with an inferior pincer grasp. Jennifer coos frequently and makes single "ma," "ga," and "ba" sounds. Her hearing seems subjectively better than hearing tests show, in that she did turn to the sound of the bell and rattle.

FROM THE DIARY OF SUSAN BERKOWITZ

Susan Berkowitz started keeping a diary for Jennifer a few days after she was born. She made entries a few times a week and wrote a summary of Jennifer's progress every month. With Susan's permission, her entry for Jennifer's 10th month is shown below.

October 31st

Ten months old today! It is also your first Halloween. At 9:30 last night I began to make your Halloween costume for your class party today. I stayed up until after midnight sewing letters on a pillowcase. My goodness, Jennifer, I felt like a real mother!

At 10 months you weigh about 15 pounds and are a little over 26 inches long. It's hard to believe that you're so close to being 1 year old. This has been the most traumatic year of my life. But, everytime I look at your sweet grin, I can't imagine my life without you. You have given my life so much more meaning and direction.

I've seen such a difference in you this month. You are so active and roll or scoot on your back all around the room getting into everything in sight. You delight in playing in front of a mirror, imitating yourself non-stop. You are getting a much louder voice now and have learned to make a few new sounds. . . . especially "da-da-da." You love to clap your hands, hold your own toes, pull my hair, grab my glasses, and play with books and paper. Sitting is getting much better. You can sit, holding yourself up with your arms for 3–4 minutes. Then, you get excited (or mad) and fall over sideways. Occasionally, you can even catch yourself on the way down. Your favorite sport is teddy bear wrestling. This month you have struck up quite a relationship with a red and white bear that is bigger than you are. It's wonderful to see you wrestle with it and yell at it. You are also laughing more (out loud) and you still pat me on the shoulder when I pick you up—I love it!

Separation anxiety has also struck! I can't stand it when I leave you at Lucy's and you cry. Mostly you cry if, when I pick you up at 5:30, I walk out of the room for a minute. Your sleeping habits (or I should say, lack of them) are absolutely atrocious. You love to take a late nap (4:00–5:30) and stay up until 10:30 or 11:00. That really bites into my time alone! We're feeding you 5 ounces every 2 hours.

This month has been a particularly hard one for Mommy to get through. When you reached double-digit (10) months, I realized how far behind you were and I started to think about how close to 1 year old you are. I'm so scared that you won't catch up. Yet I see a spark inside your eyes that tells me that you'll be okay. I suppose I'm frightened in a selfish sort of way. I do so want to be able to talk to you and have you under-stand me. . . . and talk back. I want to read you stories and help you explore the world. But I feel as though there is little more I could do than I'm already doing to help you. I guess we just have to give it more time, but the worrying is wearing me out.

You are such an adorable baby. And you are mine. . . at least for a while. We'll have a good life, Jenn, and a happy one. No matter what it takes from me. . . . I give you my promise on that.

"Kathy, I really need to meet this deadline at work. You don't seem to understand. . . ."

"Of course I understand," said Kathy. "I just keep forgetting! Could you meet me downtown for a late lunch one day? We could go somewhere near your office. How about this Friday?"

"That should be all right with me," answered Susan. "I'll meet you in the parking lot behind Anthem Publishers. Would 1 o'clock be late enough?"

"That should give me enough time to get there. I'll see you on Friday then. Good-bye. . . and, again, I'm really sorry about this morning."

"There's no need for you to say you're sorry," replied Susan with a faint chuckle. "See you Friday. 'Bye."

DISCUSSION QUESTIONS

1. Based upon the available information, how has Jennifer changed Susan's life?

2. What strategies has Susan used to cope with or adapt to Jennifer's special needs?

3. How might Susan's coping style have affected others (e.g., Kathy, Julie, Jennifer, Debbie, Carmen, Susan's parents, Susan's ex-husband)?

4. Did Kathy handle the issue of the fever policy in the best way? Would you have handled the situation any differently?

5. Did Ron Thompson handle the situation as he should have? Why or why not?

6. Was calling Susan that evening a wise move on Kathy's part?

7. Did Kathy handle the telephone call to Susan in an appropriate manner? What did she say or do to facilitate a productive exchange? Could she have done anything differently to improve the exchange?

8. Assume Kathy's role. It is Friday and you and Susan have decided to have lunch at a delicatessen down the street from Anthem Publishers. The purpose of the lunch meeting, as you see it, is to find out what Susan Berkowitz wants or needs before you offer alternatives.
   • What strategy would you use to accomplish your agenda for the meeting?
   • Write down at least three things (be specific) you might say to start the meeting with Susan. Which of these three do you think you would actually use and why?
   • Write down at least 10 questions you would like to ask Susan during the course of the lunch meeting. Write them using the actual words you think you would say if you were in Kathy's position.

9. If Susan remains firm in her decision to withdraw Jennifer from the classroom program, what alternatives are available? Would you present these to Susan? If so, how would you present them?

10. If Susan decides not to accept any early intervention services at the time, how would you respond?

11. Does Kathy have an obligation to ensure that Susan understands the full extent of Jennifer's disabilities? Does she have a responsibility to ensure that Jennifer is receiving some form of intervention?

Supermom

P.J. McWilliam

Wilson Jordan is a 10-month-old who has Down syndrome. With the exception of frequent ear infections and a mild heart defect, Wilson is doing quite well. His developmental progress has been promising. In this case, Wilson's mother, Ellen Jordan, concerns the early intervention professional more than Wilson himself. Ellen seems so intent on making Wilson "normal" that she doesn't appear to enjoy the little boy behind the Down syndrome. Ellen knows everything there is to know about Down syndrome and all that goes with it. She has therapists coming to their home as often as possible to work with Wilson so he doesn't fall behind in his development. And now, she is talking about cosmetic surgery, weight control, and computers.

The Jordans have been married 5 years and live in a moderately affluent development on the outskirts of a metropolitan area. Robert, age 35, is a lawyer with a growing firm. He has worked for the firm for 2½ years and has established himself as a competent attorney with the potential to become a partner in the future. Ellen is 31 and has a master's degree in English. She is employed part-time in a local bookstore and is also very active in a variety of civic organizations. The Jordans have a 10-month-old son, Wilson.

Ellen's pregnancy went full-term and was uncomplicated. Down syndrome was detected at birth, and Wilson remained in the hospital 3 additional days for further testing. During this time, a heart defect was identified. It was, however, considered to be mild and not expected to require surgery for at least 3 years. Ear infections have been a continual problem. As a result, tubes were inserted a month ago in the hope that they will provide some relief and curtail any possibility of permanent hearing loss. In addition to his recent outpatient surgery for tube insertion, Wilson was hospitalized one other time for pneumonia when he was 5 months old. Wilson's developmental progress has been quite promising for a child with Down syndrome. Now, at 10 months, he is babbling, banging and throwing objects, imitating some simple gestures, sitting independently, and on the verge of crawling.

IN PURSUIT OF INFORMATION AND SERVICES

Not unexpectedly, Wilson's parents' initial reactions to his diagnosis were shock and grief. These feelings seemed to be more sustained for Robert than for Ellen. In fact, for a time, Ellen feared that Robert's "depression" was seriously affecting his work and threatening his chances at eventual partnership in the firm. Within a few weeks of Wilson's birth, Ellen appeared to push her grief aside and "take the bull by the horns." With a flurry of telephone calls, she soon knew of nearly every local resource for Down syndrome and began seeking information and resources nationwide. Frequent trips to the university library have resulted in the accumulation of a massive amount of information about Down syndrome.

The family has received weekly home visits from an early intervention program since Wilson's birth. They were also invited to parent–child groups that meet twice a month. The Jordans have opted not to participate in these groups because of Wilson's susceptibility to colds and subsequent ear infections. In addition to home-based services, the Jordans have arranged for a number of other therapies for Wilson. When Wilson was 4 months old, Ellen was concerned that he was not rolling over yet and felt that additional physical therapy was needed. She contracted with a private therapist for additional weekly sessions. Since then, private physical therapy has been increased to twice a week. When Wilson was 8 months old, the Jordans added private speech-language therapy to his agenda. Wilson also participates in a megavitamin therapy program offered by a university clinic. This necessitates a 200-mile excursion once a month.

Visits to the Jordan's home have always been rather business-like. Ellen has the living room carefully arranged, complete with selected toys, bolsters, and other educational materials. She also has a written set of questions, topics, or concerns she wants to address during the visit. Wilson is always freshly bathed and dressed in a smart outfit. Ellen usually offers information as to how rested he is, if he has been feeling well, whether he is on any medications, and when and what he last ate. This is followed by Ellen's appraisal of how ready he is to perform that day.

PARENTAL CONCERNS ESCALATE

During the last several weeks, Ellen has made several new requests for information. Ellen has been talking about what children and adults with Down syndrome look like and how their appearances stigmatize them. She is worried that Wilson will automatically be viewed by others as having mental retardation because of his facial characteristics. She also expressed concern over his becoming overweight as it may result in his not being socially accepted by his peers. Ellen has read about cosmetic surgery for people with Down syndrome and says that she has decided she wants this done as soon as possible. She requested the names and addresses of surgeons who have been involved in this work. Ellen also requested information on weight control for children with Down syndrome and would like the names of good nutritionists in the area. She plans to prevent Wilson from having weight problems by starting diet control early. Finally, Ellen has read about the early use of computers to enhance the language and literacy skills of children with Down syndrome and wants more information so she can get Wilson started with this, too.

During the most recent home visit, Ellen asked the early interventionist if it would be possible to come twice a week instead of once a week. If not, would it be possible to arrange additional home visits on a private basis? The staff member asked Ellen why she felt this was needed. Ellen said that she was concerned Wilson would "fall behind" without concerted effort on his developmental skills. Because she worked part-time at the bookstore, she did not feel that she worked with Wilson enough. She had an in-home babysitter whom she trusted to care for Wilson, but she did not feel the sitter could provide the level of expertise needed to keep Wilson "on target." Ellen said she did not wish to quit her new job, but wanted someone to provide training for Wilson while she was at work. Already, the physical therapist and speech-language therapist are scheduled to come 1 day a week while she is at work.

A CONCERNED PROFESSIONAL SEEKS TEAM SUPPORT

The early interventionist who regularly visits the Jordans has become increasingly concerned about the family and has come to the team members for their advice. First, there is concern that the parents may be pushing Wilson too much.

"Although Wilson gets a lot of adult interaction," says the home visitor, "very little of this time is spent just playing. Instead, everything is viewed from the perspective of Wilson learning specific skills." Ellen's persistent concern over Wilson's developmental progress, coupled with her new concerns over cosmetic surgery and diet, are cause for the home visitor to question whether Ellen is really accepting Wilson's condition.

The early interventionist is concerned about Ellen's emotional well-being. Ellen is extremely well-organized and very cool and businesslike regarding Wilson's intervention program. She shows very little emotion in discussing her concerns about Wilson or expressing her own needs. Instead, she states all needs in a matter-of-fact manner and takes immediate action. "The woman never stops to take a breath," says the home visitor. "Her day is tightly scheduled down to the last minute, and she organizes everyone else's schedule as well. I find myself trembling a bit if I'm 5 minutes late for a home visit and she promptly ushers me to the door at the end of our scheduled time."

In response to the blank expressions on the faces of the other team members, the interventionist continues, "Now, don't get me wrong, she's very courteous and even quite humorous at times. It's just . . . well, I get the feeling that she's a driven woman. I don't know how long anyone can keep up the pace she has set for herself. It wears me out just to be around her!"

The interventionist is further concerned that Ellen may not be getting the level of emotional support that she needs. "I've asked Ellen about Robert's opinion several times," the interventionist tells the team, "but Ellen just says that he agrees with her. From what I can gather, she's taken over the whole show—probably more to protect him than anything else. Whatever the reason, Robert seems to be under a lot of stress at work and puts in a lot of extra time at the office."

The interventionist went on to say that parent-to-parent support has been mentioned to Ellen on several occasions, but Ellen appears to want nothing to do with it. Ellen says she's too busy, that she thinks Wilson is coming down with a cold, or she simply says, "No, thank you."

DISCUSSION QUESTIONS

1. Why might Ellen be so insistent about obtaining services to keep Wilson "on target" and want information about techniques for altering his appearance? Are Ellen's recent requests adequate reason for the early interventionist to be so concerned?

2. If you were one of the team members with whom the interventionist consulted, how would you suggest concerns about Ellen's "acceptance" of Wilson's condition be handled? Why would you propose this approach?

3. What options does the interventionist have for addressing Ellen's new concerns and requests for information about cosmetic surgery, weight control, and computers for Wilson?

4. What are the potential outcomes of each of the options you identified for Question #3? Which option(s) would you select and why?

5. The interventionist is concerned about Ellen's emotional well-being and the seeming lack of support she has from others. Based on the information available, do you think this is a valid concern? If so, is there anything the interventionist should do at this time?

6. Should the interventionist do anything more to encourage Robert's active involvement in home visits or in decisions about intervention strategies for Wilson?

7. Is it likely that Wilson will be adversely affected by his mother's strategies for enhancing his development or her plans for his future? If so, should the interventionist feel responsible for protecting Wilson from these effects?

8. Based upon your answers to the preceding seven questions, what would you suggest the interventionist do during next week's home visit? Over the next month or two?

April Must Wait

P.J. McWilliam

April Banks is 4 years old. She has cerebral palsy, resulting in very limited use of her arms and legs, and no speech. Although April does not perform well on standardized assessments, she seems reasonably bright and has a charismatic personality. Overall, she has a lot of potential, but she also needs a lot of help to realize her potential. April was enrolled in a classroom program, but Margaret, her mother, withdrew her from the program and placed her in a dubious child care situation. The staff are concerned about April's welfare and the effect this new situation may have on her public school placement in the next year or so. Margaret, a single parent, knows the importance of intervention for her daughter but she is having a difficult time balancing all of her family's needs. The case describes a visit to the Banks's home by one of the professionals who works with the family.

Rick drove to Taylor County early to pick up April Banks. He had to have her at the center by 8:30 A.M. for her audiological appointment. April's mother, Margaret Banks, couldn't bring her to the center herself because she was working the 11 P.M.–7 A.M. shift at the hospital and had classes to attend in the afternoon. The early intervention program needed an audiological evaluation of April or it would be out of compliance with state regulations and not be able to serve April and her family. Rick knew that rescheduling the audiological evaluation probably would not help. The chances of Margaret bringing April to the center were slim. Rick was actually a little surprised that Margaret had accepted his offer to take April to the center. She had also agreed to let him take April to her classroom after the evaluation and drive her back home at 5 P.M.

It was approximately 9:30 A.M. when Rick pulled into the parking lot of the classroom building. He turned to April who was belted into the car seat beside him. She had an ear-to-ear grin on her face and her arms were flailing out of control. It was obvious to Rick how excited she was to be at the classroom again.

"Well, little lady," Rick said, "I suppose you approve of my agenda for the day. Do you want to go in and see Leigh?" April's arms moved even faster and she managed to get out a sound. "Aaaaah," she said. To the untrained ear, April's grunting would probably sound like distress, but Rick knew that she was ecstatic. He could see it in her eyes. Rick stared into the little girl's deep, brown eyes and smiled. He couldn't help wondering what April would be like if she were his child. During the past year, she had won his heart and he wished her family situation was more supportive of her education.

Rick got out, walked around the car, and opened April's door. "You don't really want to go in there, do you?" Rick teased. April's arms, which had finally quieted, started flailing again. "Maybe you should go over to the office with me and help me write reports." Her arms moved faster. "Oh, so you do want to help me write reports," Rick said and pretended that he was going to close the car door. April gave a loud, "Aaaaah!"

"Oh, I'm sorry," said Rick. "I thought you wanted to go help me. My apologies, ma'am. I'll take you right in."

Rick had gotten April so excited that it was difficult to get her out of the seat harness, but soon they were on their way up the ramp to the classroom. Rick could see Leigh, the classroom teacher, waiting at the door.

A 4-YEAR-OLD WITH POTENTIAL

April Lynn Banks is 4 years old. She has athetoid cerebral palsy, resulting in very limited control of her arms and legs and she has no speech. Although April cannot walk by herself, she is able to get around by rolling or commando-style crawling on the floor. She also has a walker with wheels and a seat. By strenuously pushing with both legs at once, April can propel the walker and get just about wherever she wants to go. The walker gets April off the floor and at a level where she can reach table tops, shelves, and the play kitchen appliances—a favorite activity of hers in the classroom. While in the walker, April also has more use of her hands and arms for playing. She can grasp objects and hold onto them, but she is very limited in what she can do with the toys once she has them. For example, April's arm and hand movements are far too jerky to accurately put a spoon into a play tea cup. Nevertheless, when she was in the classroom, she loved nothing better than to spend time playing with the toy pots and pans at the tot-sized kitchen sink.

April has very few self-help skills. She relies upon adults completely for dressing, bathing, grooming, eating, and toileting. Her teacher, Leigh, had been somewhat successful in toilet training April while she was in the classroom, but she has not been in the classroom for more than 2 months. According to Rick, it doesn't appear that her mother, Margaret, has continued the toilet training program at home. Another of April's socially significant characteristics is that she drools constantly. Every time her head drops forward, the drool comes cascading down her chin and neck. She doesn't appear to have any control over it.

It is difficult, if not impossible, to get a handle on April's cognitive level of development because of her severe physical impairments and her lack of speech. The professionals on the early intervention team have tried all of the tests for special populations and adaptations of standardized tests in an attempt to get a better picture of April's potential. The majority of psychological testing has indicated that April's abilities fall within the mental retardation range of intellectual functioning. Nevertheless, the psychologist has some doubts about the accuracy of these tests for April. She may, in fact, be closer to normal in intellectual abilities than the test scores indicate. Testing conducted by the speech-language pathologist reveals similar levels of abilities in terms of receptive language.

The early intervention team is concerned about April's school placement when she reaches 5 years of age and is eligible for kindergarten in the public school system. It is the general consensus among team members that, with rather intensive intervention efforts, April stands a chance of not being placed in a self-contained, multiple disability classroom. If she could show more of her cognitive abilities and become at least somewhat independent, perhaps she could be placed in a self-contained special education class for higher functioning children in her local elementary school. There was also the outside chance that the school could be convinced to include April in a regular kindergarten classroom.

To this end, Rick had managed to work with Margaret to secure funds to purchase an electric wheelchair for April. It was hoped that April could be taught to use an adapted toggle switch to direct the chair. It would take a lot of training, but it seemed that it might be possible. The wheelchair arrived 3 months ago but couldn't be used right away because of a battery connection problem. Now the wheelchair is working well, but April has never had a chance to try it. Margaret doesn't want the wheelchair in their home because the house is too small. It would be too difficult to carry it up the steep steps to the house, and she says she doesn't have storage space for it. Consequently, the wheelchair is in the storage room in the classroom.

The speech-language pathologist had also worked with the teacher, Leigh, to develop an augmentative communication system for April. If she had some way to express her wants and thoughts, perhaps she would not appear to have such severe disabilities and would be more independent. The first communication board consisted of just a few pictures under a Plexiglas cover on the trays of April's travelchair and walker. Different sets of pictures and symbols were later developed for other activities, such as meals, free play, outside play, and music time. April seemed to catch on fairly quickly; however, it was difficult for her to accurately move her arm and hand to point to the picture she wanted. It took a long time and a lot of effort for April to indicate what she wanted to say, and when she got excited it was almost impossible. The problems escalated when Leigh tried to put more than four or five pictures or symbols on a single board. They were trying some board adaptations and looking into a computerized system when April stopped coming to the classroom.

Rick was working on the homefront. He had been providing home-based services to the family for a year. Although Margaret agreed with the use of augmentative communication in the classroom, she did not do much in the way of carrying over the programming at home. When Rick visited the home, the communication boards were usually sitting beside the kitchen door along with the travelchair, or they had been left in the classroom. Occasionally the tray, along with a communication board, was still on April's walker. When Rick brought up the subject of the communication system, Margaret typically responded by saying it was difficult to use the board when she had so much to do and that she felt as though she understood April well enough to know when she wanted something and what she wanted.

VISITING OLD FRIENDS

Rick didn't bother with the travelchair. He picked April up and carried her to the door where Leigh was waiting. Upon seeing Leigh, April's anxious arms started to pummel Rick about the head and shoulders. "Hey, little girl," he said, "You'd better stop beating me up!"

"Hi, April!" said Leigh as she opened the door for them. "It's so good to see you. We've missed you so much!" Leigh took April from Rick's arms and gave her a kiss. Rick went back to the car to get April's things.

Leigh carried April over to the big round table where an adult and four children were playing with blocks and a farm animal set. She sat April in the chair with an adapted insert and pushed her up to the table. Three-year-old Hannah got out of her seat, walked around the table, and sat a horse and a pig in front of April. She walked back to her chair without saying a word. "Hannah, that was such a nice thing to do," said Leigh. "Thank you for sharing with April. Are you happy to have April back again today?" Hannah nodded her head and grinned shyly. Leigh put the horse within April's reach and April grabbed it. Rick was coming up the ramp with the travelchair, April's walker, and a grocery bag. Leigh hurried over to the door to help him.

Leigh put April's things away and returned to the front door where Rick was standing. He was watching April playing at the table. She was trying very hard to put the horse into the barn held by the adult.

"It sure is great to see her back with friends, isn't it?" Leigh commented.

"She's as happy as a clam," answered Rick. "You'd just die if you saw where she spends her days now."

"Why?" asked Leigh. "Where's that?"

"Do you really want to know?" asked Rick, a little sorry that he had raised the issue.

"Of course I do."

"She stays with a woman named Nell," began Rick. "I had to go see April there one day to get a measurement of her so that the adaptive equipment specialist could adjust her walker. Nell lives in a trailer without air conditioning. It was hot as hell in there, even with electric fans going. When I walked in, April was just lying on the sofa with some soap opera on the television in front of her. My bet is that April spends most of her time just lying on the sofa there. Nell seems to take good care of April, physically, but I doubt that she provides any real stimulation. Nell has a baby of her own who looks about 6 or 7 months old and I didn't see her doing much with him either."

"That's terrible," said Leigh. "Does Margaret know what's going on there?"

"I don't know," replied Rick. "Actually, I suppose she does. It's not exactly a horrible place, you know. It just isn't the best place for April. Nell seems to care about April, but she doesn't seem to understand that she's not an infant or a basket case. Then again, maybe it's just her idea of what good care is."

"There must be a better place for her than there or a way to get her back here full-time," said Leigh.

"Margaret seems quite happy with Nell," said Rick. "She's dependable, available at odd hours, close by, and meets April's physical needs. Besides, it wasn't easy for Margaret to find someone locally who would keep April at all."

"I know it's been hard on Margaret," said Leigh. "I admire her for going back to school and working all of the long hours that she does. But what about April? Doesn't Margaret realize that April needs a lot more than she's getting? There must be something else."

Rick's attention was diverted to the classroom. The adult and the other four children had gradually wandered away from the table and formed a group on the floor behind April. They were all looking at and playing with some new matchbox cars that one of the children had brought to school that day. April was inadvertently left behind at the table. The farm animals and barn were now well out of her reach and she was just sitting there with a blank face and drool dripping down the front of her shirt.

"Hey, April!" Rick called out. "What's the matter? Did you get left behind in the dust?" April looked up at Rick and stared at him. "What's wrong?" Rick asked. April craned her neck trying to look at the group of children behind her. "Well, if you want to be over there, you'd better speak up," Rick said in a half-teasing manner. "Go ahead. . . . tell them," he continued. Rick stood silent for a minute.

"Aaaaah . . .," April yelled.

"All right!" said Rick. "Now, that's what I call speaking up for yourself. Rick walked over to April, picked her up, and plopped her on the floor beside the group. She was immediately included in the group's activity. Rick walked back to where he had been standing with Leigh.

"You know," Leigh said, "maybe we could arrange for transportation back and forth to school. There must be some way . . . ."

Rick interrupted, "Transportation isn't the only issue. Remember? That's just a small part of it. The real problem is Margaret's work schedule and practicum placement for her nursing program. She has to be one place or the other an hour or more before the classroom opens and often isn't finished until some time after the classroom closes."

"Did you ever talk to her about the possibility of arranging respite services for before and after school?" asked Leigh.

"I mentioned it to Margaret," said Rick, "but it didn't go over too well with her. Basically, she said that she couldn't deal with the extra stress of always trying to arrange respite services. She also said something about her taking on extra hours at the hospital to make more money, and she needed babysitting she could count on. I suppose Nell's it."

"Maybe we could take responsibility for arranging respite services," suggested Leigh. "Do you think you could talk to Margaret about it again? It's worth a try, isn't it? You know how much April regresses when she's been out for a month or two."

"I suppose I could," Rick said hesitantly. "I'll see her this afternoon when I take April back home. Maybe I could bring up the subject then. But, for now, I better get over to the office. We have a team meeting in 20 minutes. I'll see you at 5 o'clock."

TAKING APRIL HOME

Rick arrived with April at the Banks's house at 6 P.M. An accident on the interstate had slowed traffic. Rick carried April up the steep steps to the front door and knocked. Margaret came to the door, took April from Rick's arms, and put her on the floor in the living room. Rick went back to the car for her things, and Margaret followed him to transfer the travelchair from his car to hers. When they returned to the house, Margaret headed straight toward the kitchen to check on the dinner she had cooking on the stove. Rick put April in the walker and went through to the kitchen to talk to Margaret.

"Have a seat. . . . if you can find one," said Margaret. "Just put that laundry basket over there on the washer." The sergeant-like quality of Margaret's voice always took Rick back a little, but he had gotten used to it. "How'd she do on her hearing test this morning?"

"Pretty good," answered Rick, picking up the laundry basket. "The audiologist said it was hard to be sure, but April seems to have a slight hearing loss in her right ear, maybe 10–15 decibels. He said that her tympanogram in that ear was a bit flat, which might account for the loss. That means that she might have some fluid behind her eardrum. He suggested that you take April to see an

ENT as soon as you can and retest her hearing later." Margaret continued to stir the pot on the stove. Rick carried the basket of folded laundry to the washing machine on the far side of the room and then returned to sit in the chair he had emptied. He waited for Margaret's response.

"I'll take her as soon as my check comes in," Margaret finally said. She didn't even turn around to face Rick. She just kept stirring. "Is that why she can't talk?" she asked.

"No. I don't think so, Margaret," answered Rick. "Not talking is probably part of the cerebral palsy. It probably affects the muscles she needs to talk just like it affects the muscles in her arms and legs."

"Oh yeah, I just forgot," said Margaret. "Well, like I said, I'll take care of the ENT thing as soon as I can. They have a clinic at the hospital."

Margaret poured a glass of iced tea for Rick and sat it down in front of him without a word. She went back to her cooking as Rick sipped on the cool drink. From the other room, he could hear April banging a toy against the tray of her walker. He could also hear JoAnn, Margaret's 11-year-old daughter, playing with April. JoAnn was great with April. Rick was always impressed with the amount of loving and caring she provided to April. Not many 11-year-olds could be expected to show the level of altruism that JoAnn did where April was concerned. JoAnn seemed to understand her little sister in a way that nobody else did.

The clatter of a pot lid drew Rick's attention back to Margaret. She was a short, heavyset woman with wisps of gray streaking her dark, curly hair. Although she was only 37 years old, Margaret could easily be mistaken for a woman 10 years older. You could see that she was probably once a pretty woman, but now her eyes looked tired and worried. Rick looked down at his drink and the circular pool of water that had formed on the marblized formica table. The table reminded him of the one his own parents had when he was a boy. It dawned on him that Margaret had never once mentioned her own parents in the year that he had been visiting here.

Margaret didn't have a husband. She had been separated from her ex-husband, Ray Banks, for 2½ years. Rick had never met Ray, nor was he ever likely to meet him, but he had heard about him from veteran team members. Evidently Ray was an alcoholic and a mostly-unemployed carpenter. He now lived at the other end of the state with their 15-year-old son, Corey. Corey had stayed with Margaret for a year after the separation, but he was constantly in trouble at school and in the small town where they lived. Corey wanted to live with his father and eventually Margaret gave in and let him go to live with Ray. She had more than she could handle anyway with April, JoAnn, and the lack of financial support from Ray.

According to the previous team member who visited the Banks's home, it was after Corey left that Margaret decided she was going to make it on her own and enrolled in nursing school. For more than a year, Margaret had been attending classes and completing practicum placement requirements in addition to her job as a nurse's aid at the hospital.

Margaret lives on a shoestring budget and is frequently in financial straits. Last fall, one of her state supplement checks for April was stolen out of her mailbox and she didn't have enough money to make the rent. When she was threatened with eviction and couldn't get a loan from the bank, she told Rick about it and asked if he knew of any other places she might try for a loan. Rick helped to arrange a loan for her through a special funds account at the center. They had been willing to give her the money, but she insisted on the loan.

Rick suddenly remembered his mission—to ask Margaret about respite care and the classroom. He tried to strike up the conversation again. "April had a great time at school today," he began. "Leigh was tickled to death to see her. . . . so were the other kids. She ought to sleep well for you tonight."

"I'll bet she did have a good time," said Margaret. "They probably spoiled her rotten."

"Well, maybe just a little bit," said Rick, grinning. "You've got some kid there, Margaret."

"Yeah, she's something all right," said Margaret. "She's a real mess."

The conversation continued for a few minutes, but Rick couldn't seem to find an opening to bring up the issue of getting April back in the classroom. Or maybe he really didn't want to raise the issue at all. After all, Margaret had refused respite care just a month ago. Rick wasn't sure how he felt about it, but he knew that he better take action or call if off before Margaret's dinner was finished and the kids came in to eat.

AN INVITATION TO DINNER

The conversation with Margaret dwindled as she busied herself with last minute dinner preparation. Rick sat silently at the table, still debating whether to bring up the issue of getting April back into the classroom. His thinking was abruptly halted by Margaret's booming voice. "JoAnn!" she yelled, "JoAnn, come on and bring April on in with you. It's time to eat."

Rick thought the decision had been made for him. It was a pretty clear message that the home visit had ended. Rick pushed his chair back and started to stand up when a plate of food seemed to drop out of nowhere onto the table in front of him. When he looked up, Margaret had turned around and was already heading back to the stove. Rick looked down at the aqua-colored plate piled high with ham, potatoes, and green beans. He just stood there and stared, uncertain of the message that was being sent. Margaret was dishing out food onto another plate and glanced over at Rick. "You haven't eaten yet, have you?" she asked.

"Well, uh. . . . no, not yet," Rick managed to say in spite of his bewilderment.

"Sit down and eat a bite of supper with us then before you go," said Margaret. "We've got plenty." Margaret's tone of voice made it sound more like an order than an invitation.

"Okay. Um. . . . Thanks," answered Rick and he reluctantly took his seat again.

By this time, JoAnn was making her way through the kitchen door with April in tow. She guided the wheels of the walker over the threshold and pushed April to a place near the table. Then, she started getting out knives and forks and set the table while Margaret finished with the plates.

Rick rather enjoyed the dinner. JoAnn entertained him with stories about school and the kids in the neighborhood. Margaret said very little, as she was busy feeding April and eating her own dinner at the same time. Rick couldn't help noticing how well-choreographed her actions were. Margaret had a single plate of food in front of her from which both she and April were eating. She held a fork in one hand and a large washcloth in the other. Like a well-oiled machine, Margaret would eat two bites of food herself, give April a bite of chopped food she kept on one side of the plate, wipe April's mouth with the cloth, and start the cycle over. Her rhythm was only broken occasionally to give April a small sip of milk or to chop more food.

At the end of the meal, Margaret told JoAnn to take April into the bathroom, wash her face, and then play with her until she washed the dishes. JoAnn dutifully responded and wheeled April through the doorway. Rick helped Margaret with the dishes, and they were finished in a short time. Then Margaret offered Rick another glass of iced tea, which he accepted, and the two of them sat down at the kitchen table.

"How are your classes going?" Rick began the conversation.

"Not too bad, I guess," said Margaret. "Some of them are getting a little tough now though. I suppose I'd be doing a lot better if I had more time to study my books."

"It must be hard to find time to study," said Rick. "It seems to me that your schedule is pretty packed just with working and taking care of the girls."

"Yeah, I stay pretty busy most of the time. It's the practicum placements that really take up the time."

"Where are you doing your practicum?" asked Rick.

"At Taylor County General," she answered. "I'm in the maternity ward right now, and next month I move over to cardiology."

"Do you work at Taylor County, too?"

"Sometimes," answered Margaret. "I pick up some evening and weekend shifts at Taylor. Other times I work at Lynden Memorial."

"Does Nell watch the kids most of the time?"

"Mostly. Sometimes I have to put April in respite at the center when I work weekends or holidays. My sister usually looks after JoAnn then. She lives over in Weston."

"I take it that you're pretty satisfied with Nell watching the kids," said Rick.

"Well, at least I know they're going to be fed and looked after," replied Margaret. "It's better than that respite program at the center. I hate the thought of leaving her there with those kids who can't do anything. They don't even let her wear her own clothes there. They all look alike. . . . like some kind of vegetables."

"Does April like it at Nell's?" asked Rick.

"I don't know that it bothers her one way or another. I suppose she'd be a lot happier if there were some bigger kids there for her to watch. Nell's little one is a bit too young to be any fun for her. But, most days JoAnn is there with her after school."

"Do you think there's any way we could get April back into the classroom where she could be with her buddies?" asked Rick, hoping he wasn't overstepping his bounds.

"I know you must think I'm terrible, Rick, but I've got more than I can handle right now as it is."

"No, Margaret," Rick quickly responded, "I don't think you're terrible at all. I don't know how you do everything that you do. I don't think I'd have the energy. It's just that, if you really do want April in the classroom now, I might be able to help find some ways to make it easier."

"I know you talked about getting respite care before and after school," said Margaret. "But, it just wouldn't work. I know it as sure as I'm sitting here."

"How about if Leigh and I took responsibility for arranging respite care?" asked Rick.

"That's not it. People back out of respite. They're just doing it for the extra money, and, if their own kid gets sick or something else comes up, well, you're stuck. I can't afford to be stuck like that. Besides, at least when she's at Nell's, I know exactly where she is. I don't have to be traveling all over Taylor and Brock counties to pick her up. Even if the respite did work out, there are days when April's sick. They won't keep her in the classroom when she's sick. You know, she hasn't been sick nearly as much since she's been staying at Nell's."

"It sounds to me like you've pretty much decided to keep things as they are for right now," said Rick. "That's fine. I think I understand how it's easier for you this way. But, I'm left wondering if there's anything that I could be doing differently. I'd be happy to help out with anything I could. Can you think of anything?"

"I don't suppose so," answered Margaret. "I've just got to try and hold things together until I get this degree finished and can earn enough money to get us out of this hole."

"How about April?" asked Rick. "Is there anything you're working on with her that I could help out with?"

"Well, I guess I'd like to get her out of those diapers if I could." Margaret paused for a moment and then continued, "You know, Leigh told me that not being potty trained would really hurt her when she went to kindergarten next year. She said that, if I didn't get her trained, April would be put in a classroom at Iverson School with all the retarded kids who can't do hardly anything."

"When did she say that?"

"A couple of weeks ago when she called me about whether April was coming back to the classroom. I thought about what she said for about a week or so and it finally bothered me so much that I went out there to that school one morning on my way home from night shift. I just had to see what it looked like. Well, the principal didn't want me nosing around the classroom and tried to put me off—wanted me to make an appointment. But, he finally let me go look through the doorway at that class. And let me tell you, that ain't no place for my April. Most of those kids were just lying around on mats in the middle of the floor with two women shaking toys in front of them. Some of them were a little better off, but not by much. Do you think they'll really try and make my girl go into that class?"

DISCUSSION QUESTIONS

1. Based upon the information available in the case, make a list of the Banks family's priorities.

2. What do you think are the Banks family's strengths and resources? Make a list.

3. Do you approve of the way Rick has handled the situation so far? What specifically has he said or done that you admire? Is there anything that you would have handled differently?

4. What, if anything, needs to be resolved or changed to improve the situation as it stands at the close of the story?

5. What factors may have contributed to the situation the characters now face?

6. Make a list of the options or strategies that Rick might use in addressing the issues you identified for Question #4. What are the possible consequences, including both positive and negative aspects, for choosing each of the options you identified? Which option or strategy would you choose and why?

7. Based upon the option you chose, is there anything that Rick should do or say before he leaves Margaret Banks's house?

8. What should Rick's course of action be over the next few days, weeks, or months?

Piecing Together the Community Puzzle

P.J. McWilliam _____

The complicated issues faced in working with the Williams family have often taxed the abilities of Carol, a home-based early interventionist. Bobby Williams, who is almost 3 years old, has multiple and severe disabilities with associated medical needs. He lives with his mother, Joy, who is a single parent and experiences difficulties beyond those related specifically to her son's special needs. Unemployment, limited social support, conflicts with professionals, financial difficulties, and her own medical needs are just a few of the barriers that Joy Williams faces in meeting her family's needs. Common to many cases in early intervention, several agencies and professionals are involved with the family, thus calling for interagency coordination and collaboration. Finally, the early interventionist featured in this case is faced with planning for the transition of the family into another service as Bobby ages out of the program by which he is currently served.

Carol drove to Jamestown this morning to visit Joy Williams. She wanted to make sure that there were no significant changes in the family situation before she met with the team that afternoon. It turned out that everything was about the same, but Carol never knew what might happen next with the Williams family. This family was one of the most challenging she had encountered in her 3 years as a member of the Smythe County Early Childhood Intervention team. The meeting with the rest of the ECI team had been Carol's idea, but, as she drove back to Smythe County, she wondered whether it was really worth all of the bother. Would it really make any difference? Or was she just battling windmills like some Don Quixote of early intervention?

A FAMILY PORTRAIT

Bobby Williams is almost 3 years old (2 years, 10 months). He has been diagnosed as having mental retardation and severe cerebral palsy of unknown etiology. Bobby also has a seizure disorder that is only partially controlled by relatively high doses of anticonvulsant medication. Overall, Bobby's functional skills are not far beyond those of a newborn.

Bobby has dark, curly hair and big, brown eyes with unusually long, thick lashes that are quite appealing. Unfortunately, this is where Bobby's attractiveness stops. His small body reminds one of a starving infant in a drought-ridden, developing country. Not only are his arms and legs pencil-thin, but they are usually rigid and trembling from the uninhibited motor messages of his brain or as a result of unrelenting waves of seizure activity. The only time he seems at all relaxed is when he is being held in a flexed position.

Joy Williams is Bobby's mother. She is 23 years old and Bobby is her only child. Joy has never been married and has never disclosed the identity of Bobby's father. Joy didn't do very well in school—academically or socially. She dropped out when she was 16 years old. She worked as a clerk in a small discount store for about 2 years, but her employment ended abruptly when she experienced an emotional breakdown and was hospitalized in a state institution for persons with mental illness. The diagnosis was paranoid schizophrenia. At the end of a 3-month hospitalization, Joy was stabilized on medication and was released to the care of her parents, Charlene and George Williams. Joy remained emotionally stable and was able to go back to work again within 8 months. Soon after that, she decided to move out of her parents' home and live by herself in an apartment. Bobby was born a year later.

When Bobby was born, Joy quit her job and moved back home with her parents. Her younger sister, Candice, was also living there. Joy did not like living at her parents' home. She felt that her mother was too interfering, always telling her what she should or should not do for Bobby. There was also constant tension between Candice and her parents because, according to Charlene and George, Candice was a bit "wild." Even more bothersome to Joy was the tension in the home that resulted from her father's drinking and the fights that ensued between her parents when he came home intoxicated. Joy felt that she had no option but to live at home because Bobby required constant care and no one else could or would watch him so that she could return to work. She contributed financially to the family through the Supplemental Security Income (SSI) she received on Bobby's behalf.

When Bobby was 18 months old, a slot became available for him at Special Tots, a classroom-based child care program for children with special needs. With Carol's assistance, Joy enrolled Bobby in Special Tots, which is located in Jamestown, and Carol continued to provide home-based services. Joy was able to get a job working behind the counter at a fast food restaurant in Jamestown and worked while Bobby attended the classroom program. She saved her money for 4 months and then moved out of her parents' home into her own small apartment. Joy's mother, Charlene, was not in favor of her moving. She was concerned about Joy's emotional stability and her ability to provide adequate care for Bobby.

To a certain extent, Charlene's concerns were justified. Joy did have some problems living independently and caring for Bobby. There was often too much month left at the end of the money, and she couldn't get the diapers or other supplies that Bobby needed. Paying the heating bill was also a problem some months. Joy didn't want to admit to her mother that she was having problems, so she often borrowed money from friends at church and tried to repay them with her next paycheck. When Joy finally told Carol about her financial difficulties, Carol assisted her in obtaining food stamps through AFDC. This eased some of the strain, but didn't solve all of the problems. There just wasn't much money coming into the household. Transportation was also a problem for Joy. She had no car and didn't drive. Although Special Tots provided door-to-door transportation for Bobby and she was able to take a bus to work, problems arose in getting groceries, taking Bobby to the doctor or health clinic, getting prescriptions filled, and getting herself to the mental health clinic. Overall, Joy didn't do too badly given her limited resources—until the unforgettable episode at the church picnic 8 months ago.

THE CHURCH PICNIC

Looking back, Carol had noticed that Joy wasn't her usual friendly self during the weeks that preceded the episode. Joy had seemed a bit edgy and resistant to her questioning. Even so, Carol never could have predicted what happened just 3 days after her last visit to Joy's apartment.

Carol was first contacted by the staff at Eastern State Institution for Persons with Mental Retardation, which is located in a neighboring county. They told her that Joy had had a psychotic episode at a church picnic and had been committed to the state institution for persons with mental illness. Bobby had been placed by Jamestown Social Services in Eastern for emergency long-term respite care because a foster home or other appropriate placement could not be found. Joy's parents did not feel able to take Bobby into their custody because of Charlene's evening work schedule. Eastern wanted to know what type of program and medical regime was necessary for Bobby, and Carol provided them with the necessary information. Carol later talked directly with staff from Jamestown Social Services and with Charlene Williams.

Evidently, Charlene had taken Joy and Bobby to the church picnic that Sunday afternoon. Joy had been acting strangely in the car, but Charlene thought she was just angry at her about something that happened a few days before. Joy kept to herself while at the picnic until some games started. Then some friends tried to coax her into joining in the fun. In the midst of their coaxing, Joy grabbed Bobby from the blanket where he was sleeping and started yelling and screaming at anyone who came close to her.

"You can't have my baby!" she screamed. "If you come one step further, I'll kill you!" She clutched Bobby closely to her and threw anything she could lay her hands on at those who tried to get close to her. Charlene and several church members tried to talk to Joy, but she didn't seem to understand anything they were saying. Joy became more agitated. Fearful that Joy might hurt Bobby, herself, or someone else, church members physically subdued her and emergency assistance was summoned.

Joy was hospitalized for 30 days and Bobby remained in Eastern State Institution in the custody of Jamestown Social Services. According to Charlene, the psychotic episode was most likely the result of Joy not taking her medication or not having the money to get her prescription filled. She also learned that Joy had missed several scheduled appointments at the mental health clinic. Joy lost her apartment and her job at the fast food restaurant, so she went back to live with her parents when she was discharged. Bobby was returned to Joy 2 weeks later, under the careful watch of social services. Bobby started back in his classroom program and Carol resumed providing home visits.

ROUSING THE IRE OF THE COMMUNITY

Soon after her discharge, Joy seemed quite stable, as if nothing had ever happened. A few months later, she began to talk to Carol about wanting to get out of her parents' home and live by herself with Bobby. She said she had tried talking to her mother about it and to the social worker who came to the house once a week, but neither of them would discuss it with her. They said she couldn't manage on her own. Nevertheless, Joy really wanted to move out on her own. She felt capable of caring for Bobby by herself, but she didn't know how she could manage it financially. She didn't think that she would be able to get a job. Even if she did, she was afraid that too much stress might trigger another psychotic episode.

Carol provided Joy with information about possible sources of financial assistance and together they explored sources of income and planned the budget needs for Joy to live on her own with Bobby. Six months later, Joy was approved to receive partial disability income for herself on the basis of her mental disability. She also got approval for Medicaid for Bobby. Joy managed to find an affordable apartment and moved out of her parents' home with Bobby. Charlene and the social worker from Jamestown did not approve of the move. In fact, both tried to talk Joy into institutionalizing Bobby if she was determined to live on her own. According to Joy, several church members have also visited her and tried to talk her into moving back with her parents. Joy thinks her mother, Charlene, is behind these visits.

Carol became the target of much criticism from the Jamestown human services community. Staff from the Department of Social Services blamed Carol for Joy's decision to move out of her parents' house and said that Joy wasn't mentally competent to live by herself and take care of Bobby. The social worker told Carol that it was easy for her to encourage Joy to live on her own, but it was the DSS who was ultimately responsible for looking after Bobby's welfare. They felt that it would be better for Bobby to be institutionalized. According to the social worker, Joy wasn't in touch with reality because she couldn't see the extent of Bobby's mental retardation. She also said that Bobby would receive better physical care in the institution and, as far as Bobby was concerned, he wouldn't know the difference. Carol felt that the real problem was that it was more work for them if Joy lived by herself.

The relationship between Joy and the teacher at Special Tots wasn't much better. Even before Joy's breakdown at the church picnic, the teacher seemed to be constantly complaining about Joy when Carol visited the school. She complained that Joy didn't send enough diapers, brush Bobby's teeth properly, keep Bobby home when he had colds, or call the school to cancel transportation when Bobby was sick. Joy's psychotic breakdown just intensified the teacher's complaints. Now the teacher looked at everything Joy did

or said with a slanted eye. Nothing that Joy said was taken seriously, rather it was just chalked up to her "mental condition." They
took good care of Bobby at Special Tots in terms of meeting his
physical needs. They also provided some "stimulation activities,"
but Carol felt that neither the teacher nor the aides showed any real
sense of warmth or caring for Bobby.

A GOOD MOTHER

Carol feels that Joy is fairly capable of living on her own and caring
for Bobby when she has a reasonable level of support. Bobby obviously means the world to Joy. She loves him as much as any
mother could love any child. Joy talks to Bobby constantly, rocks
him, and tries to play with him by showing him toys and books. In
some ways, her low-key personality, patience, and lack of expectations for him provide a better environment than the fast-paced environment of most homes and preschool centers. In short, she knows
how to wait for a response from him and is capable of repeating an
activity over and over again.

Carol thinks quite often about what she observed while watching the interaction between Joy and Bobby during a home visit at
the apartment. Joy had been telling Carol about Bobby's ability
to talk. Carol didn't usually pay too much attention to these sorts
of comments because Joy always showed an unrealistic assessment
of Bobby's abilities. But this time Carol felt sorry for Joy as a result
of all the criticism she was getting about moving into the apartment. She decided to humor Joy and attend to her comments, so
she asked Joy to show her what Bobby could say. What Carol saw
then was surprising.

Joy held Bobby in her arms in the rocking chair and began to
talk to him in a soothing, adult fashion about what they were going
to do later that day. Bobby turned his head slowly and oriented
toward Joy's face. His large eyes seemed to stare intently at her and
his body was still. Then, Joy stopped talking and just stared back
into Bobby's face for what seemed to be the longest time. The silence was rather uncomfortable for Carol, who decided to just wait
out the display. Then Bobby began to make cooing sounds while
maintaining his stare into Joy's face. Joy didn't say a word, but just
maintained the face-to-face pose. After a minute, Bobby stopped
cooing and Joy started talking back to him as though he had said
something quite responsive to the original words she spoke. The
turn-taking interaction continued for several more minutes.

Carol remembers her astonishment at Joy's ability to wait for

Bobby to respond. What amazed her more was the fact that Bobby only cooed when Joy stopped speaking and that he seemed so intent upon Joy's face. Carol had to laugh at herself as she drove home in the county car that afternoon. Was psychosis contagious? Was she the one hallucinating now? Or did what she thought she saw really happen? It certainly looked real enough to her. Although she didn't believe for a minute that Bobby actually said the things that Joy said he did, he had definitely been engaged in turn-taking interaction. This was a skill far beyond any he had ever been given credit for. Carol wondered what the social services professionals in Jamestown would think if they saw what she had seen. But then, she thought, they would never have taken the time to watch. They were too busy telling Joy what she should do.

IN SEARCH OF SUPPORT

Regardless of how capable Carol thought Joy was of taking care of Bobby, she knew that Joy could not live independently without assistance. Both Joy and Bobby had many needs, and Carol knew that she alone could not meet all of their needs. Even if she could, the time she would be involved with this family was limited. The Smythe County ECI program only served children from birth to 3 years of age, although, under special circumstances it could extend its services until the child's fourth birthday. When Bobby was discharged from the ECI program, the Williams family would be completely in the hands of the services available in Jamestown. Bobby's education programming would consist solely of that provided at Special Tots. This concerned Carol a great deal. If the present attitude toward Joy by the Jamestown community continued, she probably stood little chance of succeeding.

Carol hoped that she could get a support system in place for Joy fast enough to ensure at least a temporary buffer against emotional and financial stress. She thought that Joy's mother and the Jamestown professional community might alter their opinion of Joy if they could see that she could manage on her own with their help. Unfortunately, home visits to Joy and Bobby involved a 45-minute drive each way for Carol. Her caseload also included 10 other families, who lived across the eastern part of the county. Once-a-week visits to Joy were about all that she could handle and still be fair to the other families. Other ECI team members could possibly make an occasional visit to Joy, but their caseloads were equally full. Even if the ECI program could provide the majority of support, Carol wondered if that would be the best thing to do. After all, the services available in Jamestown would be the only source of support for the family within a year. Shouldn't that support system be put into place now?

THE MISSING PIECES

Carol thought a great deal about what it would take to keep the Williams family intact and not overly burden any one source of support. Considering Bobby's and Joy's special needs, their chance of succeeding could be jeopardized by any of a number of possible cracks in their support network. Listed below are some of the issues that Carol considered.

Respite Care

In terms of respite care, Eastern State Institution was probably the only facility that would take Bobby, and it had some respite care slots for 1-week stays. If regular respite could be arranged (e.g., 1 week every month), this might relieve Joy of the constant strain of caring for Bobby and give her a chance to attend to her own needs.

Joy's Mental Status

Joy's mental status was Carol's biggest concern. Joy would probably do quite well providing she kept regular appointments at the mental health clinic and stayed on her medication schedule. Once Joy started becoming delusional, she wouldn't trust anyone and would not seek help at the mental health clinic. Things would only snowball, and another hospitalization—or something worse—would result. It seemed to Carol that having someone who made regular contacts with Joy and monitored her mental status might serve to prevent another episode like the one at the church picnic. It wouldn't necessarily take a professional to do this. Another option was an adult day program sponsored by the mental health clinic, but Carol wasn't sure that Joy would even consider this.

Bobby's Health Needs

Bobby needed his seizure medication on a regular schedule. As long as he was receiving regular doses, he did about as well as could be expected. It was also important for his blood levels to be checked periodically by the seizure clinic at the hospital to ensure that his dosage was correct. As long as Joy was emotionally stable, she seemed to be competent in administering his medication. However, it probably wouldn't hurt to have someone checking in on Joy and occasionally reminding her of the importance of regular administration.

Making and keeping appointments at the seizure clinic was another issue, with the biggest obstacle probably being the lack of transportation.

Carol had several other concerns about Bobby's health. Bobby was susceptible to respiratory infections (i.e., bronchitis, pneumonia, throat infections, and common chest colds). He was also particularly prone to ear infections. Carol wasn't confident about Joy's ability to detect these illnesses at an early stage and they might progress to more serious bouts of illness than they should before treatment was obtained. Here again, transportation was an issue. Joy had to have a way of getting Bobby to a doctor when he needed attention. Proper diet and dental care (in light of the effects of his seizure medication) were additional concerns related to Bobby's health.

Bobby's Orthopedic Needs

Bobby was developing severe contractures in his hips and the orthopedist recommended hip release surgery to provide some relief. This surgery would involve Bobby being in a cast for 6–8 weeks after surgery and thereby make caring for him difficult during the recuperation period. The orthopedist was concerned about Joy's ability to handle this situation. Carol had mixed feelings about it. She knew the orthopedist did not think highly of Joy, but she also wasn't very certain about Joy's ability to take care of Bobby during his recovery. She did, however, think that Joy could manage if she had some help. There was also the possibility that Eastern State Institution for Persons with Mental Retardation might be able to keep Bobby during this period, though Carol didn't know if they could keep him that long or how Joy would feel about his staying there.

In light of Bobby's severe spasticity and the progressive development of contractures, the physical therapist at the ECI program recommended that a Mullholland wheelchair be purchased for Bobby. The Mullholland chair has far more adjustment capabilities than other travelchairs and would provide superior positioning for Bobby. Bobby would be easier to feed in the Mullholland and the positioning it would provide would help to reduce the development of contractures and perhaps prevent severe scoliosis. The problem with the Mullholland is that it cannot be used as a travelchair for car travel. The chair does not readily collapse for storage in the trunk, but rather must be partially disassembled. Carol was concerned that Joy didn't have the mechanical aptitude needed to appropriately use the Mullholland wheelchair. She remembered the difficulty she herself had in learning to use one with another child on her caseload.

Special Tots had a van for transporting the children to and from school. They might be able to transport the Mullholland wheelchair in the van without disassembling it. Even if they couldn't, the staff should be able to learn how to work with the chair. The major hurdle would be coming up with ways that Joy could use it for Bobby at the apartment. A set of six steps led up to the front door of her first floor apartment. Joy couldn't possibly take Bobby up them while he was still in the wheelchair. She would have to take Bobby first and then the chair. While this was quite manageable now, Carol wondered what it would be like in a year or two as Bobby got bigger. After all, Joy was not a very big woman. A ramp would be nice to have, but the landlord certainly would not put out the money or labor for building one.

The Mullholland wheelchair would pose a big problem when it came to taking Bobby places other than school (e.g., orthopedic clinic, seizure clinic, doctor's office, or on other outings). Taking the Mullholland wheelchair in a private car, in a taxi, or on the bus would require partial disassembly. Carol was afraid that the difficulty involved might deter Joy from taking Bobby places he needed to go and might reduce Joy's social contacts. She couldn't help but think that getting out of the house, with or without Bobby, would be important for maintaining Joy's mental health. Right now, Joy used his old travelchair when going in a car and carried Bobby whenever a trip involved going in a taxi or a bus. But how much longer would she be able to do this?

Transportation

There was a shopping center not too far from Joy's apartment where she did her grocery shopping, bought most of the household supplies, and picked up a few clothes for herself and Bobby. Rain or shine, she usually walked to and from the shopping center. If she had to, she took Bobby along in his travelchair even though it could be a bit difficult managing the travelchair and the packages.

Getting to places further away often posed a problem. Joy was reluctant to ask her own family for rides for fear of them throwing it in her face that she couldn't handle living alone. Occasionally, she would ask a church member to pick her up on the way to church so she could attend. But Joy wasn't certain how some church members felt about her after the episode at the picnic and therefore hesitated to ask them for much help with other transportation. Her social worker in Jamestown provided some help with transportation when it was needed to meet Bobby's health needs, but Joy avoided this woman whenever she could. She said the woman always talked to her like she had mental retardation and told her she was doing everything incorrectly. Joy told Carol that on several occasions the social worker made her wait in the car with Bobby while she went into a fast food restaurant for her lunch break in the middle of driving them to the hospital clinic.

Bobby's Birthday

Although it might seem trivial to others, Joy's major concern at the moment was having a birthday celebration for Bobby when he turned 3 years old in 2 months. She wanted to have a decorated cake, ice cream, balloons, and a proper birthday present for him. She talked about it every time Carol visited. Joy was barely making ends meet with her limited budget and was afraid that she wouldn't have enough money for Bobby's birthday. Carol was almost ashamed to bring up the issue to the rest of the team, but it seemed to mean so much to Joy. Surely, it must be important. Carol was also angry at the social worker in Jamestown for what she said to Joy about the birthday. According to Joy, she mentioned the birthday party to the social worker and the social worker told her that Bobby didn't know what a birthday was and that she needed to spend her money on more important things.

PLANNING FOR PREVENTION

Carol felt confused and a little frustrated about the Williams family. She couldn't understand why the professional community in Jamestown wasn't more supportive of Joy wanting to make it on her own and take care of Bobby. Joy loved Bobby and tried her very best to do the right things for him. Was it her fault that she had a mental disorder and few resources of her own? Besides, Joy responded well to medical treatment of her disorder. When she took her medication, was properly monitored, and wasn't under too much stress, she was stable enough to care for her son. Carol felt that she was the only one who believed in Joy and was willing to be truly supportive. She was afraid that Joy would fall apart and lose Bobby soon after services from the ECI program ended. Carol felt as though she needed the support and advice of her teammates, so she called a meeting to discuss the Williams family.

DISCUSSION QUESTIONS

1. Given Joy's history and diagnosis, is Carol justified in her support of Joy's expressed desires? Was it appropriate for Carol to go against the opinions of Joy's mother and the Jamestown social worker in helping Joy to live on her own with Bobby?

2. What factors have contributed to the difficulties Joy Williams now faces? Could Carol have done anything differently to eliminate or reduce the impact of any of these factors?

3. If you were writing an IFSP for Bobby Williams and his family, what would you list as the family's strengths or resources?

4. Based on the information available, what do you think Joy's priorities or concerns might be? What strategies would you use to further clarify family priorities and establish goals for intervention?

5. Carol has some concerns that Joy may be unaware of or consider unimportant. How should Carol deal with these issues?

6. If you were one of the other members of the Smythe County ECI program, how would you counsel Carol on proceeding with the Williams family?
   - What would you suggest Carol do during her home visits to Joy and Bobby?
   - What strategies would you recommend for dealing with the dissension among the members of the Jamestown professional community?
   - What, if any, assistance should Carol enlist from other members of the Smythe County ECI program?

7. If you were Carol, and responsible for developing an IFSP for the Williams family, who would you involve in its development and how would you proceed in accomplishing this task?

8. It is mentioned that "under special circumstances," the Smythe County ECI program can extend its services until the child's fourth birthday. What would the advantages and disadvantages be of extending the ECI program's services for an additional year? Would there be advantages in making the transition to Jamestown services sooner? How might the decision

regarding when Bobby's transition takes place affect the strategies you would choose in preparing Bobby, Joy, and the Jamestown community?

9. What will be required to ensure Joy's ability to live independently and care for Bobby over the next 5–10 years?

10. In general, what toll is exacted on a professional when he or she is confronted by other professionals or agencies who do not adhere to a family-centered philosophy of service provision? Does he or she have an obligation to influence how others provide services? If so, what can an individual do in such situations?

Recommended Readings

ADOLESCENT PARENTING

Anastasiow, N.J. (1987). Programs developed in response to teen pregnancies. *Infant Mental Health Journal, 1*, 65–75.

Dunst, C.J., Vance, S.D., & Cooper, C.S. (1986). A social systems perspective of adolescent pregnancy: Determinants of parent and parent–child behavior. *Infant Mental Health Journal, 7*, 34–47.

Garcia-Coll, C.T., Vohr, B., & Hoffman, J. (1986). Maternal and environmental factors affecting developmental outcome of infants of adolescent mothers. *Developmental Behavioral Pediatrics, 7*, 230–236.

Helm, J.M. (1988). Adolescent mothers of handicapped children: A challenge for interventionists. *Journal for the Division of Early Childhood, 12*, 311–319.

Jones, D.J., & Battle, S.F. (1990). *Teenage pregnancy.* New Brunswick, NJ: Transaction Publishers.

Ware, L.M., Osofsky, J.D., Eberhart-Wright, A., & Leichtman, M.L. (1987). Challenges of home visitor interventions with adolescent mothers and their infants. *Infant Mental Health Journal, 8*, 418–428.

CHILD ABUSE AND NEGLECT

Aberman, J., & Russell, T. (1990). A constructivist approach to working with abusive and neglectful parents. *Family Systems Medicine, 8*(3), 241–250.

Chandler, L.K., & Lubeck, R.C. (1989). The appropriateness and utility of a child-focused view of jeopardy: A family-focused alternative. *Topics in Early Childhood Special Education, 9*, 101–116.

Fantuzzo, J.W., Wray, L., Hall, R., Goins, C., & Azar, S. (1986). Parent and social-skills training for mentally retarded mothers identified as child maltreaters. *American Journal of Mental Deficiency, 2*, 135–140.

Kelly, J.A. (1983). *Treating child-abuse families: Intervention based skills-training principles.* New York: Plenum.

Lutzker, J.R. (1984). Project-12 Ways: Treating child abuse and neglect from an ecobehavioral perspective. In R. Dangel & R. Polster (Eds.), *Parent training* (pp. 260–297). New York: Guilford Press.

CHILD ASSESSMENT

Fewell, R.R. (1991). Trends in the assessment of infants and toddlers with disabilities. *Exceptional Children, 58,* 166–173.

Kjerland, L., & Kovach, J. (1990). Family–staff collaboration for tailored infant assessment. In E.D. Gibbs & D.M. Teti (Eds.), *Interdisciplinary assessment of infants: A guide for early intervention professionals* (pp. 287–297). Baltimore: Paul H. Brookes Publishing Co.

Linder, T.W. (1990). *Transdisciplinary play-based assessment: A functional approach to working with young children.* Baltimore: Paul H. Brookes Publishing Co.

McWilliam, R.A. (1992). *Family-centered intervention planning: A routines-based approach.* Tucson, AZ: Communication Skill Builders.

Murphy, A. (1990). Communicating assessment findings to parents: Toward more effective informing. In E.D. Gibbs & D.M. Teti (Eds.), *Interdisciplinary assessment of infants: A guide for early intervention professionals* (pp. 299–307). Baltimore: Paul H. Brookes Publishing Co.

Rosetti, L.M. (1991). Infant–toddler assessment: A clinical perspective. *Infant–Toddler Intervention, 1*(1), 11–26.

Sheehan, R. (1988). Involvement of parents in early childhood assessment. In R. Sheehan & T. Wachs (Eds.), *Assessment of young developmentally disabled children* (pp. 75–90). New York: Plenum.

Wachs, T.D. (1988). Environmental assessment of disabled infants and preschoolers. In R. Sheehan & T.D. Wachs (Eds.), *Assessment of young developmentally disabled children* (pp. 321–346). New York: Plenum.

CHILDREN SUPPORTED BY MEDICAL TECHNOLOGY

Condry, S. (1989). *A literature review of topics concerning children who are technology supported and their families.* Lawrence: University of Kansas Beach Center on Families and Disability.

Council for Exceptional Children. (1988). *Report of the Council for*

Exceptional Children's Ad Hoc Committee on Medically Fragile Students. Reston, VA: Author.

Graff, J.C., Mulligan, M.M., Guess, D., Taylor, M., & Thompson, B. (1990). *Health care for students with disabilities: An illustrated medical guide for the classroom*. Baltimore: Paul H. Brookes Publishing Co.

Haynie, M., Porter, S.M., & Palfrey, J.S. (1989). *Children assisted by medical technology in educational settings: Guidelines for care*. Boston: Project School Care, The Children's Hospital.

Monahan, C. (Producer). (1989). *Educational planning for the child with special health care needs* [Videotape]. Chicago: Home Health Care Management System, Illinois Division of Specialized Care for Children.

Walker, D.K. (1986). Chronically ill children in early childhood education programs. *Topics in Early Childhood Special Education, 5*(4), 12–22.

FAMILY-CENTERED PRACTICES

Able-Boone, H., Sandall, S.R., Loughry, A., & Frederick, L. (1990). An informed, family-centered approach to Public Law 99-457: Parental views. *Topics in Early Childhood Special Education, 10*(1), 100–111.

Bailey, D.B. (1987). Collaborative goal setting with families: Resolving differences in values and priorities for services. *Topics in Early Childhood Special Education, 7*(2), 59–71.

Bailey, D.B., & Simeonsson, R.J. (1988). *Family assessment in early intervention*. Columbus, OH: Charles E. Merrill.

Deal, A.G., Dunst, C.J., & Trivette, C.M. (1989). A flexible and functional approach to developing individualized family support plans. *Infants and Young Children, 1*(4), 32–43.

Dunst, C.J., Trivette, C.M., & Deal, A.G. (1988). *Enabling and empowering families: Principles and guidelines for practice*. Cambridge, MA: Brookline Books.

Foster, M., Berger, M., & McLean, M. (1981). Rethinking a good idea: A reassessment of parent involvement. *Topics in Early Childhood Special Education, 1*(3), 55–65.

Hanson, M.J., Lynch, E.W., & Wayman, K.I. (1990). Honoring the cultural diversity of families when gathering data. *Topics in Early Childhood Special Education, 10*(1), 112–131.

Harry, B. (1992). *Cultural diversity, families, and the special education system: Communication and empowerment*. New York: Teachers College Press.

Lynch, E.W., & Hanson, M.J. (Eds.). (1992). *Developing cross-cultural competence: A guide for working with young children and their families.* Baltimore: Paul H. Brookes Publishing Co.

McGonigel, M.J., & Garland, C.W. (1988). The individualized family service plan and the early intervention team: Team and family issues and recommended practices. *Infants and Young Children,* 1(1), 10–21.

McGonigel, M.J., Kaufmann, R.K., & Johnson, B.H. (1991). *Guidelines and recommended practices for the individualized family service plan* (2nd ed.). Bethesda, MD: Association for the Care of Children's Health.

Nash, J.K. (1990). Public Law 99-457: Facilitating family participation on the multidisciplinary team. *Journal of Early Intervention, 14,* 318–326.

Norton, D.G. (1990). Understanding the early experiences of black children in high risk environments: Culturally and ecologically relevant research as a guide to support for families. *Zero to Three, 10,* 1–7.

Slentz, K.L., & Bricker, D. (1992). Family-guided assessment for IFSP development: Jumping off the family assessment bandwagon. *Journal of Early Intervention, 16,* 11–19.

Summers, J.A., Dell'Oliver, C., Turnbull, A.P., Benson, H.A., Santelli, E., Campbell, M., & Siegel-Causey, E. (1990). Examining the individualized family service plan process: What are family and practitioner preferences? *Topics in Early Childhood Special Education,* 10(1), 78–99.

Vincent, L.J. (1992). Families and early intervention: Diversity and competence. *Journal of Early Intervention, 16,* 166–172.

Vincent, L.J., Salisbury, C.L., Strain, P., McCormick, C., & Tessier, A. (1990). A behavioral-ecological approach to early intervention: Focus on cultural diversity. In S.J. Meisels & J.P. Shonkoff (Eds.), *Handbook of early childhood intervention* (pp. 173–195). Cambridge: Cambridge University Press.

HOMELESS CHILDREN AND THEIR FAMILIES

Bassuk, E., & Rubin, L. (1987). Homeless children: A neglected population. *American Journal of Orthopsychiatry,* 57(2), 279–286.

Chavkin, W., Kristal, A., Seabron, C., & Guigli, P. (1987). The reproductive experience of women living in hotels for the homeless in New York City. *New York State Journal of Medicine,* 87(1), 10–13.

Grant, R. (1990). The special needs of homeless children: Early intervention at a welfare hotel. *Topics in Early Childhood Special Education, 10*(4), 76–91.

Hu, D.J., Covell, R.M., Morgan, J., & Arcia, J. (1989). Health care needs for children of the recently homeless. *Journal of Community Health, 14*(1), 1–8.

Kozol, J. (1988). *Rachel and her children: Homeless families in America.* New York: Random House.

McChesney, K.Y. (1986). New findings on homeless families. *Family Professional, 1*(2), 1–10.

Rossi, P.H. (1990). The old homeless and the new homeless in historical perspective. *American Psychologist, 45*(8), 954–959.

U.S. Conference of Mayors, Task Force on Hunger and Homelessness. (1987). *Report to the House of Representatives Subcommittee on Housing and Community Development.* Washington, DC: U.S. Government Printing Office.

Young, J.G., Huberman, R., Pascualvaca, D., Iyer, M., Bittel, C., Buchenholz, G., & Grant, R. (1990). Developmental status of preschool children in homeless families [abstract]. *Scientific Proceedings of the Annual Meeting of the American Academy of Child and Adolescent Psychiatry, 6,* 55.

MAINSTREAMING AND LEAST RESTRICTIVE ENVIRONMENTS

Bruder, M.B. (1993). The provision of early intervention and early childhood special education within community early childhood programs: Characteristics of effective service delivery. *Topics in Early Childhood Special Education, 13*(1), 19–37.

File, N., & Kontos, S. (1993). The relationship of program quality to children's play in integrated early intervention settings. *Topics in Early Childhood Special Education, 13*(1), 1–18.

Hanline, M.F., & Hanson, M.J. (1989). Integration considerations for infants and toddlers with multiple disabilities. *Journal of The Association for Persons with Severe Handicaps, 14*(3), 178–183.

Hundert, J., & Houghton, A. (1992). Promoting social interaction of children with disabilities in integrated preschools: A failure to generalize. *Exceptional Children, 58,* 311–320.

McLean, M., & Odom, S. (1988). *Least restrictive environment and social integration: Division for Early Childhood White Paper.* Reston, VA: Council for Exceptional Children.

Odom, S.L., & McEvoy, M.A. (1988). Integration of young children with handicaps and normally developing children. In S.L. Odom & M.B. Karnes (Eds.), *Early intervention for infants and children with handicaps: An empirical base* (pp. 241–267). Baltimore: Paul H. Brookes Publishing Co.

Odom, S.L., & McEvoy, M.A. (1990). Mainstreaming at the preschool level: Potential barriers and tasks for the field. *Topics in Early Childhood Special Education, 10*(2), 48–61.

Peck, C.A., Odom, S.L., & Bricker, D.D. (1993). *Integrating young children with disabilities into community programs: Ecological perspectives on research and implementation.* Baltimore: Paul H. Brookes Publishing Co.

Peterson, C.A., & McConnell, S.R. (1993). Factors affecting the impact of social interaction skills interventions in early childhood special education. *Topics in Early Childhood Special Education, 13*(1), 38–56.

Salisbury, C.L. (1991). Mainstreaming during the early childhood years. *Exceptional Children, 38,* 146–155.

Sexton, D. (1990). Quality, integrated programs for infants and toddlers with special needs. In E. Surbeck & M.F. Kelley (Eds.), *Personalizing care for infants, toddlers, and families* (pp. 41–50). Wheaton, MD: Association for Early Childhood Education International.

NATURALISTIC CHILD-LEVEL INTERVENTIONS

Bailey, D.B., & McWilliam, R.A. (1991). Normalizing early intervention. *Topics in Early Childhood Special Education, 10*(2), 33–47.

Bailey, D.B., & Wolery, M. (1992). Designing and arranging environments for infants and preschoolers with disabilities. In D.B. Bailey & M. Wolery (Eds.), *Teaching infants and preschoolers with disabilities* (2nd ed., pp. 197–227). New York: Charles E. Merrill.

Bricker, D., & Cripe, J.J.W. (1992). *An activity-based approach to early intervention.* Baltimore: Paul H. Brookes Publishing Co.

Carta, J.J., Schwartz, I.S., Atwater, J.B., & McConnell, S.C. (1991). Developmentally appropriate practice: Appraising its usefulness for young children with disabilities. *Topics in Early Childhood Special Education, 10*(2), 48–61.

Giangreco, M.F., York, J., & Rainforth, B. (1989). Providing related services to learners with severe handicaps in educational settings: Pursuing the least restrictive option. *Pediatric Physical Therapy, 1,* 55–63.

Hart, B., & Risley, T. (1975). Incidental teaching in the preschool. *Journal of Applied Behavior Analysis, 8,* 411–420.

Hershberger, P. (1991). A naturalistic approach to home-based early intervention. *Infant–Toddler Intervention, 1*(2), 83–92.

Linder, T.W. (1993). *Transdisciplinary play-based intervention: Guidelines for developing a meaningful curriculum for young children.* Baltimore: Paul H. Brookes Publishing Co.

McWilliam, R.A., & Bailey, D.B. (1992). Promoting engagement and mastery. In D.B. Bailey & M. Wolery (Eds.), *Teaching infants and preschoolers with disabilities* (2nd ed., pp. 229–256). New York: Charles E. Merrill.

Noonan, M.J., & McCormick, L. (1992). A naturalistic curriculum model for early intervention. *Infant–Toddler Intervention, 2*(3), 147–159.

Warren, S.F., & Gazdag, G. (1990). Facilitating early language development with milieu intervention techniques. *Journal of Early Intervention, 14*, 62–86.

PARENTS WITH MENTAL RETARDATION

Booth, C.I., Mitchell, S.K., Barnard, K.E., & Spieker, S.J. (1989). Development of maternal social skills in multiproblem families: Effects on the mother–child relationship. *Developmental Psychology, 25*, 403–412.

Espe-Sherwindt, M. (1991). The IFSP and parents with special needs/mental retardation. *Topics in Early Childhood Special Education, 11*(3), 107–120.

Espe-Sherwindt, M., & Kerlin, S.L. (1990). Early intervention with parents with mental retardation: Do we empower or impair? *Infants and Young Children, 2*(4), 21–28.

Feldman, M.A. (1986). Research on parenting by mentally retarded persons. *Psychiatric Clinics of North America, 9*, 777–796.

Graziano, A.M., & Diament, D.M. (1991). Parent behavioral training: An examination of the paradigm. *Behavior Modification, 16*, 3–38.

Greenspan, S., & Budd, K.S. (1986). Research on mentally retarded parents. In J.J. Gallagher & P.M. Vietze (Eds.), *Families of handicapped persons: Research, programs, and policy issues* (pp. 115–127). Baltimore: Paul H. Brookes Publishing Co.

Llewellyn, G. (1990). People with intellectual disability as parents: Perspectives from the professional literature. *Australia and New Zealand Journal of Developmental Disabilities, 16*(4), 369–380.

Lubeck, R.C., & Chandler, R.C. (1990). Organizing the home environment for infants with handicaps. *Education and Treatment of Children, 13*, 347–363.

Pharis, M.E., & Levin, V.S. (1991). A person to talk to who really cares: High-risk mothers' evaluations of services in an intensive intervention research program. *Child Welfare, 70*(3), 307–320.

Tymchuk, A.J., Andron, L., & Rahbar, B. (1988). Effective decision making/problem-solving with mothers who have mental retardation. *American Journal of Mental Retardation, 92*, 510–516.

Tymchuk, A.J., Andron, L., & Unger, O. (1987). Parents with mental handicaps and adequate child care—A review. *Mental Handicaps, 15*, 49–54.

PLANNING FOR TRANSITIONS

Affleck, G., Tennen, H., Rowe, J., Roscher, B., & Walker, L. (1989). Effects of formal support on mothers' adaptation to the hospital-to-home transition of high-risk infants: The benefits and costs of helping. *Child Development, 60*, 488–501.

Diamond, K., Spiegel-McGill, P., & Hanrahan, P. (1988). Planning for school transition: An ecological-developmental approach. *Journal of the Division for Early Childhood, 12*, 245–252.

Fowler, S.A., Schwartz, I., & Atwater, J. (1991). Perspectives on the transition from preschool to kindergarten for children with disabilities and their families. *Exceptional Children, 58*, 136–145.

Hains, A.H., Fowler, S.A., & Chandler, L.K. (1988). Planning school transitions: Family and professional collaboration. *Journal of the Division for Early Childhood, 12*(2), 108–115.

Hanline, M.F., & Knowlton, A. (1988). A collaborative model for providing support to parents during their child's transition from infant intervention to preschool special education public school programs. *Journal of the Division for Early Childhood, 12*(2), 116–125.

Hanline, M.F., Suchman, S., & Demmerle, C. (1989). Helping parents make the transition to special education preschool. *Teaching Exceptional Children, 21*(2), 61–62.

Rosenkoetter, S.E. (1992). Guidelines from recent legislation to structure transition planning. *Infants and Young Children, 5*(1), 21–27.

PREMATURE INFANTS AND HOSPITAL-BASED SERVICES

Als, H. (1982). Toward a synactive theory of development and support of infants' individuality. *Infant Mental Health Journal, 3*(4), 229–243.

Als, H., Lester, B.M., Tronick, E., & Brazelton, T.B. (1982). Towards a research instrument for the assessment of preterm infants' behavior (APIB). In H.E. Fitzgerald, B.M. Lester, & M.W. Yogman (Eds.), *Theory and research in behavioral pediatrics* (Vol. 1, II, a, pp. 35–63). New York: Plenum.

Als, H., Lester, B.M., Tronick, E., & Brazelton, T.B. (1982). Manual for the assessment of preterm infants' behavior (APIB). In H.E. Fitzgerald, B.M. Lester, & M.W. Yogman (Eds.), *Theory and research in behavioral pediatrics* (Vol. 1, II, b, pp. 64–133). New York: Plenum.

Brazelton, T.B. (1984). *The Neonatal Behavioral Assessment Scale* (2nd ed.). (I and II). Clinics in Developmental Medicine, No. 88, Philadelphia: J.B. Lippincott.

Cardone, I.A., & Gilkerson, L. (1992). Family administered neonatal activities: An adaptation for parents of infants born with Down syndrome. *Infants and Young Children, 5*(1), 40–48.

Gilkerson, L., Gorski, P.A., & Panitz, P. (1990). Hospital-based intervention for preterm infants and their families. In S.J. Meisels & J.P. Shonkoff (Eds.), *Handbook of early childhood intervention* (pp. 445–468). Cambridge: Cambridge University Press.

Long, C.E., Artis, N.E., & Dobbins, N.J. (1993). The hospital: An important site for family-centered early intervention. *Topics in Early Childhood Special Education, 13*(1), 106–119.

Ploof, D.L., & Feldman, H.M. (1992). Organizing early intervention services in a hospital setting: The Developmental Support Project as a parallel organization. *Infants and Young Children, 5*(1), 28–39.

PRENATAL DRUG EXPOSURE

Crites, L.S., Fischer, K.L., McNeish-Stengel, M., & Siegel, C.J. (1992). Working with families of drug-exposed children: Three model programs. *Infant–Toddler Intervention, 2*(1), 13–24.

Gustavsson, N.S. (1992). Drug exposed infants and their mothers: Facts, myths, and needs. *Social Work in Health Care, 16*(4), 87–100.

McDonald, C.C. (1992). Perinatal cocaine exposure: Predictor of an endangered generation. *Infant–Toddler Intervention, 2*(1), 1–12.

Myers, B.J., & Kaltenbach, K. (1992). Cocaine-exposed infants: Myths and misunderstandings. *Zero to Three, 13*(1), 1–5.

Schutter, L.S., & Brinker, R.P. (1992). Conjuring a new category of disability from prenatal cocaine exposure: Are the infants unique biological or caretaking causalities? *Topics in Early Childhood Special Education, 11*(4), 84–111.

Trad, P.V. (1992). Toddlers with prenatal cocaine exposure: Principles of assessment, Part I. *Infant–Toddler Intervention, 2*(1), 285–306.

SERVICE COORDINATION AND INTERAGENCY COLLABORATION

Bailey, D.B. (1984). A triaxial model of the interdisciplinary team and group processes. *Exceptional Children, 51,* 17–25.

Bailey, D.B. (1989). Case management in early intervention. *Journal of Early Intervention, 13,* 120–134.

Briggs, M.H. (1991). Team development: Decision-making for early intervention. *Infant–Toddler Intervention, 1,* 1–9.

Dunst, C.J., & Trivette, C.M. (1989). An enablement and empowerment perspective of case management. *Topics in Early Childhood Special Education, 8*(4), 87–102.

Harbin, G.L., & McNulty, B.A. (1990). Policy implementation: Perspectives on service coordination and interagency cooperation. In S.J. Meisels & J.P. Shonkoff (Eds.), *Handbook of early childhood intervention* (pp. 700–721). Cambridge: Cambridge University Press.

Lowenthal, B. (1991). A new role for the early interventionist: Case manager. *Infant–Toddler Intervention, 1*(3), 191–198.

Lowenthal, B. (1992). Interagency collaboration in early intervention: Rationale, barriers, and implementation. *Infant–Toddler Intervention, 2*(2), 103–111.

Moore, S. (1992). Case management and the integration of services: How service delivery systems shape case management. *Social Work, 37*(5), 418–423.

Peterson, N.L. (1991). Interagency collaboration under Part H: The key to comprehensive, multidisciplinary, coordinated infant/toddler intervention services. *Journal of Early Intervention, 15,* 89–105.

Swan, W.W., & Morgan, J.L. (1993). *Collaborating for comprehensive services for young children and their families: The local interagency coordinating council.* Baltimore: Paul H. Brookes Publishing Co.

Zipper, I.N., Weil, M., & Rounds, K. (in press). *Service coordination in early intervention: Parents and professionals.* Cambridge, MA: Brookline Books.

STRATEGIES FOR CONSULTATION

Fine, M. (1990). Facilitating home–school relationships: A family-oriented approach to collaborative consultation. *Journal of Educational and Psychological Consultation, 1*(2), 169–188.

Hanline, M.F. (1990). A consulting model for providing integration opportunities for preschool children with disabilities. *Journal of Early Intervention, 14,* 360–366.

Hanson, M.J., & Widerstrom, A. H. (1993). Consultation and collaboration: Essentials of integration efforts for young children. In C.A. Peck, S.L. Odom, & D.D. Bricker (Eds.), *Integrating young children with disabilities into community programs: Ecological perspectives on research and implementation* (pp. 149–168). Baltimore: Paul H. Brookes Publishing Co.

Johnson, L., Pugach, M., & Hammittee, D. (1988). Barriers to effective special education consultation. *Remedial and Special Education, 9*(6), 41–47.

Nevin, A., Thousand, J., Paolucci-Whitcomb, P., & Villa, R. (1990). Collaborative consultation: Empowering public school personnel to provide heterogeneous schooling for all—or, Who rang that bell? *Journal of Educational and Psychological Consultation, 1,* 41–67.

Peck, C.A., Killen, C., & Baumgart, D. (1989). Increasing implementation of special education instruction in mainstream preschools: Direct and generalized effects of nondirective consultation. *Journal of Applied Behavior Analysis, 22,* 197–210.

Phillips, V., & McCullough, L. (1990). Consultation-based programming: Instituting the collaborative ethic in schools. *Exceptional Children, 56,* 291–304.

Acronyms

AFDC	Aid to Families with Dependent Children
AIDS	acquired immunodeficiency syndrome
APIB	Assessment of Preterm Infants' Behavior
BDI	Battelle Developmental Inventory
BOCES	Board of Cooperative Educational Services
CMV	cytomegalovirus
CPD	cephalopelvic disproportion
CPR	cardiopulmonary resuscitation
CT	computed tomography
DAP	developmentally appropriate practice
DEC-CEC	Division for Early Childhood of the Council for Exceptional Children
DSS	Department of Social Services
ECI	Early Childhood Intervention
EKG	electrocardiogram
ENT	ear, nose, and throat specialist—otorhinolaryngologist
G-tube	gastrostomy tube
HIV	human immunodeficiency virus
IEP	individualized education program
IFSP	individualized family service plan
ITP	individualized transition plan
MDI	Mental Development Index
MRI	magnetic resonance imaging
NBAS	(Brazelton) Neonatal Behavioral Assessment Scale
NG	nasogastric
NICU	neonatal intensive care unit
OT	occupational therapy
PDA	patent ductus arteriosus
PDI	Psychomotor Development Index
PL 99-457	Education of the Handicapped Act Amendments of 1986

PL 102-119	Individuals with Disabilities Education Act Amendments of 1991
PT	physical therapy
PTA	parent–teacher association
SIDS	sudden infant death syndrome
SSI	Supplemental Security income
TE	tracheoesophageal
WIC	Women, Infants, and Children

Index

Individualized services
  community structure and, 24
  importance of, 21
  recommended practices and, 13
Individualized transition plan
  (ITP), recommended practices and, 6
Individuals with Disabilities Education Act Amendments of
  1991 (PL 102-119)
  coordinated service delivery and,
  15, 16
  recommended practices and, 5–7
Infant
  with chromosomal abnormality,
  227–233
  with Down syndrome, and
  mother intent on making
  child "normal," 251–254
  exposed to drugs, 147–153,
  203–214
  mother with mental retardation
  and, center-based program
  and, 87–95
  premature, see Neonatal intensive care unit (NICU); Preterm infant(s)
Information
  mother's increasing pursuit of,
  child with Down syndrome
  and, 252–254
  types of, provided to family, 13
Inner city
  teenage mother in, 63–72
  welfare hotels in, 109–119
Instructional strategies, based on
  case studies, 34
Insurance agencies
  policies of, recommended practice implementation and,
  27–28
  see also Medicaid
Integrated therapy, 14
Integration, see Inclusion
Intellectual abilities, limited
  in parents, 191–199
  see also Mental retardation
Intensive care unit, neonatal, see
  Neonatal intensive care unit
  (NICU)
Interagency coordination
  problems with, 271–281

see also Coordinated service delivery
Interdisciplinary team
  disagreement among, about
  child's needs, 219–224
  see also Team approach
Intervention(s)
  effectiveness of, indicators of, see
  Quality indicators
  plan of action for, consultant
  and, 57–58, 59–60
  selection of, decisionmaking and,
  35–36
Interventionists, see Professional(s)
ITP, see Individualized transition
  plan

Job requirements, affecting service
  delivery, 26–28
Job training, substance abuse program and, 210, 214

Kindergarten, regular class in, see
  Regular education; Transitions
Knowledge, professional, service
  delivery and, 28–29

Larsen syndrome, educational
  placement of child with,
  121–136
Least restrictive environment, see
  Inclusion
Legislation
  recommended practices originating from, 5–7
  see also specific legislation

Mainstream, inclusion in, see Inclusion
Massage therapy, for infant exposed to drugs, 150–151
Medicaid
  recommended practice implementation and, 27
  substance abuse treatment and,
  206, 210
Medical problems, see Health history; Health problems, in
  child; specific problems
Meetings
  disagreement among team mem-